IT'S NOT (ALL) YOUR FAULT

IT'S NOT (ALL) YOUR FAULT

Self-Help and the Individualization of Oppression

Sharon Podobnik

MANUSCRIPTS
PRESS

IT'S NOT (ALL) YOUR FAULT
Self-Help and the Individualization of Oppression

ISBN
979-8-88926-841-3 *Paperback*
979-8-88926-729-4 *Hardcover*
979-8-88926-842-0 *Ebook*

To the ones who inspired this book,
who are the least likely to read it.
We wouldn't be here without you.

And, to you.
We really need you.

CONTENTS

INTRODUCTION

I'm one of the lucky ones.

I own a successful leadership development firm. I have a husband who adores and supports me and friends who love and challenge me. I live in a cozy little condo in Seattle with a view of glittery, snow-capped mountains from my kitchen sink.

And yet, I sometimes still wonder if this whole living thing is worth it.

Because even though I'm "one of the lucky ones," I still feel like shit on a regular basis. I'm always tired. I'm perpetually worried about money. I'm self-conscious about my smile, my body, my hair, and my clothes. I have never felt like I was doing enough. Ever.

Unfortunately, I know I'm far from the only person feeling this way. Things aren't working the way we were promised they would.

We are told if we go to school and study hard, we'll get a great job, be paid well, and earn our slice of the American Dream. We are told if we play by the rules, we'll be thin, and beautiful, and beloved. We are told that health, happiness, and success are all within reach for all of us, regardless of who we are or our circumstances. We are told if we're feeling down, or anxious, or not quite where we want to be in our lives, we can turn to spirituality, psychology, and self-help, and they'll get us where we want to go.

We are told again and again we are in control of our destinies.

So we eat less and work more. We play the part and fake it 'til we make it while trying to convince ourselves we're being our most authentic selves. We try so hard to do everything *right.*

But you and I know something's up, don't we?

Because we can study hard, work hard, and still not be paid what we deserve or achieve our own fairy tale version of the American Dream with a beautiful home, a golden retriever, and a 401k that overfloweth. We know health, happiness, and success are not guaranteed and are achieved by some more easily than others. We can play by the rules and still not feel great about our bodies, our relationships, or our career. We can do everything we were told to do and still feel lost, lonely, sad, conflicted, and confused.

We know even if we "have it all" on paper, we can still feel depressed and anxious and just... deeply unsatisfied.

Many of us internalize this as not doing enough and strive like hell to do more, better.

It feels like it's all our fault.

It isn't.

The painful truth is that education socializes us into societal roles, only some of which are meant to lead to traditional success. When it's not enough, we resourceful, resilient things turn to self-help. Self-help promises to give us everything we've been missing and, in the process, confirms what we've been taught to believe: everything we're struggling with is, in fact, all our fault. If only we had enough willpower and worked hard enough, we could be different, and all our problems would be solved.

Self-help, with all its shiny promises and beautiful intentions, says, "Whether you want to be a badass or have a rockin', badass bod, we can teach you how." It suggests the reason you're not feeling like a badass with a badass bod is entirely within your control and, therefore, within your control to change.

Instead of questioning whether or not "being a badass" or having a badass bod is a worthy pursuit, self-help assumes everyone wants to and should want to. Instead of asking why we want this or how we got here, self-help says, "You're the problem, but don't worry, I can fix you." Instead of leaning into our own wisdom and intuition, most self-help and self-love "experts" prescribe, "Do what I did, and you can be just like me!"

Self-help promises to help you be "the best version of yourself you can be," in a game in which "the best version of yourself" is strictly defined by someone else, not by you.

My journey with self-help started as most do—while I was in desperate need of guidance. The first self-help book I ever read was called *You Can Be Happy No Matter What* (Carlson). I don't remember anything about the book, but I do remember asking myself over and over in the shower, then in the car, and later in a flood of tears in the fetal position on the floor, "What if this is as good as it gets?"

Oddly enough, I've always been a deep believer in a better way. I've been the person rallying for possibility and potential where others see none. Driving around my old neighborhood in western Pennsylvania, where old sheds and farmhouses are unceremoniously abandoned by the roadside, I see moss- and ivy-covered frames and imagine what splendor and life might have once existed there. I think about what *might be* if only we let what *is* return to nature as a nurse log, supporting the life of plants and animals in generations to come.

I meet women bursting with genius, passion, incredible depth, and intuition who are playing it safe and playing second fiddle to fragile, hostile, overconfident, and underqualified men as well as creative, kind, and caring men withholding their fullest, most vulnerable, and feeling selves in relationships and careers that demand and perpetuate toxic masculinity and misogyny. I immediately see—and cannot unsee—what could be: congresswomen, nomadic wild women, and millionaires creating generational wealth for their families; purpose-driven artists, social workers, and advocates; people making the impact they were meant to have on the world.

This penchant served me well as a poor kid. I trusted my upbringing was not my destiny and that hard work and education would save me. I threw myself into education. My studies in psychology introduced me to the concepts of trauma, human development, neurodivergence, and abnormal psychology, which helped me to better understand myself, my family dynamics, and the people I came into contact with every day. My studies in sociology introduced me to discussions of power, privilege, inequality, and socialization, which helped me to understand the role politics, the media, our school systems, and social institutions play in shaping who we are and how we exist in the world. My multiple stints studying abroad took me to more than twenty cultures and countries, where I learned the ways religion, culture, and education systems socialize us in vastly different ways. I discovered no one way of being was inherently better than another.

I worked with thousands of students and teachers across multiple states during my decade in schools, carrying with me the belief that if we just worked hard enough, we could all achieve our potential. Eventually, my successes as a classroom teacher led me to instructional and leadership coaching, where I supported folks in being the best damn educators and leaders they could be.

I had come so far, yet was still so miserable. After a massive waking up (read: breakdown) on my honeymoon left me feeling excruciatingly untethered, I took a long look at my life and asked if I was living the life I wanted. The answer was painfully clear—I just wasn't. I was working my ass off every day, and I was still feeling fat, poor, lonely, anxious, insecure, and unsuccessful. I knew I wasn't on the right track, but I didn't know what the right track was.

I assumed if I wasn't happy and wasn't living up to my potential, it must have been work related. After all, we are what we do, right? I got to brainstorming.

I dreamt of a community of people willing to Do the Work that would enable us to realize the ways we hold ourselves back, to heal what was broken in us, and to do the hard things that would help us to be successful. I dreamt we would evolve into peaceful, centered humans who would recognize the hurt in others and with a mighty sigh, say, "Oh, sweet thing, you need to go ahead and love yourself," when we might otherwise suggest they go fuck themselves.

After six weeks of market research and rapid-fire prototype testing, I launched Go Love Yourself—a monthly self-help book subscription box for women. We'd read self-help books, get implementation support from coaches who "got it," and grow in community. We'd calm the fuck down, find the badass boss bitch confidence that had been eluding us, and go after our dreams together!

Brilliant!

I grew the company from a measly handful of customers in the month of our launch (thanks, friends and family!) to hundreds of monthly subscribers joining from more than twenty-five countries around the globe. As a part of our curriculum development process, I read more than fifty self-help books per year. I partnered with all the major publishers, receiving early editions and connecting directly with authors. I facilitated dozens of book discussions and women's circles where we shared our most intimate hopes, dreams, fears, and insecurities. I published more than twenty-five self-coaching workbooks designed to help women support themselves on their self-improvement journey with topics ranging from imposter syndrome, perfectionism, and self-love to forest bathing, digital detoxes, and sexual empowerment. Along the way, I coached hundreds of women as we walked our journeys together.

It became exactly what I dreamt it would be and was exactly what I wanted while I was mid-burnout as a teacher: Self-help! Self-care! Community! But after investing hundreds of thousands of dollars and years of my life into the hand-crafted job of my dreams, the same issues remained. I was deeply unhappy.

I closed the doors on the business I built from scratch just shy of her third birthday.

Hundreds of us were reading books monthly. We put the ideas from the books into action with great intent, passion, desire for change, and fidelity. Yet, for most of us, our lives were basically the same. We were in the same relationships and the same stressful jobs, with many of the same worries of wallet and waistline we had before.

What started as the solution to one breakdown became the impetus for another.

How was it possible so many intelligent, driven, accomplished, and diligent women could strive so valiantly for another way of being, and for all intents and purposes, see no great meaningful change?

Easy.

We were solving the wrong problems.

When we need to change ourselves to belong, to gain acceptance, approval, and love, we often end up using aggressive and dehumanizing levels of self-control. We voluntarily submit ourselves to full-fledged thought reprogramming to fit our culture's expectations about who and how we should be in order to be successful. We need to call this what it is—complicity in our own oppression.

Self-help gives us ways to fit ourselves into a society that wasn't built for us. It is a capitalist religion that helps us to navigate and participate in our own oppression.

For years, I turned self-help books into actionable workbooks for my community. I combed through their advice to determine which reflection questions would spark the "aha!" that would make all the difference. As I vetted texts, I found nearly half of them had such palpable shaming or harmful recommendations that I vetoed them immediately. The other half routinely lacked actionable ideas, or were so action oriented there was little to reflect on. The most powerful ones changed our perspectives, inspiring action without prescribing it.

Later in this book, you'll read about my drinking problem.

I didn't quit drinking because I hit rock bottom and needed to make a change or because I read a book detailing the six easy steps for reclaiming my life. I quit because the book I read (at a bar, beer in hand) invited me to step back from everything I believed about alcohol and examine it from a safe, supportive distance. I created new awareness around a problem I had, analyzed the true source of the problem, and solved *that* problem at its source. For the first time in my life, I didn't try to force a change. I didn't try at all.

In this book, I also hope to inspire action without prescribing it. It's meant to serve as an invitation, a conversation, and a catalyst for transformation. Along the way, I bring in lots of other voices—those who have opened the door for new ways of thinking and being in my own life. Their perspectives and contributions to the larger conversation feel absolutely invaluable to me. I hope they will feel inspiring to you, too.

I aim to include and amplify a variety of diverse voices, and I am committed to doing so in a respectful and responsible way throughout this book. I'm aware of the limitations of my perspective and welcome feedback and critique as I continue to learn and grow.

There's a funky conundrum here because I am perpetually at risk of falling into the many traps embedded in the self-help industry as I reveal them to you. Some I embed on purpose so they can be experienced as they are exposed. We'll learn more about what those are and what that means, but suffice to say that in this moment, the world is complex and kind of fucked up sometimes, and I'm doing my best as I trust we all are. I deeply desire to do right by you, reader, and all the voices that are gathered in this book. I'm no model of perfection, nor do I aspire to be.

The many stories, examples, and studies in this book are meant to support us all in recognizing our common humanity and developing what transformation expert, author, and activist Dr. Barbara J. Love calls a liberatory consciousness. A liberatory consciousness helps us purposefully navigate oppressive systems and institutions rather than submit to our socialization (2013). Our journey together will parallel my own, starting from a sleep state and progressing through the four elements of Dr. Love's framework: awareness, analysis, action, and accountability/allyship.

Along the way, we will question the beliefs, practices, and values embedded in self-help that keep us participating in systems of oppression in order to release ourselves from being cogs in the machine making us miserable and step into the enduring integrity of our own values. This, in turn, will allow us to act intentionally, interrupting systems, demanding change, and supporting others in their liberation.

We could have considered many frameworks for this purpose. I encourage you to dig into and learn from different frameworks and find the ones that speak to you. Some of my favorites include Paulo Freire's critical consciousness and bell hooks' feminist education for critical consciousness (Freire 2014; hooks 2014).[1] Multiple paths can take us where we want to go. Dig in. Swim around. See what resonates.

I also encourage you to consider thoughtfully all beliefs, practices, and values explicit and implicit in these pages. I aim to cite other books, research, philosophical positions, sociological observations, and historical information while being abundantly clear that all knowledge is socially constructed; all data is collected by and interpreted by humans with distinct and particular perspectives. Explore primary sources I cite. Look for bias and perspective taking in my and others' interpretations. After thoughtful consideration,

---

1 You'll notice some names throughout this book that are lowercase on purpose. Some writers do this as a form of artistic expression, others for personal preference, and others as a form of protest against societal norms. bell hooks uses lowercase letters in her pen name as a way of shifting the focus from herself to her message.

dismiss not that which solely conflicts with your individual lived experiences, as we all have extraordinarily different experiences, but that which insults your soul.

We are all at different places in our liberation journeys. I am under no delusion I've got this all figured out. Far from it. Every day, I find myself realizing new and different ways my socialization has failed me and ways in which I am perpetuating harmful systems through my own beliefs and actions. While I continue my learning journey, I'll share what I've learned from the lens of someone deeply embedded in the self-help world in order to support us in examining the ways systems like racism, sexism, and classism show up in our everyday lives and specifically how they manifest in the self-help books we read.

We will learn more about what is being communicated to us and why in order to make informed decisions about whether the "help" being offered is well-intentioned, predatory, or both. We'll explore how self-help came to exist as well as its current function in society in order to decide what can and should be done to right the wrongs pervasive in the self-help community. We will determine what actions to take in accordance with our own individual values that aim to create a more just world and invite ourselves to take responsibility for taking those actions individually and in community.

True empowerment requires us to have a safe space to process our learnings. Because of this, I highly recommend reading this with a friend or group of friends. Resources to support this experience can be found at www.itsnotallyourfault.com.

In this moment, I have great hope.

I see not only the explosion of the self-help industry, which tells me we believe change is both possible and worth pursuing, but also a growing collective discontent and intolerance with the way things are for all of us.

As a collective, we have the opportunity to pick our heads up and recognize that not only are we not alone in our discontent, but it can't possibly be all *anyone's* fault. When 77 percent of Americans feel anxious about their financial situation (CapitalOne 2020), up to 60 percent of *elementary-aged* school girls in the US are concerned about their weight (Smolak 2004), and working women in the US are among the most stressed employees *globally* (Gallup 2022), it becomes clear these issues are no individual failing but a collective failing to support individuals. When hundreds of millions of Americans are experiencing the same things, it's not a coincidence–it's a failing system.

When we realize we're not alone, we can press pause on our cycles of shame and loneliness and move into deep, radical curiosity, compassion, and change. From this expanded perspective, we realize many of the problems we are facing aren't actually the result of personal shortcomings or individual moral failings. We get to imagine a world in which our depression and exhaustion are not seen as a sign of how shitty we are but a reflection of living in a shitty collective reality.

These things we're facing on a daily basis? They're just not (all) our fault.

I hear you, already, telling me what you could be doing to do better. I hear you saying, "Sure, Sharon, it's not *all* my fault, but surely some of it is. Surely I feel this way for a reason?" I feel your hesitance and your hope. I also feel your despair as you ask, "Well then, shit. What was all of this for?"

And I'm sorry. I'm not sure just yet. Only time will tell what role this chapter will have played in our collective story.

Until then, know this, dear friend: I am writing this book for you.

You, who sit here and think about the stress that never fully dissipates, the things you thought you'd accomplish by now, and the ways you would like life to be different—I wrote this for you.

This book is for every one of us who has picked up a self-help book with an intense, burning desire and hope that life could be better *if only.* If only we could feel more confident; if only we could lose the weight; if only we could kick our perfectionism to the curb.

This book is for anyone who has seen a self-help title and thought, "For fucks sake, really?" It's for anyone who has read a self-help book on a Kindle or listened to the audiobook out of embarrassment while desperately wanting to be different. It's for anyone who has spent hard-earned money on a "life-changing" retreat or workshop or coaching program only to go back to a shitty workplace on Monday, binge on ice cream that night, and still feel awful later, as if it were all for naught. This is for everyone who has come back to self-help time and time again.

I see you.

I am you.

I've shelled out thousands for coaching programs. I've paid hundreds to be hypnotized for weight loss. I've read *The Hoarder in You* and *Why Men Marry Bitches* on my Kindle to avoid sideways glances. I've raised eyebrows at titles while walking down the aisles of my local bookstore before slipping the offending books under my arm to buy.

I've done the waking up at 5 a.m., the writing it down, the affirmations, the visualizations, the decluttering, and the diets. I've set the goals and done the work and gotten the help meant to help me overcome my limiting beliefs. I've meditated and reflected and done the exercises.

This is for all of us who have wanted to be better versions of ourselves and placed our trust in people and programs and systems who we believed would be here for us and help us.

This is for all of us who trust there must be a better way.

This is for us.

SECTION I

ASLEEP

CHAPTER 1

WAKING UP

I was six years old the first time I learned I was "no fun."

It was Thanksgiving, and while my grandma, mom, and aunts were dutifully preparing our feast of boiled potatoes, boiled corn, and roasted turkey, the men chatted and the children played amongst themselves. My uncle was making fun of me and chased me into the family room while pinching my ass. It hurt. I didn't like it. I apparently forgot to smile and laugh it off like I'd done a million times before. I remember him being at eye level, scrunching his face into a mock pout, narrowing his eyes, and saying, "Oh... you're no fun."

A video exists of me at Christmastime 1987. I'm just over two years old, and as one of the earliest grandchildren, I'm showered with love, affection, and toys. In the video, I'm playing with some of my new stash. I bang on the keys of my tiny xylophonic piano, scream-singing, "I love you!" I pour make-believe water from one child-sized plastic pot into another and direct that same uncle to make corn. "No! Coffee!" I say. "Wait! Those are the green beans!"

It's cute. I'm cute. The whole thing is so sweet and innocent it makes you want to gouge your eyes out. It could have, and should have, stayed a sweet little memory of play and joy and youthful innocence.

But it didn't. Because year after year, every Christmas, from the age of two until I was bringing partners home to meet my family in my twenties, the video was played. We would pack a dozen adults and a dozen children into a room that could comfortably fit six. Together we'd watch me pound the keys and pour the coffee and tell my uncle what to do. They'd laugh, and they'd mock me, and they'd laugh some more. They'd throw their heads back and cackle 'til they cried as I curled into my mother's lap, wanting to die.

I'd cry, and they'd see me crying, and they'd tell me it was just a joke as they ejected the tape, put it in the rewinder, and plopped it back into the VCR to watch all over again. Eventually, Grandma would holler in from the kitchen, "Leave her alone," or, "Dinner's ready!" and I would slink into my seat at the kids' table, sleeves soaked through with snot and tears.

As children, we are wonderfully observant, astute little humans. We begin responding to the people around us before we are even born. A study showed twin fetuses interact and even reach for and comfort each other while in the womb (Weaver 2011). We naturally yearn for and seek out social interaction from our earliest moments. We are completely dependent on the adults in our lives to provide for our most basic needs and will do whatever it takes to be seen, noticed, taken care of, and taken seriously (Miller 1979).

When we don't get what we need—whether it's food, attention, loving connection, or otherwise—we have an impossible choice to make (Eisenstein 2013). We can either assume the people we rely on for every aspect of survival are unable to meet our needs and, unable to strike out on our own, fall into despair, or we can assume it's all our fault and change ourselves in response to the people we rely on.

We make the tough, unconscious decision that the adults in our lives are good, caring people who didn't mean to hurt us, determine we caused the negative reaction from others, and act accordingly. For many of us, this results in a special sensitivity to the needs of others as we turn to people pleasing in order to win favor with the caretakers in our lives (Miller 1979). We all do our best to fit into whatever scenario we happen to be born into. We try to be who our caretakers need and want us to be and do what we have to do to get what we need from them.

From the people around us, we learn how to navigate the world we are born into. We learn who we are and how to belong or, alternatively, how to earn love and acceptance each time our caretakers praise and punish us. We internalize what we learn as truth, accepting as fact what we are told: the sky is blue; you're being too sensitive; you're asking for it.

The messages we learn about ourselves and how to be in the world become our playbook. Unquestioned and unexamined, they remain the rulebooks we live by for life. We do what we need to do to fit in, gain love and acceptance, get and keep a job, and get and keep a partner. When dissonance arises, as it inevitably does when the way we *are* feels at odds with who we are told we *should be*, we assume *that* is our fault too, feel shame for being different, conform as best we can, and carry on.

Because of course we do. What's the alternative?

To survive, my young mind learned I was wrong to protest injustices. I internalized that I was no fun. When I then stopped participating during family gatherings, I was called out for being too quiet and shy.

It wasn't until my therapist issued me the insurance codes "Generalized Anxiety Disorder" and "Social Anxiety" in my thirties that I had something other than "shy" and "quiet" to call myself.

"Yes, you're too shy and far too sensitive," the diagnoses seemed to agree, "but it's okay. It's not your fault! Your brain just doesn't work right. We can fix you!"

My therapist explained that everyone experiences nervousness or anxiety at some point in their lives, but that mine was pervasive and interfering with daily life. Most of us experience anxiety in response to specific events like public speaking, which also motivates us to prepare and practice. The millions of adults with anxiety disorders in the United States, on the other hand, display excessive worry about any number of issues for *months*.

And I was displaying an *excessive* amount of worry.

For years, I carried around my diagnoses as a badge of explanation. I used them to make sense of why I'd never been comfortable in any group setting and why I needed to be nearly black-out drunk to be the bubbly, social person I knew I could be. I read every *Buzzfeed* and *Psychology Today* article I could find and forwarded my partners listicles to help them understand me and support me in social situations. I read books on the prevalence of autism in adults and wondered if that could explain my awkwardness, too.

The news felt like a jolt of awakening—a positive revelation on my journey toward self-understanding. My diagnoses woke me up from the shame of being a painfully shy person and helped me to understand what I simply didn't have words for before. It was, in fact, because I had a faulty brain.

I called it, "I'd rather be at home reading." My family called it "shy." My therapist called it "debilitating social anxiety."

Without the expertise my therapist offered, I would have continued to feel the shame of feeling like an outsider everywhere I went, with no explanation why. My therapist helped me understand that it wasn't a personality flaw, per se, my brain just didn't work the way *normal* people's brains did. It wasn't my *fault*, but the problem was still *me*.

As we grow and evolve, we move from taking our cues about ourselves and the world around us from our parents and begin to take them from the other trusted folks in our lives—our friends, teachers, and trusted professionals, like my therapist. We rely on others to be our mirrors and reflect back to us who they see. As they do, we develop new theories about how and why things are the way they are and add to our ever more complex self-concept.

Over time, this becomes a complicated web of other people's opinions floating around in our brains—often to the point where we hear their voices in our heads and mistake them for our own, subverting how we would otherwise feel.

The first expensive winter coat I ever purchased was a luxurious, down-filled black coat that went to my knees. It didn't just zip up the front, it had Michael Kors emblazoned buttons adorning a lapel that closed across my torso for extra protection from blistering winter winds. When I popped the hood up over my head, faux fur hung just over my eyes. It fit perfectly, flattered my frame, and kept me warm, cozy, and dry in the brutal winters in Pittsburgh and DC. At sixty dollars, it was the most money I'd ever spent on a single item of clothing.

For a while, I felt like a fool wearing it. It felt too fancy for me. What would my family think of the stupid faux fur? Who did I think I was anyway? Eventually, I got used to it simply by wearing it enough. The coat made me feel like a queen.

In reality, I could make it through the snow-filled streets of campus feeling toasty and warm, and that was enough for me. I wore it through most of my classes—a fully acceptable comfort blanket.

Over the years, I wore that jacket so much—it was the only winter jacket I owned—friends and colleagues joked I slept in it. They weren't far off.

After a while, she began to age. Her hair grayed and frayed. Her shiny black exterior dulled and her insides came apart at the seams. I paid to have her stitched and fixed and prettied up so I could have more time with her.

One crisp fall day, twelve years into our relationship, I caught a gust of wind and shivered. I went to zip her up, but the zipper wouldn't budge. I sucked in and contorted my body and pulled the zipper up over my hips to try again. No avail: it wasn't zipping. I made a mental note to lose ten pounds, crossed my arms for warmth, and picked up the pace to generate some heat. Heat and calorie burn! Double win, ya dumb bitch! Maybe let's skip dinner tonight, shall we?

I spent that entire winter cold. I doubled up my bottoms, layering leggings and jeans, and tripled up my tops, layering knits, scarves, and hoodies under a coat that would not close. Each time I added the final layer, I condemned myself, shaming myself and reminding myself I'm not simply fat, I'm fat *and* lazy *and* poor. It wasn't just that the jacket didn't fit, it was also that I wasn't prioritizing going to the gym, getting a new coat, or eating better. It was that even if I did, it wouldn't matter because I was a shy, anxious, failure of a human, and no coat could cover that up. And even if I could find a coat big enough for my bloated body, it would be ugly and shapeless like me and far too expensive for my failing entrepreneurial self anyway.

My wardrobe malfunction symbolized everything that was wrong in my world.

I spent whatever energy I had convincing myself it wasn't so bad: Seattle's winters were more temperate than those in my hometown of Pittsburgh or DC, where I'd spent many years. I'd probably lose weight over the summer and fit into it next year. And hey! If I've got enough fat for the coat not to fit, it's surely enough to keep me warm! I downplayed my misery and shoved off my shivers and found excuses to stay inside.

I hung on to that coat two years too long. I refused to admit I'd outgrown her, despite every ounce of evidence proving it time and time again. I've always been a believer in potential, and I reasoned I could totally make her work. I'm resilient, damn it! Determined! Stubborn.

Over time, my beloved coat has come to serve as a metaphor in my coaching practice for all the things we put up with, all the things we tolerate and make excuses for that we know we've outgrown, even if we're not yet willing to admit it.

Just like I kept my coat even though it no longer fit, I kept going to Grandma's year after year, holiday after holiday. I tried so hard to be a good daughter, sister, niece, cousin, and granddaughter, smiling and laughing along and hugging every adult around the dinner table, even when my body recoiled and even after I realized years of freezing and fawning had left me numb and empty in these situations.

In my coaching practice, I've come to recognize a familiar pattern: It's not until we let ourselves *feel* how small a coat, person, relationship, job, or situation feels that we will also allow ourselves to fully feel and accept the deep pull to make a change. Until then, we find reasons to explain these things away, to rationalize how they didn't mean it like that, or it's not really so bad. We dismiss our own complaints as being too sensitive, or reading too much into something, or not worth it. We ask ourselves to be far, far too resilient.

When we stop making excuses for ourselves and others and quit criticizing ourselves for the discomfort we're feeling, we get to feel and truly recognize what our bodies and brains have been telling us all along: "This shit ain't right."

In my experience, when we allow ourselves to embrace, embody, and fully feel just how bad something is—whatever we're rationalizing—we can move from shaming ourselves about our own discomfort into asking questions. Once we build the awareness we're dismissing ourselves, we can remove the self-judgment and censure long enough to make the situation neutral, determine what that discomfort is trying to tell us, and decide what to do about it.

In April of 2015, two years before I began my official foray into the self-help world, the Archbishop Desmond Tutu traveled to Dharamsala, India, for the occasion of His Holiness, the Dalai Lama's eightieth birthday. The two men—each sacred, spiritual leaders—gathered together to celebrate their friendship, reflect on their long, joyful, and challenging lives, and to answer a question that would become the foundation for their book, *The Book of Joy* (Dalai Lama and Tutu 2016).

As I listened to the men banter back and forth via audiobook, I was struck by the way the two carried on. They reminded me of eight-year-olds with the hard-earned wisdom of eighty-year-olds. They reflected on the great challenges and difficulties of their lives in prison and in exile with reverence and an unmistakable lightness—a peace and acceptance.

Every word landed like a prayer on my ears. But what's most fascinating is the lesson that stuck with me. It wasn't how to find joy in the hardest of times or to believe in the good of humanity in the face of oppression, though they talked about that, too. What stuck with me was their gentle, insistent teasing. The two verbally poked and prodded and giggled like schoolboys. It was just so damn clear how much love there was between them and how beautifully it played out as playfulness and joy.

"You know, there are cameras on us," the Dalai Lama smiled and said. "Try to act like a holy man" (Dalai Lama and Tutu 2016).

I was most struck by what felt like an offhand comment by the Dalai Lama about their playfulness. "To tease someone is a sign of intimacy and friendship," he said, "to know that there is a reservoir of affection from which we all drink as funny and flawed humans."

I replayed the idea over and over in my mind—a reservoir of affection. That's what felt wholesome about their playfulness. There was a preestablished measure of mutual love and respect. It was not simply understood but also explicitly announced and concretely demonstrated. There was love, compassion, and caring between the two men, which enabled the playful jabbing and lighthearted teasing.

It's exactly what was missing from my lifetime of teasing.

It was never mutual, which meant it never felt playful. There was no world in which I felt it would be safe or appropriate for me to respond in kind—to go around pinching my uncles' asses or to play embarrassing videos of them during the holidays. It simply wasn't an option without ridicule, reprimand, or judgment, so for me, it wasn't an option.

Teasing is only teasing when it's conducted similarly to the Dalai Lama and Desmond Tutu's—in a lighthearted, playful way, reciprocal in nature, wherein both partners give and take and do so in an attempt to make both parties laugh with no intention to harm. When a line is accidentally crossed, or one party objects or becomes upset, the behavior immediately stops and reparations are made (Coloroso 2003).

When the teasing is one-sided, it becomes taunting. The person being laughed at feels demeaned, embarrassed, and ridiculed. The behavior is often delivered with sarcasm, eye rolls, and directions to "lighten up, it's just a joke." The unwillingness to stop and make amends is an indication of the seriousness and one-sidedness rather than lighthearted, reciprocal playfulness.

When any kind of power dynamic comes into play, such as physical size difference, control over one's career or sense of belonging, or when the offender refuses to stop the behavior despite having clear indications of the harm being caused such as crying or verbal objections—it's bullying. Bullying doesn't come from a reservoir of love—it comes from the satisfaction of having the power to harm someone else.

Only after listening to the playful jabs between the two holy men and being curious and angry and confused did I realize at the ripe old age of thirty-five that what I'd experienced every Christmas was my annual family bullying.

This realization was a wake-up call for me and enabled me to get curious about all the other ways bullying and power dynamics showed up in family affairs. I remembered the aunt who was "teased" for being the baby, the youngest of seven children. The sister whose name was "teasingly" followed by a pig call. One niece who was made fun of for being a "ditz" and another a "snob." Quickly and easily, dozens of memories of men bullying women under the guise of joking flooded my system. I could not think of one instance of a woman attempting this in return.

In situations of bullying, the victim, feeling powerless, does what their coping mechanisms allow them to do. They often experience extreme stress that leads to a lack of interest in school, family, and friends, as well as a reluctance to be in public and groups for fear of bullies in other spaces. Victims suffer from stress illnesses, depression, loneliness, low self-esteem, and anxiety (Coloroso 2003).

Suddenly, it made sense why I might be silent and chronically, debilitatingly anxious. I lived in a family with a culture of bullying. It was the air I breathed. It was the water I swam in. It was the life I went to sleep in and woke up to every day. I called it "normal."

All of us live and work in cultures of bullying. We call it "normal."

While bullies and assholes come in all shapes and sizes, more often than not, we expect them to look like the bullies we see in movies, Regina Georges or Draco Malfoys, ruthless in their scrutiny. The reality is, they also come in the form of grandparents, aunts, uncles, mothers- and fathers-in-law, cousins, parents, teachers, bosses, neighbors, friends, partners, and more. And whether we experience taunting, bullying, harassment, or straight-up oppression, we, especially us women, tend to look for reasons the offending behavior was justified.

But like my family's justification that "It was just a joke, Sharon," we explain away the pain while still experiencing the very real shame of public humiliation.

"It must be my fault," we're primed and then encouraged to think. "I shouldn't have been so foolish. If I weren't so dumb/fat/frivolous/smart/stupid/old/young/slutty/prudish/loud/quiet/ambitious/lazy/kind, I could've avoided this treatment/situation/pain."

Before we have the skills and awareness to fully recognize the harm we do to ourselves and each other in this line of thinking, we function from a sort of unconscious sleep state. We do what we have to do and find ways to survive in whatever culture we're born into, whether that's a penthouse on Madison Avenue or a farmhouse outside of Madison, Wisconsin. We conform, consciously and unconsciously, changing ourselves to fit in.

In our efforts to feel better and fit in better, many of us turn to supports like self-help. Sometimes, they are helpful. Often, they reinforce the idea that the crappy way we're feeling is justified, that the treatment we received was justified, and give us their personal strategy for dealing with it in the future.

"Yes, of course you're feeling that way," self-help books seem to say. "And yes, it is your fault. But we can help you."

"Yes, obviously men are going to be dicks sometimes. That's just boys being boys! Here's what you can do to avoid their wrath while trying to get ahead in the male-dominated workplace!"

"Yes. You are absolutely too fat. Let's get you some willpower, shall we?"

"Yes, I can see you're stressed. Let's get you some meditation techniques to help you temporarily forget how stressed you are so you can get back to work."

"Yes! Your lack of confidence is holding you back! Here's how I got my confidence back while juggling my full-time modeling career, and you can, too!"

Books like this keep us asleep to the real injustices and travesties being perpetrated. Instead, they offer us more and more ways to, as Brené Brown would say, "hustle for our worthiness" (2012). Eventually, we again get that nudge, that inkling in our gut that says, "Something's not right here." We finish our twelfth fad diet, gain all the weight back, yet again, and finally realize our degrees and work ethics and the fact we've not yet killed our bosses, children, or spouses are more than enough evidence to prove we've got willpower in spades. Maybe the fact these strategies haven't been working isn't actually (all) our fault.

Or we attend our sixteenth webinar on confidence and imposter syndrome, dutifully list out all of our accomplishments, recite our affirmations in the most powerful of power poses, only for Jim or John or Chad to cut us off midsentence yet again, and finally think, "Maybe this lack of confidence thing isn't (all) my fault to begin with."

And maybe, we take a look at our social anxiety, years of fear and hypervigilance and silence, and think... yeah, no... maybe it's just not my fault at all.

So, whose fault is it?

CHAPTER 2

SOCIALIZATION

A few years ago, my husband and I attended a family wedding in picturesque Positano, Italy. My cousin's venue was perched high on the cliffs of the Amalfi Coast overlooking the Mediterranean Sea. The cool salty breeze ruffled the bouquets adorning the dinner tables and kissed our cheeks as the couple danced their first dance in the glow of golden hour. In every direction, stars and strung lights twinkled. It was magical.

The gathering was intimate—there were just twenty of us—so mingling was easy. We were never more than a few seats away from anyone, and everyone was jubilant to be celebrating the wonderful couple. Conversation flowed like wine, and laughter erupted over the sounds of the waves crashing below.

My husband, Mark, has a powerful ability to connect with people. He's innately curious, kind, and gregarious with a gentle, inviting smile and a magnetic, hearty laugh. These are some of the things I love most about him, and as predicted, he spent the evening charming everyone. So, as you might imagine, we both found ourselves bewildered and upset when I started kicking him under the table.

Had he broached a taboo topic? Was he dominating the conversation? Was he getting drunk, loud, and obnoxious? No, none of these. So what was it?

I was terrified for him. I was scared he would speak and he'd say something silly or playful and other people would think he was silly and stupid. I was afraid he'd share too much or have an unpopular opinion, and there'd be an unkind, undeserved judgment levied against him. I was fearful he'd bring up in casual conversation a topic other people didn't feel like talking about.

Why the hell was I so fearful of people judging his behaviors, especially ones I love and admire about him?

Because he had the audacity to do these things around my family. He had the gall to have opinions around my aunts and uncles. He was brazen enough to speak openly around them, to let himself be seen, and to put himself at risk of being known, and therefore, disliked.

I stomped his foot under the table, sending frantic telepathic messages that never arrived. I pleaded with him internally, "You fool! In this family we don't speak unless spoken to! What are you doing inviting this attention? You're putting us in danger!"

I silently feared for and confused the hell out of him. I praised the pope, gelato, and all things holy once speeches started. This temporary reprieve from the onslaught of potential threats let me breathe long enough to see what was happening—I was projecting all of my fears and anxieties onto him. I was shocked by his innocence and openness and saw my silence for what it was—my conditioned responses to years of bullying and trauma.

I had learned to be silent, so I could be safe.

My kick was my way of showing him the ropes as discreetly as I could, given our impending doom. The messages never arrived, but I wonder—what if they had? What would have been the best-case scenario?

Would the ideal outcome be that Mark also learns to not show up as a fully present, whole-hearted human around my family? Would success here mean letting the "adults" run the conversation while the rest of us sip our soups quietly until we can break away to safety? Is the ideal scenario really to let things play out the way they always have before?

Of course not. That's what led to decades of my own silence and abuse of alcohol.

But that's how intergenerational trauma—the trauma we learn from our families and pass down to our children—works. That's how the internalization of and participation in oppression works. They function at the unconscious level.

From the moment we are born, our well-intentioned parents and guardians try to do their very best by us. They encourage us to fix our hair, chew with our mouths closed, and be good little boys and girls. They push us to study hard and fit in. To not create too many waves or upset other people. They strive to impart the hard-earned lessons they've learned in their own lives about how to be happy, healthy, and successful.

Unfortunately, too many well-intentioned souls simply pass on the messages and strategies they've learned without stopping to question whether they are worth passing on at all. As little girls, too many of us are reprimanded by our mothers and teachers for being too hungry, too loud, too messy, too opinionated, or too brazen. Little boys are reprimanded for being too soft, too sensitive, too tender, too emotional, and too weak. We learn that's just *the way it is.*

Unless we take a good step back to see the bigger picture, we're simply passing down fears and projections from our parents, their parents, and their parents' parents. Before we know it, we're teaching our children the social constructs, expectations, fears, and projections from the 1800s. We push them onto our partners, our work colleagues, our children, our students, and our friends without giving it a single thought.

Earlier this year, I started working with a stylist. I wanted to elevate my professional image and look the part of the successful business owner I am. Together, we discussed my style choices, past and present. I lamented that since moving to Seattle, I had the double whammy of not having many clothes fit, thanks to recent weight gain, coupled with not really having any idea of what I wanted to wear.

We talked about my previous wardrobes: the jeans and Steelers hoodies I still had from growing up in Pittsburgh, the club wear and sky-high heels I had from my time in Miami, and the super preppy clothes I bought when trying to prove to my future husband I could hang with him and his bougie ass DC friends. We discussed the dozens of sheath dresses and blazers I'd amassed in DC, and the unnecessarily authentic cowboy boots I bought at a flea market in Oklahoma to fit in for my summer there, the ones that only make appearances during country music festivals these days.

We realized I've never had an actual style of my own. I'd never in my life bought an item of clothing simply because I wholeheartedly loved it or felt it expressed my style or personality. Each and every piece was a tool in my arsenal of impression management. With each addition to my wardrobe, I'd consider what impression it would leave people with and what boardroom or bedroom doors it could open for me.

Over the last few years, as I've intensified my commitment to being "my authentic self," it's meant recognizing all the ways I've shape-shifted for the sake of being accepted. Most of us are no strangers to changing ourselves to gain favor and acceptance, whether we're buying the clothes that'll help us to fit in or changing our personality to do so. This is common in the workplace, where those around us experience our "work self." We work hard to cultivate the image that we are credible, competent, and confident, even if that's not at all how we're feeling.

The companies we work for aren't helping. They encourage us to leave familial identities and responsibilities at the door. We're encouraged to abandon personal quirks, differences, and preferences in the name of "professionalism." And lately, we're even encouraged to build a "personal brand," one that is ostensibly not the same as who we really are.

And then we wonder why imposter syndrome is rampant in the workplace.

While I focused on being my authentic self, I held strongly to the question, "Who are you when you aren't trying?" I assumed you must be *who you really are*. Recently, though, I've come to realize when we're not actively contorting ourselves to fit in, we default to who we have been trained to be and call *that* our personality.

We often try to explain who we are by using labels like "perfectionist" and "introvert" to make things easier for ourselves and others. Though many assume our personalities are fixed from birth, studies show they are not (Harris et al. 2016). Instead, our personalities are most clearly expressed in how we respond in interactions with others. The circumstances we are in drastically affect how we show up, as demonstrated by my ever-evolving wardrobe. What we call our personalities are actually patterned responses to circumstances rather than a reflection of fixed identity.

A personality is one of the many components that we categorize and label to form our understanding of the self.

While no one can point to a self and science can't find it, it hasn't stopped our best thinkers in the fields of psychology, sociology, religion, and philosophy from trying to define, explore, and explain it, and self-help from trying to help it.

Some schools of thought, like Internal Family Systems, suggest we are born with an innate "self energy," or core self that is inherently calm, compassionate, confident, curious, creative, and courageous (Schwartz 2023; Schneiderman 2020). Others explain that the self, like personality, is socially emergent. Rather than being present at birth, it develops over time through social experiences (Mead 1934). The greater likelihood is that it's a combination of both. We are born with an innate sense of self that is kind, and curious, and impacted by our experiences. We come to understand "who we are" through our interactions with the world in a journey known as socialization.

Socialization is the method by which we are taught to become acceptable members of society. It is how we learn what is considered "right" and "wrong" and acquire the values, habits, beliefs, practices, and attitudes acceptable to those around us. According to Charles Cooley, former president of the American Sociological Association, we don't actually form opinions about aspects of ourselves until we come into contact with others who have opinions about us (1908). Until then, we see ourselves neutrally.

As children, we often draw, sing, and dance with wild abandon. It is only once someone labels us as "good" or "bad" at these things that we conceptualize ourselves as being a good artist, a bad singer, or a bad dancer. We then carry these beliefs and allow them to impact our behavior. If we believe we are a good drawer, we might put more effort into drawing and expect our art to be impressive. If we believe we are a bad singer or dancer, we may abandon these activities, even if we enjoy them. Unexamined, these beliefs impact us, our self-concept, and what we're willing to do forevermore.

Through socialization, we learn to compare ourselves to an ideal version of who we think we should be. Our ideals, too, are socially constructed—that is, provided by and defined by the society around us. We try to be the "right" version, the "best" version of our self, one aligned with the values given to us by our families, schools, religions, friends, and workplaces. Even when we exert our agency in our teenage years, rebelling against what we've been conditioned into, we still recognize it as a rebellion rather than an act of courageous authenticity and feel the sting of our difference. While the pressure to conform may be conscious, the majority of this happens unconsciously, even well into adulthood.

And when the context around us changes, and we leave our families of origin, attend schools with different cultures, and assimilate into the cultures of our workplaces, it makes sense we would do what we need to do to fit in. After all, we've been taught the individuals in that place will judge us based on our adherence to their values, beliefs, and attitudes about who we should be. So, we shoot the tequila, and buy the blazers, and work harder and harder, all the while telling ourselves it's exactly what we want to be doing with our lives.

We see this all the time in ourselves, our families, and our friends. The friend who takes gorgeous photos and comes alive behind the camera but downplays her work and refuses to pursue it because "that's not real life." The cousin who stopped traveling to settle down and have children because it's "just what you do."

In the US, we spend around fifteen thousand hours at school, even more if we go on to higher education. We look to schools and the education system to prepare us and empower us for full, fulfilling, and meaningful lives. While educators have the power to drastically change students' lives for the better, the educators who do are often an exception to the bureaucratic, archaic rule.

I have worked directly in nine school systems across five states and the District of Columbia as a classroom teacher, instructional coach, and school administrator. I've supported teachers in dozens more as an adjunct professor of education. I have worked for a handful of different teacher preparation programs and observed school systems in a handful of countries. Over and over, I see administrators praising silent obedience rather than active participation. Sterile classrooms are routinely favored over the organized chaos of passionate debates and riveting science experiments gone awry. And sure, those classrooms are maybe a bit louder and less predictable, but the relationships, memories, and understandings built there last a lifetime.

And I get it. As a first-year teacher, I was determined to demonstrate my effectiveness and my authority and had internalized that authority is best demonstrated as power over others. In our oppressive systems of control and hierarchy, what the person with power says, goes, or else. We sell obedience as the only way students can be successful on their end-of-year exams, which is the only way they can get into college, which is the only way they can get a decent job and be paid a decent income, which is the only way they'll be a respectable human, live a life worth living, and achieve the "American Dream."

Just like my attempt at keeping Mark safe during dinner, our educators are worried about our students' futures, and do their best to teach them the lessons that will keep them safe and successful. We end up teaching obedience and compliance in oppressive systems.

The way we led our classrooms was routinely the only way we knew. Most of us recreated our school experiences for our own students. Aside from the integration of technology and laptop-learning into some of our schools, our practices were remarkably similar to the experiences we had. Like me kicking Mark under the table, this is how socialization in the school system works—by consciously and unconsciously recreating "the way things are" or how they've always been.

Our school system hasn't changed meaningfully in hundreds of years, despite the massive evolution in technology, industry, and science. Our "industrial era schools," based on the "factory model" of education, "batch" kids by their "date of manufacture" and require them to sit quietly in rows, memorizing and regurgitating the information given to them (Robinson 2009), all in service of making them obedient and accustomed to working for someone else in the future. Rather than prioritizing collaboration and communication, the system demands attendance and compliance. Through this process, we learn to prioritize external knowledge and expectations. In turn, we learn to distrust our own intuition, wisdom, and bodily systems, as well as the earth, her wisdom, and her systems. Creativity, spirit, and different ways of thinking, knowing, learning, and demonstrating our intelligences are actively discouraged.

It's also one of the primary places of socialization via shaming in our young lives.

Shame is a devastating technique. It is first levied upon us by parents and teachers as a way to keep us in line. It teaches us there is a "right" way of being and a "wrong" way and that our love, belonging, and approval are contingent upon us being the "right" way. As Brené Brown notes, shame is the feeling we are bad, as opposed to guilt, which is the feeling of remorse that we have done something bad (2012).

Nancy Flanagan, a retired career educator, notes there's a strong urge to embarrass uncooperative students in the American edu-psyche. Teachers—this former teacher included—often resort to shaming when they are frustrated, overwhelmed, and struggling to maintain control of the classroom. Public shaming runs rampant in schools and is evidenced in the use of public behavior charts as a method of discipline and control. This type of control means less nuance, less explaining, and less back-and-forth. When using shame as a classroom management and "motivational" technique, the child is unlikely to engage in self-reflection. Instead, she will assume *she* is wrong rather than analyzing why *her behavior* was considered wrong (Flanagan 2017).

This teaches children that some people are good and others are bad. It reinforces that good children with good behavior are loved and accepted, and that noncompliance is bad and shame-worthy. It reinforces that good and bad are determined by authority figures, not something we intentionally choose and decide for ourselves.

I often think back to the students I had in the classroom who were labeled "bad." What made them "bad" was the way they made our jobs as teachers harder. They asked too many questions. They had too much energy. They let me know when I wasn't helpful, clear, or engaging. They wanted to read something else, or draw, or be playing outside. Most of the time, I was thinking, *Me too, kid, me too,* and then deducted points from their classroom character tally or dollars from their classroom store account.

I often think about one student in particular. He slept during class, was prone to outbursts of tears and anger, and received very low grades. *He's not applying himself,* we all said. *He's a smart kid, we just need him to try harder,* we told his parents. He failed and was held back as all his peers went to third grade. After he was diagnosed with dyslexia, given appropriate accommodations and the support he needed to catch up from years of inattention and blame, he began to thrive. He became my best student and best classroom leader.

He hadn't failed as a student. I had failed him as a teacher by not giving him what he needed.

As kids, we don't get all that context. Even as teachers, we often miss the message behind students' actions and just label based on how we see them and the effects they're having on our days. We train kids to respect our authority, regardless of whether or not we're doing right by them. They then go on to be employees who are expected to respect supervisors' and politicians' authority, whether or not their supervisors or politicians are doing right by them. Our socialization sticks with us.

In each new situation we encounter, whether at home, school, or church, we learn the guide-rails for social cohesion and add to our ever-evolving playbook of "how to be" while ascribing morality to conformity. We are rewarded with the promise of acceptance and success in exchange for participating in the cultures and systems as they are and living as we've been trained to.

Some norms are useful and benefit everyone, like wearing a mask during a pandemic, keeping our hands to ourselves, or letting people off the elevator before we get on. Other norms, like learning "if you don't have anything nice to say, don't say anything at all," prioritize the status quo with no real benefit other than sparing feelings and enabling bad behavior. It's important to learn the difference because the latter creates much more harm.

One deeply harmful impact of our socialization is the pressure to be perfect. Young people today feel so much pressure to succeed they adopt perfectionism as an essential requirement for achieving their goals (Curran and Hill 2019). It's only human to want to be proud of high-quality work, a commitment to excellence, and a strong work ethic. But after having known and coached so many self-proclaimed perfectionists, I now see perfectionism for what it is—a deeply ingrained need to protect ourselves from the shame of not getting it right. Our socialization encourages us to embrace perfectionism as a lifestyle in order to control the outcome in every facet of our lives. If that's the case, it seems absolutely common sense to want to do things the "right" way.

But as we know, when we commit to doing things the "right" way, we're actually committing to doing things someone else—typically the people in power—determined to be "right." This is known as paternalism. Paternalism occurs when the people in power, whether parents, teachers, bosses, or policy-makers, assume they are qualified and entitled to define "right" and "wrong" on behalf of other people. They act as missionaries and regulatory agents, converting and requiring others to subscribe to their version of the "right" way of being, thinking, and living, ostensibly for our own good.

Conformity becomes a prerequisite for acceptance by those in power; *doing* something "wrong" in the eyes of the people in power becomes synonymous with *being* "wrong."

Talk about feeling shamed.

Whether we feel better than other moms because we feed our kids organic foods, or feel better than our neighbors because we mow our lawn every week, or have a fancier car, or whatever the case may be, we are playing into the idea we need to be a certain way to be accepted and that some actions and things make you better than other people.

When we are committed to doing things "right" for the sake of being seen as the "right" kind of person, rather than because we personally believe our actions to be morally just, we are doing so as a way to prove our acceptability to society. This suggests some people are the good, right kind of people, whereas others are the bad, wrong kind of people. When we act in a way that we believe makes us better than *those other people* who are doing it "wrong," we have internalized a need for and a commitment to being superior.

A commitment to being superior to someone else is a commitment to supremacy.

If I believe thinner people are better than fatter people, wealthier people are better than poorer people, and educated people are better than uneducated people, I have internalized the beliefs of a supremacist culture. When that is the case, even subconsciously, I will do anything and everything in my power to make sure I'm one of the "good" people.

In a culture that prioritizes a single "right" way of achieving success defined by mostly white, Western standards, we're not just dealing with supremacy, we're dealing with white supremacy. The pressure to measure up to the standards put in place by an outside power in exchange for your acceptance as a human being of worth is an established manifestation of white supremacy culture (Okun 1999). This symptom of white supremacy culture is reinforced by every self-help book that encourages us to gain favor, acceptance, and success by changing ourselves.

Every book that helps you to change yourself to fit in or gain acceptance perpetuates a culture of white supremacy. By my estimation, that's nearly all of them.

We call the content of self-help books "the keys to success." The keys to success, then, are to abide by the rules that tell us how to be the "right" kind of woman in the workplace, how to get the "right" body, and how to be the "right" kind of leader. The keys to success in our culture are abiding by and passing on internalized supremacist beliefs.

As we use self-help to increase our efforts to do and be better, we become more and more socialized into this way of thinking. We become oversocialized.

Oversocialization is the result of internalizing the social norms of our society so deeply we feel nearly powerless to decide for ourselves. Stricken by conflicting "right" ways given to us by different agents of power and gatekeepers of acceptance, the binary thinking we're trained to use no longer works, rendering us paralyzed by indecision. So many of us rely so deeply on using other people's standards we become mired in anxiety, wondering what we "should" do. We call that analysis paralysis and perfectionism, and it is the result of our socialization, full of contradictions, working unconsciously below the surface of our awareness.

Many of us, especially the cisgender white folks among us, aren't told explicitly we're being trained to conform to a system and society that values some people and lives and ways of being over others. For white folks, this supremacist conditioning and how to function successfully within it is implicit. It's implied.

Others of us, though, learn this lesson explicitly and directly.

The way we are socialized to think about race is highly dependent upon the racial contexts in which we live as children and the contexts our parents created for us (Hagerman 2014). White children who spend time in primarily segregated white spaces, like I did, often do not notice their whiteness. We are brought up not talking about race, using coded language instead of explicitly discussing race, or using "colorblind" language, suggesting we "don't see color" or "we're all children of God."

For most white people, this means our socialization is invisible. We aren't trained to see it or the way power functions in our society. As with my uncle, who was never directly given permission to harass me, it wasn't explicit. It was simply "the way it is." When white children are taught to see the world through a "color-blind" lens, whiteness, and therefore, privilege and biases, become invisible and normalized. Without seeing the role privilege, belief, and bias play in one's own life, we fail to see the way they play out in our systems and structures.

In comparison, families who live in more diverse neighborhoods and send their children to more diverse schools often have more explicit conversations about race, inequity, and injustices and choose to foster critical thinking around ideas of privilege and the ways social systems, such as schools, socialize us into belief systems. Children in such families have more opportunities to learn about other people and cultures, to reflect on biases with their parents, and to more thoroughly and accurately analyze power structures, inequality, and challenges to social mobility (Hagerman 2014).

Non-white parents and parents of non-white children don't have the luxury of not addressing race, inequity, injustice, and biases. Instead, children are prepared to be aware of and cope with discrimination and to understand the racial barriers they may face. While parents may also promote egalitarian and humanitarian values, teaching their children all people are created equal, they also bring awareness to the ways they may not be treated as such, especially when a setting or event makes race highly salient, such as involvement in communities that are highly integrated or highly discriminatory (Hagerman 2014).

In 2016, I was on the leadership team of an arts-focused charter school in Washington, DC. The morning after Trump won the election, our school's executive director made it clear we were not to opine on the matter. As a publicly funded institution, we could not take sides on this. Our job was to teach our students what was happening impartially, neutrally, as objective fact.

The thing is, our school served primarily Black and brown children. Trump's win was not neutral at all. His victory had real implications on all our lives, especially our students and colleagues of color and LGBTQ+ students and colleagues. In reality, that meant just about all of us.

As I popped into classrooms that day, a typical part of my day, I was met with nervous glances from teachers. Many were creating safe spaces for their students to share deep concerns for their safety, their family's safety, and the future of the country. Young students cried and drew pictures about their fears. Older students pressed their teachers for more information. The entire building felt on edge. Not discussing the implications of the election results would not make them go away. Leaving students' fears unaddressed would only mean them having to process without the support of teachers they trusted and loved. I was expected to redirect them, but I didn't. They deserved their humanity, however inhumane the system.

Our systems, and especially publicly funded institutions, like to pretend elections and policy decisions don't have much of an impact on our daily lives. The reality is, however, they might not have much of an impact on the lives of the people protected by those same institutions. They have major implications for the lives and well-being of the people most marginalized by our society. Our teachers and students knew that immediately.

Folks of color know whether they choose to talk about racism directly or not, the effects and impacts will be there. Not shining a light directly on it does nothing to reduce the effects. In fact, it exacerbates the violence, pain, and injustice. For many of us white people, though, we hope if we don't talk about it, don't learn about it in school, and don't address the impacts in our workplaces and societal systems, it won't exist, or it'll just go away.

But that's how socialization works: it impacts us whether or not we choose to shine a light directly on it. Socialization operates under the cloak of our subconscious belief systems and ingrains itself into our interpersonal relationships and social systems. Unchecked and unexamined, our socialization seeps into all the ways we love and learn and lead without our direct consent.

And the perfect irony of socialization is we end up thinking we've made the decision for ourselves.

Most of us operate from an unconscious system we hardly recognize churning under the surface. We make decisions and believe we've made them for ourselves while totally underestimating the effects of our families, friends, churches, and schools. We tell ourselves we were born perfectionists, or we've always been workaholics, that it's just who we are. But that's our socialization talking.

Interrogating our habits, patterns, and beliefs allows us to inspect our socialization and its influence on our lives.

Rather than living on autopilot or buying into the self-help industry's messages that serve to further socialize us within these systems, we get to choose who we want to be and what we want out of life for ourselves.

We get to ask ourselves, "What do I really want?" instead of chasing what we are told we should want—the American Dream.

CHAPTER 3

AMERICAN DREAMING

I first became conscious of my culture while studying in Germany. My friends took me to an American-themed diner. We sat in giant, candy-red booths and perused the colossal plastic menus. I vibrated with the excitement of anticipation, nostalgia, and comfort food with friends. Some of my friends, however, looked absolutely queasy. Suddenly, I saw what they saw—an overwhelming number of options, most of which were fried, gigantic portions, and pages and pages of meat. I felt the shock of seeing my own culture through someone else's lens. I suddenly understood what American culture must look like from the eyes of anyone else in the world.

A few years later, I found myself studying abroad again, spending months in more than a dozen non-Western countries. This time, my culture shock came upon reentry. I popped into a grocery store to grab a loaf of bread and was absolutely overwhelmed by the sheer number of bread options on the store shelves. We'd spent time in communities whose entire grocery stores could have fit into the square footage of our bread aisles. Seeing the absolute excess of food, most of which I knew would be wasted, I broke down in tears.

My reentry from German life into the American diner and from my time exploring non-Western countries back into American grocery stores gave me the opportunity to see and experience everything anew, as if exploring someone else's country and culture for the first time. As I readjusted to life back home, I found myself feeling very aware of so many things I'd taken for granted as "how life is" before. These experiences made culture become conscious for me.

To see our culture anew is to see our socialization anew. Sometimes we benefit from explicit guidance, which is what I aim to provide in this book. Other times, disruption reveals the unfamiliar. Leaving and reentering a culture or experiencing trauma can interrupt our assumptions and give us a chance to approach our culture with fresh curiosity.

We rarely get a chance to do this while simply moving through our lives. It often takes a significant change to create the space and distance to do so. For me, it was a reverse culture shock. For others, it may be an empty nest, "hitting rock bottom," or a job change.

For many of us, it was the pandemic.

Thanks to the massive, collective disruption in our experiences, environments, and routines, the pandemic allowed us to effectively see our lives through a new lens. We recognized we saved money by not going to obligatory social outings we didn't like that much anyway, or that we had more time to spend with family without the hour commute to work. We realized our employers don't value us, or we don't love what we do, or we don't want to work at all. We realized our partners don't support us in the ways we need, or conversely, that they are our rock during hard times. We collectively had the opportunity, invitation, and in some cases, requirement to slow down, stay home, and pay attention to our lives in ways we hadn't before.

Many of us realized we spend a third of our lives toiling away in jobs on behalf of other people's dreams, making other people money, and missing out on living our own lives. This interruption of "life as usual" allowed many of us to realize we've been sleepwalking through our lives and living them according to other people's standards and expectations. Many of us are realizing the American Dream isn't actually our dream at all. It's not my dream, and it's not necessarily your dream. It was one given to us through our socialization.

We are, in fact, American Dreaming.

The first time I met Mark's parents, I was ridiculously nervous. He and I had very different childhoods. I grew up on the cusp of poverty in the Rust Belt. He grew up affluent in the Silicon Valley. I was terrified they'd smell my poverty and assume I wasn't a worthy partner. I remember trying to play things off, as if I belonged in the conversations and in the family, while the whole time being both excessively self-conscious and taking furious mental notes.

I wanted to learn how I could be wealthy, too. And if there was an opportunity to learn from actual wealthy people, I wanted to take advantage of it. Mark may come and go, but those lessons would be with me until death do us part.

I wanted to know what they talked about at the dinner table, how they made decisions, what they cared about, and what secrets they knew about success. I wanted to learn to be like them.

I grew up as many of us had, surrounded by the promises and lure of rags-to-riches the American Dream is famous for. I thought, if only I could be more like them, I could *be* more *like them*. I wanted to believe if I tweaked my priorities, or read the right newspapers, or thought about things the right way, I could make it, too. I started studying people like a self-help researcher might, looking for cheat codes to help me win big. I thought if only I could learn what the right clothes were, I could buy them, and the right people would see me as *one of them* and welcome me into their social circles, businesses, and heck, even families.

And then, I studied friends who were trying out their own versions. I watched some friends add "a touch of gray" to give themselves an air of refinement and a leg up in business while others covered their grays so they could stay young and attractive and promotable. I watched women hide their pregnancies from their employers so they wouldn't be fired or looked over for a promotion. I watched men parade around their wives and children so they'd be seen as trustworthy and dependable. We're all just trying to be in control.

The idea that our character, disposition, and individual actions are entirely responsible for our successes are a huge part of both our socialization and the mythology surrounding the American Dream. We need to believe we can overcome poverty to achieve wealth, escape oppressive living conditions to find happiness, and transcend obscurity to find fame and fortune. This hope keeps the American Dream alive, and the promise keeps us working our tails off.

To believe we are in complete control means with the right efforts, we can have everything we've ever wanted. We want it so badly we will overlook mounting evidence about the impact of contextual factors in order to be able to attribute folks' success to their character, disposition, and individual actions. This is what psychologists call misattribution error, the tendency to attribute to the individual that which may be more accurately attributed to circumstance.

For rich folks, this is a boon. In a culture where self-worth is measured by net worth, rich people get to say their wealth and success are of their own creation. "All it took was hard work and dedication," they claim, even if they also began with a massive head start. This cultural belief system also soothes the guilt of having so much while others have so little; they get to chalk it up to effort and encourage others to just work harder.

This is what Professor Siegrist of the University of Düsseldorf calls the effort-reward imbalance (Szalavitz 2018). The effort-reward imbalance aims to describe the effects of unjust compensation: we can do a little and receive a lot, or we can do a lot and receive too little; our efforts don't necessarily equal our reward. The super-rich, feeling the conflict, take solace in the justification they've earned every penny, even if they haven't. The poor, also feeling the conflict, take solace in the belief that if they just worked harder, they too could achieve the American Dream. There's hope.

This internal misattribution error not only allows the rich to ignore the privilege and effects of things like inherited capital, social capital, and systemic advantages but also blame those who don't experience wealth for their own circumstances. The working class, poor individuals, and people receiving social support are blamed for being poor, for not working hard enough, and for not "picking themselves up by their bootstraps" regardless of how hard they actually work.

Ironically, only in the past few generations has this phrase come to mean "doing whatever you have to do to make it without any help from anyone else." In the 1800s, the phrase was used mockingly to describe something knowingly impossible, "as gross an absurdity as he who attempts to raise himself over a fence by the straps of his boots" (Kristof 2020). Despite describing absurdly impossible acts, it has unironically become part of American mythology. Similarly, terms like "welfare queen" are created to stereotype and vilify poor women, especially single mothers of color, despite the majority of recipients being white (Cammett 2014).

More often, though, the second case Professor Siegrist outlines is true: folks do too much and receive too little in compensation (Szalavitz 2018).

In a study on the health of the American Dream, participants from twenty-seven countries were studied to determine their *beliefs* about socioeconomic mobility compared to the *actual* socioeconomic mobility in their country. The study found that people in the United States believed in the existence of a meritocracy more than any other nation in the world, and data indicates the belief is actually getting stronger over time. We're more certain we'll be rewarded for our individual effort and skills than people in other countries (Isaacs 2008).

Growing evidence, however, suggests we have less economic mobility in the US than in other industrialized countries. Unfortunately, most US citizens who are born on the bottom rung of the wealth ladder will stay on the bottom while most folks born on the top rung will stay on top.

As Michael Hout, Professor of Sociology at NYU, noted, many Americans falsely believe they have more social mobility in the US than they would in other countries. He says our circumstances at birth, especially our parents' occupations, shape our futures much more than we previously thought. The US doesn't necessarily live up to its image as the land of opportunity (2018).

Despite the American Dream being unrealistic or unattainable for most of us, everyone I know is doing their very, very best to thrive in our broken system with all of the tools at our disposal. The tools of choice are most often a combination of education, hard work, self-control, and self-help.

On paper, I am evidence the American Dream works. My great-grandparents were immigrants. I received a college education despite neither of my parents having done so, and went on to earn my masters as well as certificates in executive leadership coaching and leadership studies from Georgetown University and Harvard University. I had a successful career in education before launching my own businesses, and each of my businesses surpassed one hundred thousand dollars in revenue in their first two years. I have a husband who loves me, a cute little condo in a beautiful neighborhood in Seattle, and a passion for travel, which I do often.

In theory, I have it made. It's everything I always thought I wanted. Yet rather than reveling in the contentedness of having achieved the American Dream, I spend the vast majority of my time dreaming about retirement and nothingness.

My first few years as a working professional, I contemplated suicide as the only viable way to get out from the mountains of student debt I was under. I owed various lenders more than a hundred thousand dollars but had pennies left after my bills were paid. Despite being on income-based repayment, the monthly payment felt overwhelming and impossible. I couldn't understand how other people could afford groceries, let alone bottle service in South Beach to blow off steam after a long week of teaching in Miami. I was so painfully afraid my new friends and colleagues would judge me for being poor that I said nothing while I quietly calculated what I'd need to cut to be able to justify a day out with friends. I made loan payment after loan payment while watching my principal and interest remain nearly unchanged month after month. I was constantly tired and perpetually broke. My life felt utterly hopeless and my efforts ultimately useless.

Now, more than fifteen years later, those problems have been replaced with newer, shinier ones. I've been able to replace my hundred-thousand-dollar student loans with a half-million-dollar home loan, but I still feel trapped in the incessant rhythms of work-chores-sleep. I fear no matter how much I work and save and invest in my retirement, our economy will tank and it'll all be gone, and there'll be nothing I can do about it. I protest and vote and recycle and scroll through the news telling me that even if I live a perfectly sustainable life, corporate interests will still doom our planet. My life still feels pretty hopeless and my efforts ultimately useless.

Most of us learned in school that the American Dream was the United States' unique value proposition as a country: everyone is welcome here, and everyone has a chance to thrive.

"And it's true!" American Dreamers will tell me. "You're living proof!"

But a few things are true.

First, I am more of an anomaly than the average. People will point to me as evidence it can work for everyone without recognizing the incomprehensible number of people who work just as hard without the results to show for it. I also have massive amounts of nonmonetary privileges that have made sure my uphill battle wasn't any harder. I have not been discriminated against because of my skin color, religion, sexual orientation, or abilities. I am tremendously fortunate to have a mother who would do literally anything to make sure I had what I needed to be successful. I had the privilege of access to decent public schools as a child and friends who have supported my business and book launches through crowd-funding support. Even a quick peek under the hood demonstrates how non-self-made I am. I have worked hard, and I am community made.

Secondly, the American Dream I'm living out is a holdover from the 1950s. Since World War II, the concept of the American Dream has been co-opted so thoroughly by brands and marketing that it's virtually unrecognizable. Our perception of success has been so fully hijacked by brands that even when we're meeting an earlier definition of success, it no longer feels like success.

Prior to World War II, one was sufficiently successful with a partner, a house, a stable job, and enough disposable income to cover the necessities and maybe a few extras. And this was often doable on just one income. As our means of production became increasingly automated, however, workers who had been relatively hands-on and connected to their work product were replaced by machines and efficient processes. The quality of the products became relatively high and relatively standardized across the board while becoming less expensive to produce. The average American family could afford all their necessities.

The manufacturing jobs that were no longer needed were replaced by jobs in marketing. Quality was no longer sufficient to set one's company and product apart, and the shift from selling a product to selling a lifestyle began. As a result, since the 1950s, companies have focused more and more heavily on selling a promise, a hope, and a way of life. Coca-Cola could no longer simply sell soda—other companies were making equally high-quality sodas, and the product provided no health benefit—so they began selling nostalgia and a relationship with an anthropomorphized brand that would enhance customers' self-image.

I notoriously do not like or care about technology. That didn't stop me from diving into the world of iPhones in 2017 so I could join the ranks of the yuppies who saw themselves as more attractive, sophisticated, and techie than the average cell phone user (Peterson 2020). Achieving the American Dream wasn't just about having a phone—it was about having the phone that would allow me to be associated with wealth. By buying an iPhone, I saw a way to buy entry into that world. Never mind that it was a hand-me-down, I got to join that club.

In today's version of the American Dream, it's no longer enough to have our needs met. We now need to buy and find satisfaction in the things that confirm and demonstrate our success, wealth, and prestige to others. We're expected to find happiness in excess and image.

It seems so obvious. If we have more, our lives will be better. If we get a fun thing, we'll have more fun. If we have more money, we'll feel wealthier. If we pursue pleasure, we'll feel pleasure. Unfortunately, studies show humans are far too adaptable for that to be true.

Humans return to a relatively stable level of happiness throughout our lifetimes. When we make more money, for instance, our spending often increases at the same rate as our income, and former luxuries become perceived as necessities. What used to be novel and exciting becomes normal, our expectations rise, and we experience no long-term gain in happiness. Having an iPhone used to be a big deal. Now it's just my phone.

Furthermore, constant pleasure-seeking may not actually bring about happiness, at least for folks in the US. This is for two reasons. First, folks in the US typically pursue happiness by seeking happiness and pleasure for themselves. Citizens in Russia and East Asia, on the other hand, attempt to increase their personal happiness by serving other people—and are successful in doing so (Ford et al. 2015). Secondly, constantly pursuing pleasure and happiness interferes with actually experiencing it. We might give up on something worthwhile but challenging because it's not fun *yet*, or we might be swept out of the present, happy moment by deliberating how to make things *more* enjoyable or focusing on what *next* thing will bring us *more* happiness.

Neither of these facts stop the marketers from pushing us to spend more to feel happier. We're convinced the perfect wardrobe, newest tech, and fancy homes will bring us happiness even though we know—and often tell others—the truest joy and long-term happiness comes from serving and connecting with others.

At the height of my American Dream success story, I'd just gotten a promotion and a raise and was making twice the salary I'd received in Florida. Moving in with Mark had reduced my living expenses enough for us to go to boozy brunches with our friends and out to dinner every Wednesday on what would become our date night tradition. I started getting monthly manicures and weekly therapy sessions. Our friends still laughed at our frugality, but I felt like I was living the yuppie dream.

While my life looked good on paper, I really needed that weekly therapy session. Most nights, I'd be up responding to work emails until 2 a.m. and back on the bus to work by 6 a.m. My work stress came home with me, and Mark and I were fighting about everything. My boozy brunches with friends typically involved drinking an entire bottle of cheap champagne by myself, followed by entire Sundays spent nursing pounding headaches and hangovers while working on lesson plans.

Ah, yes—the real American Dream: work hard, play hard. Glorify overwork and high-functioning alcoholism. That's how you know you've made it.

But, of course, it still wasn't good enough. We wanted to get married, and the average wedding was nearly thirty thousand dollars (The Knot 2023). We wanted to buy a home, and prices for starter homes began at four hundred thousand dollars in the area. We constantly had a new goal, so the finish line kept moving. The promised land always seemed to live just over the next horizon. We needed to somehow earn more or spend less to save for them and *finally* be happy.

I looked at how hard I was already working and wondered how I could work any harder. I took a look at people with houses, and cars, and good god—kids!—and wondered how they could be that much smarter and harder working than me. I took a look at our relatively frugal lifestyle and wondered if we were being extravagant, knowing that cutting back any more would strip us of the few joys we actually spent money on.

I continued to fall prey to internal misattribution error, assuming I wasn't doing enough or wasn't doing it right, and that it was all my fault. I'd head back to my goals and the drawing board and double down. I'd commit to working harder, doing more, and doing whatever it took to get ahead. I'd pop Xanax to make it through the day, and pop open a bottle of wine as soon as I got home. Every moment, even the happiest ones, were plagued by anxiety and foreboding joy. I couldn't enjoy my life in the moment because I was constantly striving for more.

The harder we work toward the American Dream, the harder it is to be happy. For folks struggling at the bottom of the socioeconomic ladder, we feel the immense shame of not being good enough by our society's standards and the weight of feeling like our lack of "success" is all our fault. For those at the top of the economic ladder, we feel the weight of knowing we have not worked proportional to our income and face the realization that the material things we have don't bring us the happiness we hoped it would.

But realizing it's all a dream has an upside: we can wake up.

CHAPTER 4

SELF-HELP IS INEVITABLE

For my thirty-fifth birthday, I decided to put my vision for retirement to the test by vacationing at Lake Stevens outside of Seattle. We started the trip with a kayaking excursion, admiring the abundant natural scenes around us. Over the course of a few hours, we explored the entirety of the lake, pausing to marvel at ducks as they navigated the water lilies and a bald eagle as he devoured his catch of the day atop a neighboring boat house. We cruised along the coast, admiring the expansive gardens adorning the waterfront mansions.

Ugh, would you look at those terraces? I mused. *Are those Greek statues? Oh my god—does that guest house have its own guest house?*

The more wealth I noticed, the more wealth I saw until I stopped watching the wildlife altogether. I only noticed the stunning architecture and the gnawing pit in my stomach. Sure, our rental was fine. But did you see that garden? Did you see the terrace on the boat house? How fun would it be to have our friends over for a barbeque on that roof deck!

As I sat down to write for the afternoon, I caught myself engaging in one of my favorite anxiety-fueled pastimes, something I call "aspirational math." I Zillowed nearby properties and divided their million-dollar price tags by my hourly rate to determine how many hours I'd have to work to afford the new home. I calculated the number of clients I'd need to serve and the number of years it'd take to get there.

In some cases, it would take literal lifetimes.

Any other day, if you'd ask me about my dreams, I'd tell you all about the tiny A-frame I fancied along a creek, or the old stone cottage I'd restore, or the cute little home on a lake where we'd ride the waves of the seasons. I'd tell you about my desire to wake with the sun and write in the wee, misty hours of the morning, wrapped in blankets and sipping hot tea. I'd tell you how excited I am to learn to garden, and grow my own food, and be a good steward of the land, and pick everything we need for lunch out of our backyard. I'd tell you about the hours and hours I'll sit on the water's edge, naming ducklings and making friends with squirrels.

But placed in an environment of big, showy homes, I felt powerless and small. My quaint visions of living close to nature felt crunchy, homely, and lazy. I felt plebeian and resentful of myself for setting my sights so low.

I imagined the condescension of people I didn't even know, whose opinions I didn't actually care about, and I was frozen with shame.

We often base our self-respect and self-worth on how we believe others see us, comparing ourselves to their values instead of our own. When I do not have a robust enough social circle to remind me of my inherent value as a person and of *my* priorities in life, I am vulnerable to the shame that comes from comparisons to countless others, some real and some imagined.

It is a deeply painful and confusing experience. To feel less worthy than another human being—even on a metric we do not inherently care about—hurts. The potential for disconnection and isolation feels immense. Shame makes us fearful we'll be rejected by others and leaves us feeling inadequate and alone. We will do anything to avoid this level of pain and disconnection.

We feel the pull between wanting to do our own thing and wanting to feel up to par with society's standards for success. Most of us strive to meet society's collective expectations and standards, even when we say this is not the biggest influence in our lives simply because the shame associated with being different, and therefore ostracized, is too great. We look to the tools we've been told would help us in the past: hard work, drive, and education.

For decades, women and people of color have been told education was the answer—the great equalizer. We've been told if we just studied hard, applied ourselves, and got our education, we could achieve equality with white men and live out our version of the American Dream.

I believed in this promise so thoroughly I committed the first ten years of my career to the idea. I taught and served in schools in historically oppressed and systemically under-resourced communities. Embarrassingly and regretfully, I was naïve enough to believe that with the right academic support, the rest of the community's problems would solve themselves.

As more and more of us do exactly as we've been told to do, though, we realize the education we were promised would help us is woefully inadequate. Not only does it not fully prepare us to be successful, conscious, functioning adults in today's society, it is wildly insufficient for overcoming the immense systemic and structural barriers marginalized folks and communities face. In fact, the use of property taxes to fund local schools means our policies are set up to perpetually reinforce and exacerbate these structural barriers.

As we discussed in chapter 2, schools socialize us toward antiquated expectations and antiquated jobs. They prioritize compliance, obedience, and adherence to standards over innovation, creativity, resourcefulness, and emotional intelligence. We graduate with fancy diplomas and expensive degrees but without the necessary problem-solving and leadership skills required for today's economy. We graduate without a basic understanding of how to navigate our systems or a satisfactory answer to life's most basic question: "How should we live?"

We see our lack of upward social mobility and stagnating wages and, assuming it's all our fault, do our best to be resourceful. Accustomed to religions and schools that teach us to defer to all-knowing authority figures, we do what we have been trained to do and look to the experts. We put our trust in the people we're told know better than we do—from doctors and authors to self-proclaimed lifestyle gurus. The less upward mobility exists, the more resourceful we need to become, and the more we turn to outside sources for help. We find self-help. We treat self-help as a manual for navigating the American Dream, looking for answers to help us understand why it isn't working and what we can do about it.

Self-help steps into the void between our preparation and aspiration and offers answers.

The term "self-help" originated in the 1800s in a purely legal context, suggesting one could help themselves to right a wrong done to them by any lawful means at one's disposal (Carlyle 1831). In essence, self-help was used as a way to enforce one's own rights, especially when the law may not have served justice or served it in the way you liked. Self-help was used as a way for injured parties to take the law into their own hands.

In some respects, we've simply expanded its scope. We use self-help as a way for parties not served by any system—whether law, medical, social, or otherwise—to take their lives into their own hands.

In that way, the self-help industry is the bastard stepchild of the American Dream and our awful marketing system. The self-help industry reassures us, saying, "Those other things didn't work out, but you can still be as successful as your wildest dreams! The only thing stopping you is you. Let me show you how." We find the folks who confirm what we've been banking on all along: success is totally within reach. We just have to make it happen for ourselves.

Critics of the genre love to attribute the popularity of self-help books to how self-obsessed and helpless current generations are (Salerno 2005; Storr 2018). Books of this kind, though, have been around as long as the written word itself because the desire for guidance and lack of self-trust have existed equally as long.

Thousands of books have been published educating the average person on social norms and how to be. Such books were extraordinarily popular throughout the eighteenth century and known as conduct books or conduct literature. Like religions and modern self-help books, conduct books promote specific ideologies. Though they weren't all explicitly religious or political in nature, conduct books, like self-help books today, often had religious and political biases, promoted political ends, and enshrined ways of being that became a sort of "natural law," or common ideology for how to be without noting where their influences came from.

American conduct books pre-1900 were generally written for inexperienced young adults. Like most self-help today, they described and prescribed morals, appropriate behavior, and gender norms for their white, middle-class readers. They created and regulated desire and served as an authority on life. Men were expected to value ambition, self-reliance, self-improvement, honesty, and punctuality, and exhibit discernment regarding their choice of friends and wives. Women were expected to value domesticity, education, and the ascribed feminine qualities of cheerfulness, humility, and submission, including to one's duties to husband, children, and home.

In "Conduct Books for Women, 1830–1860," author Jane Rose shares that many of the conduct books of the time centered the topics of women's domestic, religious, and wifely duties, health, fashion, dating, mental improvement, education, conversation, and harmonious marital relationships (1995). They set limits to women's autonomy, literacy, and vocations. They glorified what was known as the "Republican Motherhood," the belief before, during, and after the American Revolution that patriots' wives and daughters were responsible for upholding ideals of republicanism: liberty, individual rights, and sovereignty (Kerber 1976, 187–205). This usage of the word "Republicanism" refers to its usage during that time wherein "republic" was synonymous with "representative democracy" and women were tasked with their part in ensuring the success of "the Republic," or the fledgling, nonmonarchical country.

Women were expected to be custodians of civic virtue and religion. While the belief system reinforced the longstanding separation of men in the public sphere and women in the domestic sphere, it newly encouraged the education of women and valued their investment in building the country, infusing a new dignity that had been lacking in women's work.

This valuing of domesticity for women became known as the "Cult of Domesticity" or the "Cult of True Womanhood." They defined what a "true woman" was: she is white and middle class. Black, working class, and immigrant women were intentionally excluded as they weren't considered "true women" in the sexist, racist, classist culture of the time. A "true woman" was expected to be the center of her family, a pillar of strength and virtue, yet frail, delicate, weak, and dependent on the men in her life to protect and shelter her. She is fit, active, involved in her community, accomplished artistically, and educated, yet completely reliant on her husband for resources and money. She works hard, yet may receive no compensation for her labor (Smith-Rosenburg 1998; Welter 1966).

These books, like all self-help books, reflect their historical context. They provided clear answers to the question of "how to live" that reflect the behaviors deemed appropriate and acceptable, bolstered by the beliefs and norms of the times.

It's the same with self-help books today. What we see on the shelves is a perpetual, real-time reflection of our collective anxieties, concerns, and challenges, as well as the best answers we have for dealing with them. Next time you're in your local library or bookstore, notice how the titles on the shelves reflect contradictory belief systems about who women should be, even today. Titles over the years reflect the different waves of feminism and what it looked like to be the "right" kind of woman during each era. Notice both the conflicting advice within each era as well as the evolution over time.

The year 1961 brought us Charlene Johnson's *Beautiful Homemaking*, a guide for good Christian women who want to access heaven via a tidy home and decent Midwestern meals (Kelly 2019). In 1965, Arlene Dahl encouraged women to be helpless and pretty in *Always Ask a Man: The Key to Femininity* (Kelly 2014). Compare these titles to Chimamanda Ngozi Adichie's 2014 *We Should All Be Feminists,* Sonya Renee Taylor's 2018 *The Body Is Not an Apology,* and Florence Given's 2020 *Women Don't Owe You Pretty.*

The titles on the shelves appear to be changing before our eyes because the world is changing rapidly, and our problems far exceed what our socialization has given us as solutions. We still need to know how to live. As we see a rise in technology, data, metrics, and optimization, we also observe an increase in books advising us to optimize the self using apps, trackers, and the quantification of results. We're implored to optimize and even "hack" the self. We are encouraged to "biohack" our biology and "neurohack" our brains. As consumerism kicks into ever higher gears, we're able to watch in real time advertisers promoting new things to be dissatisfied with so they can sell us happiness through new things. Self-help does the same, sensationalizing and cherry-picking "research" to reveal secret new problems we didn't even know we needed to care about, just so they can sell us a solution.

I like to think I'm not writing a self-help book, rather a book shedding new light on a longstanding problem, creating new awareness and consciousness that will help us to eliminate the problem at its source. But who am I kidding? I hope this book helps you. And in the process, I'm giving you something else to care about; something you might not have seen as a problem in the past, yet another problem to solve.

In my writing process, I spend a lot of time thinking about the best ideas, examples, and solutions I have to offer. Even in critiquing the self-help industry and attempting to share with you what I think are more constructive ways forward, I am neither immune to its impact, nor sure I have a better way to share my thoughts with you than through the vehicle of self-help. I find myself in moments of writer's block, being so aware of how this book, too, is a reflection of the times, the needs, and the strategies we have available for dealing with them.

I'm grappling with so many tensions—wanting to give us a way to take life into our own hands while recognizing I'm asking us to solve yet another problem; the desire (and pressure) to provide guidance and wisdom, thereby putting myself in the place of being yet another external source of information; taking a big gamble in even participating in the genre as I expose it and opening myself up for critique, too.

It's risky, but it's worth it to me because the titles on today's shelves reveal readers still care deeply about how we are perceived and want guidance on how to get it "right." We want to know how to get ahead at work, how to lose weight, how to find a partner, and how to get rich. But one of the biggest problems in self-help is that our solutions are being written through the same thinking that caused the problems in the first place. Books and authors that encourage us to change ourselves to gain favor, acceptance, and success don't help us to transcend our systems, only navigate them.

These books reach an incredibly large audience. In 2021, the personal development industry was estimated to be worth nearly forty-two billion US dollars. Research indicates the industry will be worth an unimaginable sixty-seven billion in 2030 (Grand View Research 2022). Folks who believe they have figured out the American Dream and others who are ready to die trying will do anything to sell you their solutions.

But here's the truth: self-help stands on a bed of oversimplified, faulty foundations.

It stands on the premise of the American Dream and the belief that life is entirely within our control, which means it is entirely our fault if things aren't working out for us. Self-help suggests we can fix everything ailing us with the author's wisdom, and that if we try hard enough, everything we want will be at our fingertips. While we can control some things in our lives, too much self-help neglects the bigger picture, the complexity and interconnectedness of our systems, and the realities of the big bad world outside. It's myopic and singularly focused to the point of oversimplification.

The American Dream is unrealistic. Self-help as an industry was inevitable.

With the right support, we can achieve great things. But so much is outside of our control—from tremendous systemic and institutional barriers to simple luck of the draw. To suggest we could simply buy a few self-help books and magically be able to afford a multimillion-dollar lake house adorned with Greek statue-lined terraces or overcome generations of trauma and decades of socialization is unconscionable—yet somehow exactly what I'd expect of someone selling manuals for the American Dream.

The unquestioned pursuit of the American Dream is keeping us far too busy to reflect on it and consider for ourselves whether it's a worthwhile goal at all. We ignore evidence about its unattainability while reassuring ourselves *we* are different. *We* are willing to work harder than everyone else, so it'll work for *us*. We delay joy and happiness in exchange for the promise of a future when we can finally have everything we've ever wanted.

We throw ourselves into solutions like self-help without stopping to ask: "Is it even working?"

SECTION II

AWARENESS

CHAPTER 5

IT'S NOT WORKING

Even when we do everything "right," we are "wrong."

My first real, true, committed foray into self-help began when I started dating my now husband. I was desperate to know what a woman was supposed to be like in order to keep her partner's interest. I bashfully read Sherry Argov's *Why Men Love Bitches* on my Kindle during my morning commutes.

I'd read through the no-nonsense, crystal clear, exacting language about who I was supposed to be to win my man's love and respect. I made mental notes to try this and experiment with that. *If men date bitches*, I thought, *well, it's time to become a bitch.*

If I'm being honest, I've always wanted to be a bitch.

I imagined reveling in not caring what others thought. I daydreamed of saying things I was thinking without fear. I pictured a powerful woman, who you didn't dare cross. She wore an immaculately tailored black blazer and pencil skirt with sky-high heels that didn't hurt and dark sunglasses that barely hid her unimpressed expression. I fantasized I'd one day be her. Impervious to insult. Unaffected. Unbothered. Imperturbable.

As a little girl, I was just terrible at it. I would get into arguments with my mother, go to sleep, and totally forget to hold a grudge against her the next day, as bitches are supposed to. I took to scrawling "YOU'RE MAD AT MOM" on a Post-it Note I hung on the backside of my bedroom door before sleep. A self-help note, perhaps. I'd wake up, read it, and try to remember throughout the day.

When middle school and high school came around, the energy required to hold all the grudges I was supposed to hold was overwhelming. Eventually, I gave up. The desire made a reappearance, however, when I enrolled in college. Penelope Trunk, via the website *Brazen Careerist,* reminded me I wasn't there to be liked; I was there to get ahead. I fashioned myself in the image I held of success and wore a blazer and heels to class most days. Instead of looking like a bad bitch on a mission, I looked responsible and nerdy in my librarian glasses and clunky Target heels. My professors loved me. "Mission: Bitch" failed again.

When the possibility of love finally came around, though, I made a commitment. I promised myself this time I would do it. I would follow through. This would be my year: *I would finally learn how to be a bitch!*

I was twenty-seven years old. I had just moved to Washington, DC, to be with my boyfriend and was painfully aware of my lowly social status as an elementary school teacher as I commuted on trains next to Hill staffers from elite universities who looked every bit of the professional bitch I aspired to be. The women were mostly young, white, and blonde and looked the part of my powerful woman archetype. I assumed they were all rich, happy, and had brunch plans. I, on the other hand, felt like a little kid playing dress-up. I felt poor, lonely in my new city, and very, very not good enough.

In my conception of womanhood, I had two choices: to be the rich bitch, happy, successful, and unbearably sexy with friends and lovers aplenty or to be a common woman, chubby, drabby, and poor, a powerless pawn in the chess game of life.

If self-help books are to be trusted as an accurate mirror to reality, they, too, would have me believe those were my only options. Both acknowledge women's unfavorable position in the patriarchal hierarchy and indicate we have a choice: we may either adjust ourselves to gain economic parity and therefore equality with men, or we are doomed to live sad, powerless lives. Because we have a choice, self-help feels like empowerment. We are given options to cope with our inevitable, unenviable situation as women as we try on a new lifestyle as a form of resistance.

I took to self-help for exactly that reason. I appreciated authors that leveled with me, reminded me I wasn't alone in feeling less-than, and promised me salvation. This promise was dependent on my renunciation of myself in pursuit of a femininity that was equal parts femme fatale and brazen careerist. I could be successful, if only I changed everything about myself.

This, I was led to believe, was the best way to make sure we were given a seat at the table. The table was, of course, still owned and operated by men, but if I played my cards right, I could show them I was smart and hardworking enough to be there but not so strong of a threat I'd usurp anyone's position. After all, girls can't be threatening when we're smiling, can we?

But the double bind of being a woman is there's no way to do it "right" by our society's standards. What is "right" is socially constructed—neither objective fact, nor universally agreed upon. As a result, when you're meeting one person's standards for being driven enough, you're failing someone else's standards for being family-oriented enough. When you're effectively assertive to one person, you might be domineering or controlling to another. Beyond the conflicting opinions of individuals, what this really points to is the collective belief that to be a woman is to simply be wrong.

We're told we need to be stronger, skinnier, more confident, less stressed, more relaxed, and somehow able to accomplish more and more every day. Mothers are expected to be superwomen, balancing work, motherhood, household duties, and wifely duties without stress. Those who choose to do so without complaint are seen as the gold standard and complimented for taking on the responsibilities and burdens without acknowledging how unfair and unequal the distribution of labor is. We focus on how "she can do it all," rather than acknowledging she shouldn't have to do it all on her own.

Those of us who can't live up to this unrealistic standard—which is, of course, most of us—struggle with feeling like failures. Hell, even those of us who outwardly exhibit the signs of meeting the standard struggle with feeling like failures *and* frauds for leading people to believe our lives are perfect when they aren't. What many of us just aren't realizing is that we're not failures—no one can live up to these expectations alone.

In Western culture, femininity itself is marked as problematic and in need of change. Femininity is pathologized, especially in self-help. To be a woman in society is to be scrutinized and deemed inadequate in every way—from how we eat, to how we dress, how we look, how we participate in relationships, and how we show up in the workplace and in the home. To be a woman is to constantly be failing in some regard.

Lucky us! Typically, there's a book you can turn to for direction in each of these topic areas—usually dozens if not hundreds. Most of them are in utter conflict as to the right way to be.

Because in a society that centers men, and the preferences and gaze of the man, the correct way to be a woman is, in fact, to be *wrong*. To be a woman is to be *The Second Sex* (de Beauvoir 2012). It is to be the Other. In a cultural belief system wherein everyone who is not a rich able-bodied straight white man occupies a position of social inferiority, no amount of changing ourselves will be good enough for the people in power (read: those same rich white men) to consider the rest of us "good enough."

There will always be a new reason we're not good enough to be considered equal—and none of it has anything to do with us. The power structures created by white supremacy rely on the myth of meritocracy and our belief that if we just met the right standards, we would finally be deserving of respect and equality. Each time we meet the bar, those in power push it a little farther away, point to our continued inadequacy, and use that to explain why we aren't yet good enough.

From birth, we're told, "boys will be boys." Girls, however, are to change themselves in every way in order to be accepted and worthy (Gonick 2004). Our wildness is tamed by the empty promises of likability and acceptance that will never truly come—acceptance will always be conditional. Conditional acceptance will always depend on our self-domestication, self-restraint, self-control, and self-doubt.

And self-help will roll with the ever-changing finish line and continue to thrive as a result. Self-help gives all of us, men and women alike, increasingly invasive ways to control ourselves for the sake of being good enough to finally be accepted in our society. Those of us who have tried it all know: No amount of force, trying, or control will be sufficient. No amount of changing ourselves will be enough. No amount of self-help will convince us or anyone else of our equality and worthiness who doesn't already see us as equal and worthy.

Because the truth is, we can't earn equality or acceptance or belonging by changing ourselves. We will never be able to contort ourselves enough for someone to accept us because the version of us they accept *isn't actually us*. To make matters worse, the acceptance is not only conditional but also temporary because as soon as we meet expectations, the expectations change. Society evolves, what it means to be the "right kind of man" or the "right kind of woman" changes, and self-help seizes the opportunity to sell us a new strategy.

Self-help by its nature keeps us striving to meet unrealistic, conflicting, mercurial standards grounded in the not-good-enough-no-matter-what-we-do belief system we all swim in. Self-help won't convince men to pay women equally. Self-help won't convince white people to share power. Self-help won't change the belief systems keeping some people hoarding power and others hustling for worthiness.

When the *right* way to be in the eyes of people in power is *wrong*, when they only accept you because you acknowledge your inferiority, self-help just won't help.

In retrospect, I realize my efforts to win my now husband's affection were entirely in vain. As each facade and contortion fell away, and I became more and more authentic, I realized he had accepted me in spite of my efforts to win him over, not because of them.

As if true love and acceptance could exist any other way.

But that message is unfulfilling and won't easily comfort those of us struggling with self-acceptance. It also won't keep us buying books.

The fact there's no right way to be a woman isn't a bug in the self-help system—it is a feature.

When I was very young, I remember my grandmother describing other women as "big" or "heavy." She meant fat, but she was a good, kind woman who would never use such *demeaning* words. When I was four or so, my mother told me I was "too heavy" for her to carry around. In all reality, her "too heavy" was likely literal. She just couldn't hold me anymore. My young brain did not catch the distinction. I've been self-conscious of my body ever since.

When I was around ten years old, I learned the following formula: to determine what your weight should be as a woman, start with one hundred pounds, and add five pounds for each inch of height you stand over five feet tall. As a five-foot-five woman, I was supposed to be 125 pounds. I'm not sure I have ever been 125 pounds. I have, though, from a young age, always been incredibly powerful. I began lifting weights on my brother's weight machine during middle school and beamed with pride when a member of the varsity football team asked me how I got my triceps so jacked.

My clean bill of health and athletic prowess, however, did not stop my pediatrician, gynecologist, or therapists over the years from noting my BMI put me in the "overweight" range. Despite the fact that BMI is an extremely faulty measurement, useless for gathering medical data, and even professional athletes would be classified as "obese" according to it (Devlin 2009), they all used it to recommend that I lose a few pounds. From the time I was ten until thirty-two, I dieted. I would ration and try to "be good," a phrase I still catch myself saying. For years, I kept obsessive tallies of my caloric intake and output.

For weeks at a time, I'd limit myself to the twelve-hundred-calorie-per-day recommendation magazines, doctors, friends, and apps told me I should be eating. Eventually, I'd feel utterly famished, break down, and eat. Or I'd go out with friends, be too embarrassed to admit I was dieting, and binge. Each time, I'd hate myself a little more. I'd shame myself for not having stronger willpower. I'd promptly gain ten pounds, be more frustrated, feel more shame, and diet harder. I'd cut my calories further, take more spin classes, and tax my willpower even more. I'd be that much hungrier and fall that much harder. With each cycle, I'd gain more weight and feel more shame.

While vetting self-help books for the Go Love Yourself community, I found weight loss books by the dozens. Each month, publishers would send me catalogs full of their latest and greatest, and I'd wonder which would actually work. Which of these dozen conflicting books do they actually believe in? It's not possible for them to endorse all of them, is it?

Of course not, but that wasn't the point.

Like all self-help books, diet books, their authors and publishers don't make money if you are successful; they make money if you feel badly enough about yourself to buy their books and keep buying their books. Estimates suggest five million diet books are sold each year in the United States alone, even though no doctor has actually uncovered the solution to weight loss (Belluz 2016). The high failure rate of diets and self-help strategies also isn't a bug in the system—it is a feature.

In fact, they've figured out the perfect cycle: Capitalize on the socialization that has us believing our acceptance is contingent upon our having a perfect body. Use marketing that taps into our shame. Sell the solution. When it doesn't work, blame the reader for not trying hard enough. Devise and sell a new strategy, *one that's sure to work!*, and blame the reader when this one doesn't work either. Find a younger, hotter salesperson willing to sell pseudoscience. Rinse. Repeat.

In the months leading up to my wedding, with the threat of fat-me photos living on forever and threatening to ruin an otherwise lovely experience, I used every tactic, strategy, and shame-induced ounce of willpower I had against myself. As my coworkers can attest, I lived off carrots and sparkling water for the six months leading up to our nuptials. I lost fifty pounds. I had never been so perpetually hungry, short-tempered, and complimented in my life.

My rebound from this one was powerful. I engaged in what my new husband lovingly referred to as the Great Nacho Bender of 2018. I felt shame—deep, overwhelming levels of shame—but also loved and supported. I cried when I ate. I cried when I no longer fit into my clothes. I cried while trying to practice acceptance. I cried while trying intuitive eating and mindful eating—as diet strategies, of course—to no avail. I exhausted myself from trying so hard, being so hungry, and exerting so much self-control over every aspect of my life for years. I felt like a failure. Again.

I'm spending extra time on diets because diets are a major part of the self-help industry and growing (LaRosa 2021). They comprise the vast majority of all self-improvement book sales. Their entire premise relies on three things: us feeling enough shame about our bodies that we're willing to try nearly anything, our unrelenting hopefulness and naivety that someone has finally figured out sustainable weight loss, and our self-flagellation when it doesn't work, convincing ourselves we were the problem.

Despite knowing what I know, I still feel like a failure. I know you can be both fat and healthy. I know people don't fail on diets, but that diets fail people. I know a consistent predictor of weight gain is, in fact, dieting (Wolpert 2007; Ferreira 2021). I know prolonged calorie-restriction can lead to a slew of harmful effects on one's brain functioning, mental health, metabolism, motivation, personality, and more (Lean and Malkova 2016; Benton and Young 2017; Fraga 2018). I know there's more to weight loss than the antiquated calories in-calories out model. I know that the characteristics we think lead to weight gain, such as obsession with food and impulsivity, are actually the *result* of diet-induced starvation (Ferreira 2021; Gil 2021; Witcomb 2017). I know that social determinants of health and experiences of powerlessness are major contributing factors (Hemmingsson 2014; Omer 2020). I know it's a multifaceted problem requiring a multifaceted solution.

But none of this knowledge is strong enough to overcome my shame. We can't use logic to solve something illogical.

And none of this will stop the self-help industry from publishing another few hundred diet books this year. And next year. And the year after. Even though they are major contributors to the problem. In fact, even though some evidence indicates people were more likely to meet their health goals during the 2020 lockdown than in previous years, the prevailing narrative from the self-help and dieting industries is that the pandemic made us fatter, lazier, and unhappier (Weiner 2021). The industry intended to make back the money they lost during the pandemic and popularized a narrative that would help them to sell solutions.

The more our systems fail to help us, including our medical systems, the more we turn to self-help. The more we are swept away by the promises of self-help, the more extreme lengths we'll go to in order to get to the promised land. In self-help and dieting, this is particularly dangerous. While we typically think of eating disorders as being an issue facing thin women, the truth is less than 6 percent of all people with an eating disorder are actually underweight (ANAD 2023), and folks in bigger bodies suffer from the same internal health complications as do folks in smaller bodies (Leigh 2019). Anyone who leverages willpower to heavily restrict intake experiences the same cardiovascular complications and hormone suppression that affect fertility, menstruation, and bone density, regardless of overall body weight. And to make matters worse, folks in larger bodies have the added psychological burden of fat shaming and weight bias that itself is linked to poor metabolic health and weight gain (Vogel 2019).

The stigma of being in a bigger body is one with deep ramifications. Medical discrimination leads to malpractice when providers recommend different treatments for patients based on weight, leads to undiagnosed conditions when providers assume weight is the cause of all ills, and leads patients to avoid interacting with healthcare providers in anticipation of the discrimination they'll receive (American Psychological Association 2017). Exposure to weight bias and fat-shaming is linked to depression, anxiety, and low self-esteem (Vogel 2019). Once people internalize this antifatness and use it as a way to motivate themselves, the severity of harm actually increases. No amount of nutrition knowledge, exercise, or willpower combats this shame. Even losing weight doesn't seem to make an impact on one's own internalized weight biases (Vogel 2019).

This progression from behaviors to belief systems mirrors the increasingly invasive strategies we've seen across the self-help genre in the past few decades. Self-help interventions not only seek to control our outward appearances and behaviors but also to control our inner lives, thoughts, and feelings in increasingly invasive and complicated ways.

This is evident in the body positivity movement, where it's no longer sufficient to even feel *neutrally* about our bodies, like we do as children. We're encouraged to love ourselves while buying into the idea our bodies are inherently hard to love (Gill and Elias 2014). This messaging often distracts from the root cause of our discontent—a marketing machine that has taught us to be dissatisfied with ourselves so they can convince us we are the problem and then sell us the solution. It's disempowerment sold as empowerment.

And, of course, it's not just diets that aren't working. The self-help industry has given us a tremendous opportunity to see what happens when you experiment with controlling every aspect of our lives—voluntarily!—to see what happens.

If changing ourselves to find the perfect relationship and partner worked, more people would be getting and staying happily married. Instead, marriage rates are decreasing, which is decreasing divorce rates by default, while boomers continue to get divorced at unusually high rates (US Census Bureau 2020; Olito 2019).

Our power structures tell us women aren't in top positions because we're just not educated enough. If our education were the only thing holding us back, the number of women in senior leadership positions would finally be matching our education levels. Women now earn nearly 50 percent of all law degrees, medical degrees, and specialized master's degrees in the US. We earn 38 percent of all MBAs and more than half of all doctorates. We hold more than half of all management- and professional-level jobs (Warner, Ellmann, and Boesch 2018). We're just as educated as the men hoarding the power, yet we still don't have economic or leadership parity, so the bar moves again.

After we educate ourselves, we are told our lack of confidence is preventing us from getting ahead. As a matter of fact, in recent years, whatever the problems we're facing, the implied diagnosis is the same: we just need to believe in ourselves (Orgad and Gill 2022). Despite a massive increase in the number of self-help books and programs targeting confidence and self-esteem for women, we don't see a discernible increase in the number of women getting ahead or feeling more confident as a result.

Even when we believe in ourselves, we still suffer from unequal demands and expectations. So, we're taught we need to juggle more, better. We're given books on how to "have it all." If strategies for how to "have it all" worked, however, we wouldn't have a global population of women reporting even *higher* rates of burnout than ever, and at higher rates than men (Krivkovich et al. 2022; Cox 2021). Across the board, women are doing more to support their teams, families, and communities while being supported less, trying harder, and suffering more.

Whether we're facing discrimination and inequality in the workplace, poor body image and weight shaming by medical professionals, or a lack of acceptance and belonging in society in general, these features of our society are reframed as problems of the individual.

Each self-help book that hits the shelf is yet another mechanism that keeps us taking more individual ownership while obscuring the reasons these issues exist in the first place. The simplistic, unsubstantiated strategies they offer rarely work in meaningful or comprehensive ways, and ultimately distract us from the complex, interconnected, and often social causes of our discontent. It's clear: the more we blame ourselves and look to others for answers, the more money the self-help industry stands to make off us.

Psychology-based interventions meant to individually empower may actually prove disempowering as we take the focus away from societal solutions that could create the actual equality we seek, exacerbating the onus on us to change ourselves. When women are directed to pursue change by changing ourselves instead of organizing to change our society, we make it less likely to achieve the equality we are looking for. The expectation that we change ourselves and seek a better life through self-help, products, and consumption is what Lauren Berlant calls "cruel optimism" (2011). Our desire and efforts to achieve health and happiness can backfire, making it less likely to achieve them.

Self-help ignores external social factors and instead scapegoats our individual degree of self-control. High self-control is consistently correlated with the regulation of emotion, temptation, and impulse for the purpose of goal attainment. It is widely cited as a uniformly good thing to have. At what point, though, do we have too much of a good thing? At what point does self-control become self-neglect, self-flagellation, and self-abuse?

We can take responsibility for every facet of our lives in an infinite number of ways, leading us to search for and find a never-ending list of things that are wrong with us and deserve to be changed. The levels of control we exert over ourselves become increasingly invasive and aggressive, to the point when we are blaming and seeking to control our bodily responses, emotions, and thoughts, even when they are completely natural, human, and warranted, given our situations.

Self-help, in its current iteration, involves dehumanization through excessive levels of control. These actions would be illegal if not perpetrated *by* the self *toward* the self. We need to find a better solution than mistreating ourselves in the hope that self-flagellation will serve as penance for our unworthiness and deliver us into the promised land of worthiness and equality.

What will it take for us to admit it's not working? What will it take for us to acknowledge and accept that no amount of self-flagellation or self-improvement will change the minds of those committed to seeing us as the "wrong" kind of person?

Iteration while mired in a position of social inferiority keeps us forever cycling through incremental improvements that will never change the fabric of society or our place in it. To live the lives we actually want to live, it's insufficient to be the change and hope the world "out there" will take note and bestow upon us the respect we've always deserved. That's not how power works.

Until we break out of this mindset and cycle, the people and industries in power will continue to manipulate us and prey on our vulnerability, suggesting if we just changed this one *other* little thing, we'd finally be worthy and acceptable.

CHAPTER 6

THE VULNERABILITY TRAP

While I've already told you about my self-help business, you don't know about the spiritual awakening (read: breakdown) that got me there.

Let me tell you a story.

I've always been a fragile-on-Sundays, #Sundayscaries type.

My high-stakes day job combined with the fact I've been diagnosed with every anxiety disorder known to man has created a short-fused, no-fun-unless-I'm-drinking-past-the-ability-to-think kind of person who was absolutely insufferable. The whiplash from my weekends back into the work week was unbearable for me, and the whiplash from vacations back into the work week was even worse. Despite my husband diligently clearing my path of anything that could trip me up, I'd inevitably spiral into panic attacks.

The return trip from our honeymoon was, of course, different. Rather than the standard week-long trip to somewhere fantastic, we were returning from twelve days of newly married bliss in the most fantastic place on Earth—an over-water bungalow in Bora Bora.

We'd spent our days snorkeling and reading and exploring the island and each other in near isolation, save the fish and stingrays and sharks. It was, of course, perfect.

I don't remember much about the day we left, other than what's documented in photos or what's been recounted to me and recreated as a memory second-hand. I know we took a boat from the resort back into town because it was the only way to get there. I know they put shells around our necks to distinguish us from the newly arrived because we still have them hanging on our bookshelf. And I know every plane and airport lounge from Bora Bora to DC offered an open bar with unlimited free drinks because I wound up on a train platform in DC black-out drunk with no charges to my credit card.

I have vague recollections of staring out over the water, and later out over the wing of the plane whispering, "I can't go back."

I vaguely recall my lovely new husband responding, "I know, right?" and, "I'm going to miss this place," and, "Work tomorrow is going to suck!" and, "Oh, sure you can! We've gotta get home sometime. Besides, aren't you missing Annie?"

Fuck that cat.

And no, no, no. You're not getting it.

Somewhere between LA and DC, my quiet cry for help hardened into resolve, and somewhere between the airport in DC and our metro stop, I laid it all out. I've seen happy now. I *can't* go *back.*

Our stop came, and he stood. He grabbed the handle of his luggage and chivalrously lifted my handle for me. I stared blankly.

"C'mon, babe, this is us." He walked to the door. I stared. "Babe, c'mon. What are you doing?"

"I can't go back there."

"To our home?"

"To our home."

"You can't go back to our home? What the fuck?"

I was crying or yelling maybe. I didn't care.

"I can't go home because if I go home, I'll be home. I'll unpack, and I'll go to bed, and I'll wake up, and I'll go to work because that's what you *do* when you go *home*. I can't. Go. Home."

He started to panic, I think, or at least I assume he did, because I would have, and he pulled me up and grabbed my suitcase and pleaded: "Can we talk about it at the next stop?"

I must have agreed. Anywhere but home. I sat down right there in the middle of the floor because who the fuck cared and my life was in shambles and I hated everything and everyone so who cared if someone saw me?

I cried and we talked and maybe I yelled and maybe he yelled too and I think he had his head in his hands, or at least I assume he did because that's what I'd do if I were in his shoes.

I drink to be okay. I must have drank *heavily* because I was *really* not okay, and, it seemed, no amount of alcohol would make things okay this time.

He shepherded me into a plan and kissed me. Or at least he must have, because at some point I stood up and we got back on the train in the opposite direction, heading home, still married.

I woke up the next day with the feeling I'd done something very, very wrong. I went to work and spent my hours confused, applying to new programs and jobs, and pretending things were fine, just fine, thanks for asking. Everything was a blur of panicked texts and cover letters. I needed a legitimate reason to quit, and when I was assigned a new boss who decided to kickstart our budding love story by putting me in my place, I locked my office door and started packing.

I texted Mark: "Rent a car. Be here at 6 p.m. Bring boxes."

When he arrived, the building was quiet and my packing was nearly complete. We spent the next few hours loading every book, thank you card, and piece of artwork I'd ever received from a student or teacher into a borrowed car. I filed away ten years of lesson plans, professional development binders, and data trackers. I felt exhilarated and evil and nostalgic. By 9 a.m. the next morning, I was free.

"So, I guess it's time you write that book now," he nodded.

We got dinner and unpacked the car, and I made a vow to find a way to work for myself—to launch a business by my birthday, just six weeks away.

And somehow, I do. I research, market test, and launch a business in six weeks because as an educator and woman, that's what I have been trained to do—set a goal and work relentlessly to pursue it. I launch a crowdfunding campaign. I rally friends and strangers around it. We are fully funded. I also apply to and am accepted to Georgetown and Harvard for good measure. I decide to attend both, just in case.

For three years, I work toward my own self-care and authenticity. I sell self-care and authenticity to others. I rally women around community and self-help books in a genuine attempt to empower us all.

For three years, I am ready with a book recommendation salve to apply to every wound. Not feeling confident at work? Read *The Secret Thoughts of Successful Women* (Young 2021)! Wondering why we're all fat and miserable? Read *Busy, Stressed, and Food Obsessed* (Lewtan 2015)! I don't care who you are, read anything by Brené Brown. She surely has your answer!

And for three years, I'm bombarded with quiet whisperings and inklings that something is not right. That the business isn't quite right. That it's not where it should be. That it could be more successful, and that *I* could be more successful. A part of me squirms knowingly. This thing I've built feels silly, inauthentic, not me. But I also want to make money, and *Rich Dad, Poor Dad* (Kiyosaki 2022) says being an entrepreneur is the best way to do so, so I keep going. I work longer hours than I did in education. I make less money while convincing myself it'll be worth it in the long run. I pull all-nighters to meet absurd, self-imposed deadlines and fuel myself with carbs, caffeine, and excessive amounts of frozen appetizers.

After three years, my trusted friend and coach, laura brewer lays it out: "This isn't you. You're out of integrity, and your body is letting you know it. And you aren't even making money with it? What are you even doing?"

She's right. I don't want her to be right, but she is. It's something I've refused to acknowledge. The whispers of "This isn't right," came first as whispers, as drizzle… then as a downpour, and finally a tsunami of self-destruction and coping I couldn't ignore.

Three months after that conversation, I close my business.

"So, I guess it's time you write that book now," Mark says again.

I finally admit I have no idea what he's talking about.

"On the train platform, on the way back from the honeymoon? You made me promise you I wouldn't let you give up your dreams. That you have known your whole life you're meant to be a writer, remember?"

I blink a few times. Furrow my brows. The words don't compute, though the feeling in my gut tells me I know he's right. Hearing another human say the thing I knew but couldn't acknowledge made it real. Since I was young, I'd get a whisper, an idea, and think, "I should write a book about that." I've made lists hundreds of ideas long. They all felt frivolous and unattainable. Not something real people do.

A few months later, while Mark and I sat on the couch, something in me felt off. Something wasn't sitting well. I asked for a minute to close my eyes. We sat there quietly for just a minute when I downloaded a message clear as day: "It's Not (All) Your Fault."

Truth flooded my eyes. I knew it was true. All the things in my life, all my aches and internalized pains and shame were only partially my doing.

I decided to write the book.

If you've read self-help in the past, you're probably familiar with two of the most popular storylines:

1. "I quit my cushy prestigious corporate six-figure job to follow my dreams."

2. "I hit rock bottom, which was the wake-up call I needed to make a change."

These storylines do a few things for us as writers. First, they connect us with our readers as we share something vulnerable—something often too scary to say out loud. And I can speak from experience—it's intimidating. While we fear the repercussions that come from someone else knowing our deepest fears, mistakes, and insecurities, we feel empathy and compassion for those who are willing to share their own.

Even if we've not experienced something remotely similar to the thing they've experienced (have you ever broken down on a train platform returning from your honeymoon?), we can tap into the feelings and emotions they elicit (dread, fear, anxiety), which we've experienced in our own ways. This empathy creates a sense of intimacy, which creates a sense of trust. Reading through a book like this suddenly feels like a conversation with a good friend who has it all figured out.

And suddenly, we as readers care how the story plays out because we're invested in the author; we relate to them and can see ourselves in them. We see they've made it out alive and being the curious, resourceful people we are, we want to know how the hell they did it. To know someone used to be where we are and has gotten where we want to go is the dose of social proof we need to activate our hope that we can do it, too.

We desperately want to connect to someone who feels our pain and to know we're not alone. To see a person who used to be just like us, struggling with the same things we struggled with, now living our version of success, can feel witnessing and redemptive. It's deliciously intoxicating. And it's the exact connection the self-help industry monetizes and capitalizes on.

Relatability isn't just nice to have. Some people's entire self-help careers are built on it. It's why there was so much backlash against self-help author Rachel Hollis in 2021 when she went viral for breaking the facade of relatability (Rosman 2021). In a since deleted TikTok video, Hollis responded to a commenter who told her she was privileged for having someone clean her toilets. In the video, she cackles before saying, "What is it about me that made you think I want to be relatable? No, sis, literally everything I do in my life is to live a life that most people can't relate to." Her career plummeted.

This was after she was accused of plagiarism (Grindell 2021), co-opting African American Vernacular English (Rosman 2021), posting Maya Angelou's "Still I Rise" as her own and blaming her team for the post (McNeal 2020), and pissing off her Christian followers as she got divorced in 2020 (Griswold 2021) while simultaneously selling two-thousand-dollar tickets to couples conferences where she taught people how to improve their relationships (McNeal 2021). Her popularity transcended all her missteps and multiple tone-deaf apologies (Ashley 2021). It has not yet proven to outlast nonrelatability.

Because the truth is, authors and other people selling things to us will share as a way to make us like and trust them. Bob Burg, the author of Endless Referrals, notes that trust between humans is so low—we're worried about being scammed and taken advantage of—we'd prefer to do business with someone we know, like, and trust (Burg 2010). Folks in self-help, content marketing, and social media marketing tout this "know-like-trust" factor as a major way to grow your audience and build your reputation. It's emotional manipulation parading as connection.

Just a few months into my business, it was clear my website copy wasn't converting at the rates other subscription box websites were. Interpretation: the words on my website weren't compelling enough for people to buy. In business, this is a big problem. Well-intentioned marketers promised to help me triple my clicks, triple my "add to carts," and triple my revenue.

The way they promised to do it? Tapping into the readers' emotions.

"Tap into the life they want. The one they're desperate for," I was told by one. "You're not just selling books and bath bombs, you're selling self-care! You're selling happiness in a box! You're selling… *an escape.*"

"Tell them all the problems they're facing," I was told by another. "Find out what they'd pay *anything* to have. Remind them you, and you alone, can solve their problems with your product!"

"Make them the hero of their own story," I was instructed. "Show them how great their lives could be if they opt in *right now.*"

With their help, I changed the words on my website from, "a new self-help book shipped to your doorstep monthly" to "You, empowered!" We framed it as, "Everything you need to transform your life," and "Your monthly reminder that *you matter.*" I went from selling something customers could touch to selling a way to invest in an ideal version of themselves.

Even people who come to the industry with the best of intentions, like I did, often end up using questionable business practices. Marketers have learned that selling a lifestyle will reap exponentially more views, purchases, and revenue than selling a product. They then push business owners to embrace the strategies.

As we discussed in chapter 3, selling a lifestyle, a feeling, or a social status rather than a product is all the rage. Want to see it for yourself? Follow a few marketers on your preferred platform and see what they're encouraging folks to do to reel you in. Notice the vulnerabilities they play on. Notice what manipulation tactics they suggest. And then take a look at your favorite brands—or perhaps even better, brands that annoy you—to see what kind of lifestyle they're selling, what vulnerability they exploit, and what manipulation tactics they use. It's bonkers.

And it's effective. Unfortunately. Because the same compulsion that leads us to dig into and read self-help is the same one that gets us identifying as a Pepsi or Coke person, or a coffee or tea person. We want the promise of the lifestyle it brings via association, and that desire makes us vulnerable.

Rarely do we see marketers emphasizing specifics anymore. Industries have hit a basic enough threshold that they aren't that dissimilar in actual quality, and secondly, it's not what sells. There are tons of good-enough beers, bags, and vehicles. Instead, we clamor for the beach vibes we associate with Coronas, the rich bitch vibes we associate with Chanel handbags, or the rugged manliness of a Ford F150. Aspirational lifestyles and emotions sell. When we're promised feelings of happiness, respect, or desirability, we open our wallets.

The same thing is true in self-help and personal development. We're dazzled by promises of what our lives could look like, reminded of the ways our lives aren't measuring up, and offered ways to make our lives and ourselves better. More relaxing, or luxurious, or powerful.

At no point in my marketing efforts did anyone ask if what I was selling worked, if the promises were true, or if they even made sense. Each month, I sent women self-help books, self-coaching guides, and items from women-owned businesses that fell under the category of "self-care." That meant everything from tea, candles, and bath bombs to cookie mixes, jewelry, and affirmation cards. Do those really count as self-care? Who knows? The category feels so broad that anything could fit that label. Did it work? Did it pamper? Heal? Help women in my membership to live better lives?

I hoped so, but the reality is, I didn't know, and it had zero implications on the marketing language we used in promotions. Marketers wanted money, which they got by promising customers a more joyful, fulfilling, and peaceful life. We so badly want life to be better that we let ourselves be duped, thinking if we buy this or that, we might finally be the person we want to be, and live the life we've always wanted. To soothe our growing sense of despair, we'll set aside what we know to be true about diets, structural inequality, and the futility of changing ourselves to fit in just to be able to have things, even temporarily, under our control.

The marketing I was doing felt gross, but at the time, I didn't know why. I chalked it up to imposter syndrome and a fear of being seen, took the interviews, and launched the Facebook ads. It wasn't until a conversation with a fellow subscription box owner who was better versed in marketing, social media, and feminism that I had the language to understand what felt so gross about it. In addition to the dissonance I was feeling about tapping into women's vulnerabilities for the sake of a sale, I was also falling prey to the idea you have to be an idealized embodiment of the solution you are selling.

In self-help, to sell a solution, we have to *be* the evidence that the solution we're selling works. As a result, we project the image of someone who has it all figured out. This is particularly evident in the life coaching and wellness world we see in social media (Powers 2012). It's the common trope of blonde women in Bali flipping their perfect, beach-wavy hair or hands in prayer with eyes closed, selling the idea that if you work with them, you too could be thin, blonde, beautiful, and stress-free, gallivanting in exotic locations. After all, their intent is to sell a lifestyle and a feeling, so they have to show themselves as having attained the thing in full, even if they are also actively working around the clock to make it look that way.

To be credible as a self-help saleswoman, I was expected to be both a self-help expert *and* the image of a self-help success story. I never set out to be a self-help expert. My goal was to bring women together to read and learn and grow in community. I didn't know everything there was to know about wellness, but that wasn't the point. I saw myself as a conduit and a gatherer, yet I was suddenly expected to have answers on everything from the causes of depression to how to solve imposter syndrome in the workplace. When you've got any kind of platform, people expect you to just know things.

So, when I was asked for interviews, I did what I could. I combined my own experiences with the experiences of other women I knew and cited scientific literature to back it up. No good. I was rarely able to give the sound bites people were looking for. Local news stations aired ten-second clips from ten-minute interviews. One interviewer told me she needed "three steps, max" to keep her audience's attention. How could I simplify years of study and nuanced solutions meant to help us navigate the complex challenges we face into a ten-second, three-step solution?

Even more dissonant was the expectation that I be the proof it worked. It wasn't sufficient to be in it with my community, figuring it out together. I wanted to be deeply authentic—it's one of the pillars my brand was built on—but I never knew how authentic or vulnerable to really go, so I toed the line. I authentically waited until my hair was styled just right, so I could shoot a video while feeling confident. I authentically shared frustrations with the impossible expectations levied against women but rarely in a way that revealed the depths of my own despair. In reality, even a year after starting my business, I was the same fragile, anxious, overworking person who broke down on a train platform. I curated my imperfections and performed vulnerability in a way I hoped made me relatable and human without calling into question my credibility.

After all, can you trust anyone who admits their own mental health issues to help you with your own? Really?

Americans, in particular, love a good rags-to-riches story, but we don't want to hear it 'til it's over; 'til you have your happy ending. We love to see the individual person who faced hard times thriving. It fits our cultural myths about the American Dream, what's possible, and who is responsible for your circumstances—you and you alone.

We don't want to hear about your struggles. We *love* seeing the final product and are curious about how it happened (Gallo 2017). We're desperate to know how we can replicate it.

Social psychology tells us our brains are wired for story, especially stories that motivate us to dream bigger. Hearing the way folks reframe obstacles to give their lives purpose and meaning can be inspiring. While some say we're wired to love rags-to-riches stories, others suggest Americans, in particular, are swept away by stories affirming what we already believe about social mobility (Kiesling 2022). We love hearing about Tony Robbins' struggles growing up poor in a single-parent household before growing his life-coaching empire and becoming one of the world's most recognizable inspirational speakers (Inc Staff 2016). We're fascinated and captivated by Oprah's rise from extreme poverty and abuse into the household name she is today (Elkins 2015).

Pointing to the truth, that these household names are anomalies, or that the rich folks we look to for advice more often come from wealthy families and receive significant help along the way, contrasts with the belief systems we rely on for hope. So, billionaire memoirists write stories about coming from the bottom and making it big that are all but bogus. Often, we don't even care how they did it. We trust without verifying.

It's also how we see so many self-help books written by people like Napoleon Hill and Jay Shetty—men with troubled pasts who reinvented themselves as spiritual leaders (Itani 2021).

Napoleon Hill was born into rural poverty in Virginia in 1883. He embarked on a number of businesses that all crumbled under shady business practices and began working for a newsletter where he simply made stories up when there was otherwise no news to tell. He used this knack to fabricate tales of influence and glory for himself, claiming he helped President Woodrow Wilson negotiate Germany's surrender in 1918 and gave Franklin Delano Roosevelt his phrase, "The only thing we have to fear is fear itself." Hill created bogus colleges and dubious "charities." Ultimately, Hill became famous solely for having published *Think and Grow Rich*, a book he claims he was asked to write by Andrew Carnegie, even though there's no record of the two ever meeting (Novak 2016). Hill became an inspirational thought-leader and self-help influencer simply by convincing everyone he was an inspirational thought-leader and self-help influencer.

Jay Shetty's rise to fame over the last few decades has been equally questionable. He grew up north of London, where he got himself into drugs, fighting, and drinking. While attending business school in London, he obsessed over rags-to-riches stories and self-made entrepreneurs. He had the "eureka moment" folks use when building a brand: he heard a talk by a monk who had renounced material wealth and was so captivated he decided to train to be a monk himself. After a few years, he left to rejoin capitalism and social media as a *former monk*, and got a spirituality show on HuffPo (Wolfson 2020).

Now, as a mogul monk, he sells courses promising to increase your happiness despite one of the main tenets of Buddhism being the idea that happiness originates from within, and those trying to push outer success are misleading you and causing you suffering (Gyatso 2016). He brazenly and openly plagiarizes others' wisdom, which is a direct violation of the Five Precepts Vows Buddhists live by, and posts easily Google-able quotes as his own on social media while preying on those who could use a spiritual pick-me-up.

Now I'm no Buddha, but even this aspiring Buddhist knows that Buddhism seeks to reduce suffering, not prey on it. One of the most insidious and deceptive parts of self-help is this performed authenticity and expertise. We want to know there's hope for us, so we'll trust those who claim to be able to deliver, regardless of whether or not they can. Like Hill, many self-help leaders unfortunately often get rich and famous simply by promising to teach people how to be rich and famous. Many engage in questionable, unethical, and fraudulent practices, manipulating their audiences by exaggerating and fabricating successes for the purpose of being able to sell their solutions. At the end of the day, their customer base is left just as lost, unhappy, and confused as before, with a little (or a lot) less money in their pockets.

Here's the bottom line: as long as we buy into the American Dream, we will be vulnerable to people selling solutions that are entirely unsubstantiated. The performed authenticity of self-help leaders acts as a false lure, leading us to waste time and money on solutions that do not work and, in some cases, cause real harm. Many of us spend years hanging on to our hope, following maps to a promised land that does not exist.

What would it look like to seek wisdom and guidance while being mindful of the ways in which our vulnerability can lead to exploitation?

CHAPTER 7

THE PARADOX OF HOPE

My Current Self, my Past Self, and my Future Self are perpetually at war with one another.

I'm unsatisfied in the present. I am absolutely overburdened by work and commitments I made to myself in the past while dreaming of a better future. I set goals I think will lead me to my rags-to-riches happy ending, and draw up grand plans that require commitment, sacrifice, and tons of work. I assume I'll find the energy for it later. Time passes, and that future becomes my present. Again, I am exhausted. I resent my Past Self for writing checks I can't cash. I need a nap.

Maybe you know the feeling—staying up too late to meet deadlines and over-caffeinating to stay awake the next day, setting yourself up for a cycle of poor sleep all week. Maybe you tell yourself you'll be different in the future, the kind of person with lots of energy who can spin even more plates and juggle everything you're currently dropping. You say yes to more but end up bitter and beat, having stayed the same.

Self-help relies on today's dissatisfaction paired with the belief a different future is possible. It insists we know what makes us happy, and that, if we can make it happen, we'll be good to go.

We think we can achieve the life of our dreams; reality is more complex. We think we know what will make us happy; contentment is more elusive. We think being hard on ourselves is productive; compassion is more effective.

Let's start with articulating the life of your dreams. What does that look like to you? Where will you live? How will you spend your time? Who will you spend it with? Do the math. How much money will your lifestyle cost? Does it include more education? Vacations? Owning a home? Two? Supporting children? Parents? Don't guess. Do the math. Write it down. What would you have to do to be able to afford this kind of lifestyle? Does it seem worth it?

Most of us want more than reality can provide. Our imaginations are boundless fountains of creativity, fueled by images we're sold in media and marketing, most of which don't exist in real life. As a result, when we think about having it all, we think of the best of everything we've ever seen—the dreamy life partners from our favorite rom-coms, the flawless skin in the media, and the status of prestigious jobs. We assume when we achieve that life, everything else will just magically fall away.

We often fail to envision the whole of the future when we envision our dreams for it. We fail to acknowledge the negotiations required to build a lifelong, committed partnership, the photoshopping and genetics that go into "perfect" skin, and the dehumanizing workloads and unrelenting stress that often accompany corporate ladder climbing. To make it compelling enough to sacrifice our present, we build up the image of a fantastic future that will exist *when...*

Romanticization makes our goals impossible to live up to because even when we achieve the vision, the qualitative feelings we assumed would come with it don't always align.

Dream cars still get stuck in rush-hour traffic. When our felt reality fails to live up to the hype, the hope, and the idealized vision we had, we're disillusioned and disappointed—no matter how great things sound on paper.

When we believe life will be better *someday*, even when our conditions are met, we have set ourselves up for disappointment (Colombo et al. 2020). Disappointment is the result of unmet expectations. It often stems from a mismatch in how we expected to feel versus how we actually feel. It has very little to do with outside circumstances and whether or not things seem "objectively" better.

Technology and media aren't helping. They distort the image we have of "normal." Social media algorithms are notorious for pushing us images that receive engagement. When we linger on something, the algorithm learns to show us more of the same, distorting our conception of what's real and what's "normal." We end up thinking *everyone* has those new shoes, *everyone* is having babies, and *everyone* is happy but us. We adjust our idea of "normal" and our goals accordingly.

When Mark and I got engaged in 2015, I created Pinterest boards for every aspect of our dream wedding. I had one for dress styles I liked, for hair and makeup options, for cakes, you name it. The number of available choices was astounding. The ways to perfect the day that was already expected to be the best day of my life was as awe-inducing as it was maddening.

As I debated color schemes and themed decor, my bridesmaid Claire noted she was thankful she got married pre-Pinterest; her decisions were easy. You get a guy, a dress, and a venue, you set the guest list and hire a DJ. Done. You didn't worry about what you'd be posting to Instagram for the next several years, and what friends of friends would think, you just tried to have a good night with your loved ones.

We spent eighteen months planning our "special day." We planned for everything. Or, of course, so we thought. A bus carrying fifty guests to the venue got lost. Our cake fell over. It rained. With so many things going "wrong," we could have been deeply disappointed. We could remember all of this with wistful sadness or anger, but we don't. The overwhelmingly positive feelings of celebrating with our favorite people far outweighed any less-than-ideal external things going on. What's a little rain when you've got so much joy?

As a kid, my mother taught me that if you never expect anything, you'll never be disappointed. I embraced my own version of optimistic nihilism: I relinquished control over the day and what it was *supposed to be* and enjoyed it for everything that it was. It was *perfect.*

The more expectations we have for what something should be like, the more opportunities there are to fail to meet your expectations. The more disconnected our goal vision is from our understanding of what makes us truly happy, the more likely we are to be disappointed.

The perfect irony is we're often happier when we have no preconceived notions of what something should be like. I went to college with zero expectations—neither of my parents had gone, so they hadn't built it up in my imagination. I had no attachments to it being the time of my life. It was a neutral event, and I experienced it as I went. Marriage, for me, has been similar. My parents divorced when I was young, so I had a good idea of what I *didn't* want but no attachments to it looking a certain way—we got to create the one we wanted. At each juncture, I've had the opportunity to decide what was important to *me*.

When we approach our lives with rigid expectations, we actually narrow our sources of joy as we fail to recognize unexpected opportunities for pleasure and satisfaction. It's like going to get gelato and being devastated there's no *mango* gelato. Our very specific devastation prevents us from trying something new, and possibly something we like even better. It prevents us from appreciating the miracle that brought tropical fruit flavors from South Asia to Italian methods of ice cream production and reverence for the global cooperation that made it happen.

Our attachments to things being a certain way prevents us from accepting the goodness present in every moment. When we are so deeply invested in the larger-than-life futures that exist in our imagination, we neglect to experience the beauty and joy in living *right now.* There are very few actual necessities in life. We need to be fed, loved, and have a place to rest our heads. We need to feel alive and like our existence matters. Instead of being content to enjoy the breeze on our skin, cool water to drink, the ecstasy of laughter, and the absolute peace of lingering in a warm bed, we sacrifice today's little pleasures for the promise of a Great Big Giant Pleasure that may or may not exist tomorrow. We perpetually endure inhumane *means* (everyday overwork, self-neglect, shame, exhaustion) to achieve an *end* not likely to come and even less likely to feel good.

And that's if we *do* push ourselves to achieve this future. On the flip side, many of us hold on to a dream we'll never take the jump to pursue, making excuses and letting other things get in the way. Many of us are so afraid of being devastated by a possible truth—we're not actually that great at writing, or we'd actually make a terrible manager—we don't let ourselves find out. We keep our dream at arm's length, safe in the wistful conception of *who we could have been if only...* We prevent disappointment by hanging on to our longing as a way of protecting our dreams and our self-esteem at the same time.

Our concepts of happiness are culturally constructed in the same ways self-esteem and success are. In Westernized countries, and especially the United States, we're increasingly expected to seek happiness in achievements, superiority, and excess. Notably, the Declaration of Independence protects our *pursuit* of happiness. It in no way takes responsibility or ownership for *creating* or *ensuring* happiness. Other cultures and governments deprioritize happiness as a value unto itself, seek it differently, or even take responsibility for creating it.

Consider Bhutan: Their legal code from 1629 states, "If the government cannot create happiness for its people, then there is no purpose for government to exist." Their constitution, established in 2008, balances the needs of society and nature through the pursuit of Gross National Happiness and its four pillars: Good Governance, Sustainable Socio-Economic Development, Preservation and Promotion of Culture, and Environmental Conservation (GNH Centre 2023). Inspired by Buddhist values, happiness in Bhutan is a sense of well-being that comes from living in harmony with oneself, others, and the natural environment.

To create harmony between self and others, Bhutanese practice their values by promoting inner peace and well-being. This fosters harmony with and respect for others, regardless of status, and strong social connections. By emphasizing cultural heritage and identity, folks in Bhutan retain a connection to their past that grounds them in the present, creates a sense of belonging, and instills a sense of self, wealth, and well-being that transcends material wealth. Despite being one of the poorest countries in the world, Bhutan invests in well-being, education, and universal healthcare, balancing accessibility, preventative care, and traditional medicine.

To promote harmony between self and nature, and co-prioritize economic development with environmental preservation, Bhutan has designated 50 percent of its land to national parks, wildlife sanctuaries, nature reserves, and biological corridors (WWF 2021). This initiative provides protected areas that sustain diverse ecosystems, positive human-nature interactions through recreational opportunities for citizens, and economic development through ecotourism (National Conservation Division et al. 2004). They also promote sustainable agricultural practices that provide nutritious, healthy foods while supporting the health of the land.

Life in Bhutan is described as spiritual, slow, sustainable, and nonmaterialistic (Miller 2016). Until the 1960s, the nation was mostly rural. There were neither roads nor motor vehicles, electricity nor TVs. People lived off the land. Today, the internet and TV exists, much to some folks' dismay, as the country and culture negotiate modernity and development. As one Bhutanese elder explained, *if we have fire, water, warm food, and tasty curry, what else could we need?* (Drexler 2014).

It's not about how much you have; it's about having what you need, appreciating what you have, and having about as much as the folks around you.

Nordic countries like Norway, Sweden, and Finland also consistently rank among the happiest each year. In contrast to Bhutan, which doesn't have a ton of money, all three are wealthy countries with effective governments that also invest in their people and create a high degree of social cohesion (Yu 2023). They provide high-quality institutional services to their people, which results in a high degree of equality. Norway has a powerful welfare system and an economy built on responsible use of natural resources. Sweden builds social equality into its systems with sixteen months of paid family leave and free day care, making Sweden the best country on the planet for women. Finland has one of the best education systems in the world and focuses on experiential learning for kids rather than quantitative testing (Morton 2022).

It's not about having money; it's about investing the resources you have in ways that provide the greatest satisfaction and well-being.

Interestingly, Finland has ranked at the top of the list repeatedly, despite Finns themselves being curious and sometimes dubious about the results. Finns don't always report feeling happy, at least not in the way we often expect happiness to look with exuberance, joy, or bliss. Instead, they report feeling safe and balanced. They are content. Because what contributes to a high quality of life, Finns say, is knowing there's someone you can count on when things get hard, the freedom to make your own decisions, and trust in neighbors and strangers alike. Finland values and prioritizes compassion, human rights, and the environment (Leaver 2018).

Instead of grinding to achieve the kind of *happy* we seek in the US, Finns focus on reducing *unhappiness.* They value work-life balance, and instead of pursuing wealth for themselves, convert economic wealth into things like reducing barriers to healthcare for their neighbors.

While there's a pervasive belief that more money equals more happiness, after a certain threshold of safety and ability to provide for ourselves and our families, there's a diminishing return on factors like emotional well-being. Some studies put the threshold around seventy-five thousand dollars in the United States (Kahneman and Deaton 2010). I've heard it described as "enough for necessities, with a little left over," kind of like the American Dream of the 1950s. Others say the number is higher and location dependent (Frank 2012). Before we reach this threshold, goal directed behavior can help us get what we need to be safe and healthy. After we have our bases covered, however, we're typically looking for happiness in all the wrong places.

In Western cultures, our self-esteem, or the regard we hold for ourselves, is built in a way that leads to perpetual unhappiness. Our self-esteem is derived from being *better than average.* It is no longer sufficient to be good. You have to be *better.* You have to be *the best.*

In a society that divides people into winners and losers, average is an insult. Statistically, not everyone can be a winner, or above average. That doesn't matter. Capitalism knows they can sell you things if you hate yourself and will sell you things they promise will make you better (self-help, expensive education), make you *feel* better (prestige via consumerism), or make you *feel better* (coping or numbing).

Complicating things, there's no absolute way to prove your winner's distinction, though many try to convince us they are great because they were great *once*. Folks who topped out in high school remind us of their value by reminding us they were *once* on top, even if they aren't now. That's why the has-been high-school quarterback still bases his identity on the good old glory days—that's when his identity had value, and basing his self-esteem now on his identity *then* is more self-protective than basing his self-esteem on his value *now.*

There's no finish line after which you get to sit back and enjoy. Self-esteem is transient. As the things around us change, so does our perception of ourselves and who we need to be. Rather than satisfying a need that is either met or not, satisfying a positional hierarchy requires constant vigilance to maintain.

Even before social media, our self-esteem was tied to the people around us. We know this as "keeping up with the Joneses." Our feelings of power and worthiness are ecological—they are relative to the power of those around us. If we live in the nicest house on the block, we feel like neighborhood nobility. When we cash out and buy an average house in a nicer neighborhood, we start to feel like schmucks. It's not enough to have nice things—we must have *nicer* things than our neighbors to maintain that sense of self. There is always more to buy, always something new to tie our happiness to.

Each time, we're playing in a different sandbox. What used to feel like luxuries are now necessities in a phenomenon known as lifestyle creep. We experience hedonic adaptation, meaning after a brief spike, we return to a sort of "set point" of happiness (Tam and Aslam 2022). Our happiness was contingent on external circumstances, and once those circumstances stop being exciting, we stop being happy about it. Our status requires constant vigilance to maintain, and means we can never let up, or someone else might take our spot and, with it, our self-esteem.

Even when we don't let up, our bodies age themselves out of their socially constructed "prime." No matter what we do, there's no way to be eternally better than everyone else. There will always be a way we don't measure up, and self-help and capitalism will forever exploit that comparative dissatisfaction. Those who have hope keep trying. Those who lose hope need other options.

For some, acknowledging they will never measure up leads to behaviors they hope will at least make them the best of the worst. Narcissism and bullying are on the rise as systemic inequality is on the rise. They are not unrelated. As our economic situations become dire, folks find ways to "punch down," and find someone they perceive as even lower on the food chain to feel better than. Folks who assume inequality is baked into the structure of life will find ways to make sure they're not at the bottom of that food chain, no matter what.

Individuals who require superiority for their self-esteem assert themselves as a member of the in-group while finding "others" to push into the out-group in order to prove their power and status. As more and more people become accepted as equals in society, their island of self-assigned superiority becomes smaller and smaller. Equality is then seen as a threat to their identity, their status, and their way of life. Those who push for equality threaten the fabric that makes up their self-esteem, so those who threaten their position become a target for their bullying.

We who value equality have to find another source of esteem—one that doesn't require being better than someone else to feel good about ourselves.

Enter: compassion. Compassion leads to strong self-esteem without the pitfalls. When we are kind and compassionate to ourselves and others, we reduce the impacts of comparison and competition. We develop stronger relationships, which in turn contribute to our own internal feelings of stability, well-being, contentment, and belonging.

While we're playing the American Dream game, we're hard on ourselves because we think we have to be. Compassion enables us to be the source of our own contentment, our own soft place to land, and our own internal refuge when things are hard. It's there for us all the time, not just when we're on top. We learn we're deserving of kindness and softness always, even when we aren't "winning," even when we aren't crushing it, even when we feel like shit. We come to understand ourselves as deserving of rest without burning out, recovery time without getting sick, and relaxation without the shame of feeling lazy (Price 2021). With compassion, we can recognize we're just as human as everyone else and just as deserving of care as the people we love.

Most of us love our plants, pets, and children pretty unconditionally. Because we have no expectation that they contribute to the economy, we love them for being who they are, and for the joy they infuse into our lives. They love us, too, because they don't know what the economy is or why we would be expected to base our worth on it.

It's so much easier for us to love our pets for simply being living things—snuggly and warm and sweet, even though they don't produce anything for capitalism—than to give that respect and understanding to ourselves. We have been convinced we must produce something for the economy, or we're worthless. We're not. You are just as deserving of love as your pet thinks you are.

And when we finally see ourselves as deserving of goodness, regardless of what we contribute to the economy, we can extend that to others, too. Compassion begets compassion. It's a virtuous cycle that leads to deeper and greater acts of compassion for ourselves and others. When we strip away the stories capitalism has given us, we can feel happy independent of our statuses within capitalism. When we have compassion for *all* living beings, we can make the world a better place for all beings, not just the ones who have the means to pay for it. This allows us to envision living life outside of the hierarchy, and envision what an entire society outside of the hierarchy could look like, too.

When I allow for my own humanity, I am able to bring my Present Self and my Future Self into alignment with one another. Rather than insisting we sacrifice one for the other, we're able to honor the wants and needs of both at the same time with compassion. I'm able to explore what Present Self wants right now and take steps in alignment with her capacity to create the Future Self she also wants.

One of my favorite parables is the story of the fisherman and the rich tourist. It goes like this: A wealthy businessman comes upon a fisherman relaxing. He encourages the fisherman to work harder to expand his business. The fisherman questions why, as he has enough to provide for his family and enjoys relaxing and spending his extra time with them. The businessman argues that with enough hard work and sacrifice, the fisherman could eventually retire and enjoy a life of leisure with his family. The fisherman points out he is already living a life he enjoys and sees no point in working harder for a future that may never come.

Most of us sacrifice the pleasurable experiences of our day-to-day lives, hoping our lives will one day be *more* pleasurable. It's a future that's not promised. While we wait for the "good life" that has been defined for us, we miss out on the good life happening all around us—the simple pleasure of a delicious meal, the comfort of a cozy blanket, the awe and wonder when we observe the natural world, the sense of accomplishment that comes from learning something new, the joy of doing the thing you most love to do, and knowing there are people in the world who love you.

Self-help is the antithesis of acceptance; it is rooted in seeking and is a way of problem-solving our dissatisfaction with the present moment. As the saying goes, "Life is not a problem to be solved, it is a reality to be experienced."

The pleasure, contentment, and peace we seek live within us in every moment. By releasing our attachments to expectations, we release ourselves from the burden of hope and sink into the experiences of the moment. We're able to let go of what we *think* will make us happy by investing more in what is currently, actually making us happy. In the process, we recognize we don't have to be wealthy, or thin, or successful to be happy. They aren't prerequisites. We redefine the good life and "good enough" for ourselves. We're able to spend more time with the people who make us come alive *right now*, experience the flow of creating art not when we're famous, but *right now*, and honor our bodies, wants, needs, and even goals, *right now.*

What would you do if you knew you would never change? If you knew life would never change? What would that mean for how you use your energy? What if I told you *someday* would never come, and today is it? Or that even if you meet your goals, you won't be as happy as you think you'll be?

To practice honoring your desires, brainstorm things you do simply because *you enjoy doing them*—not for the *ends* they promise, but for the flow and satisfaction you experience now. Perhaps you enjoy going for a long walk and listening to birdsong or dancing and getting that rush of endorphins. Maybe crochet helps you relax, or you really enjoy testing new recipes, or learning about ancient history. There's a good chance these things are available to you now. You don't have to earn them, monetize them, or "win" at them. What would it take to make time for these things in your life and just let them feel good?

Step into the vision you have of life *someday* to identify what it means you want *now.* I want a giant lake house. Why? For some reason, I think time doesn't exist at the lake and it'll be one long stream of sunrises and sunsets, flowers and warm biscuits. Don't ask me why I think that, I don't even like biscuits. Stress-free, time-free life doesn't exist. The opportunity to slow down and enjoy today's flowers and sunsets do.

To balance the very real desire to plan with the paradox of hope requires we balance today's needs with tomorrows, remain open to the unexpected, and practice an openness and appreciation for the joy available in every moment.

What would it take to balance today's wants and needs with tomorrow's? To appreciate the quality of life you currently enjoy while continuing to build something meaningful for tomorrow? How will you know when enough is enough?

CHAPTER 8

WINDOWS OF UNDERSTANDING

I had hoped getting married and going on my honeymoon would change my life. I'd finally achieve my rags-to-riches fairy tale happy ending, and my days of dieting, shape-shifting, and stress would be behind me. I had no idea it'd change the trajectory of my life in the way it did.

I assumed we'd retreat as newlyweds and revel in each other's love, making eyes at each other over dinner. In reality, slowing down gave me the space to think about something other than work, wedding planning, diets, and chores—a dangerous opportunity indeed.

And I remember exactly what caused my epiphany. While Mark and I were lounging in a day bed at our resort in Bora Bora, a sweet little family peddled by on their bikes. All four were clad in the stereotypical white, flowy resort attire I imagine to be the aspiration of resort advertisements everywhere. Mom's sun-kissed, wavy hair flowed behind her. Dad's linen shirt was unbuttoned just enough to let you know he was on vacation, but not drunk. The daughter's keyhole lace dress and ribboned hair, and the son's crisp, child-sized polo completed the image.

Watching the scene from a distance, you'd think it was the portrait of luxury, relaxation, and family bonding. Instead, we were close enough to see the snot dripping from the boy's nose as he pedaled along, whining that *he didn't want to.* His shoulders slumped forward, head rolling back, tears streaming down his face. The daughter's eyes were glued to her iPhone, scrolling with one hand, steering with the other. Both were swerving all over the path, only narrowly avoiding collision. Dad sighed, the seat on his bike so low his knees almost hit his handlebars. But mama duck, leading the way, was flawless. A gentle smile, a whiff of salt air, I imagined her mentally crafting her Instagram caption for later: "Catching some Vitamin Sea in Bora Bora! We might not have Wi-Fi, but the connection is stronger than ever! #grateful for quality time with the fam in paradise! #blessed!!!" They rode up to the presidential suite of their overwater villa, crashed their bikes into a heap at the door, and disappeared inside.

I realized at that moment that this trip, the honeymoon I'd been dreaming of, the vacation we spent months saving up for, this getaway I thought we'd never see the likes of again was just… this kid's life. He was maybe six years old, yet so world-weary he was boo-hoo sobbing. The girl, no more than ten, had lost interest in the horizon that stretched on forever in all directions. I imagined vacations like this being so commonplace in their young existences they'd already lost reverence for its utter majesty.

The highlight of my life was very likely a regular occurrence in theirs. One they were so accustomed to they didn't mind squandering it away with squabbles and social media.

My heart sank. I wasn't sure if I should be embarrassed or envious. My mind swirled. Was my bar too low? Should I be dreaming higher? Was there room for me to dream bigger? Was that world open to me?

I had brought *You Are a Badass* (Sincero) and *Do Cool Shit* (Agrawal) as my beach reading material. Both books answered in a chorus of eye-rolls and yesses: "Your goals are boring and small! You are not relegated to a life that is boring and small. Dream bigger!" They nurtured the seeds of discontent that eventually sprouted on the train platform a week later as a breakdown, and matured into the multi-blossomed, multibranched tree it is today.

I see events like this one, ones where I realize *my* experience is not *everyone's* experience, and where I recognize *my* worldview is not *the only* worldview, as moments when I have access to a window of understanding. I can peer into it and see what life is like for other humans. For a brief moment, I have the opportunity to experience the world through their lens.

Taking time away from the regular humdrum of life, whether through vacations, honeymoons, sabbaticals, or even a pandemic-induced quarantine gives us the time and space to consider our lives through different lenses. The reprieve from the grind pops us out of our typical day-to-day routines, which gives us just enough space to see our lives from an arm's length—to see them a bit more objectively, with a hint of awareness and mindfulness.

Through social media, too, we're granted seemingly unrestricted access to unfiltered thoughts, feelings, perspectives, and experiences without the gatekeeping that exists in traditional media. Sometimes, it's curated to portray a fictitiously flattering image of reality, like the woman on the bike or the blonde babes in Bali. Other times, it's a vital source of information about topics routinely seen as too heavy, too personal, too exhausting, and too controversial to bring up in person. It is such an important fountain of accessibility to a plurality of first-hand vantage points, helping folks to learn more about, for example, the racial disparities in the US, what it's like to be transgender, and what to do about climate change directly from the activists themselves. Unrestricted access also means the onus of our learning can stay ours—we don't need to burden friends with questions or pry into their personal experiences if they don't want to organically share.

A few years ago, a friend started posting about her experience being neurodivergent, someone whose brain doesn't work in the same ways we're told it's "supposed to" work. At first, I read her stuff because I cared about her. I was aghast and impressed by her willingness to speak so openly about what I considered to be her admission of abnormality. As she shared her experiences and what she was learning about neurodivergence and the autistic community, I read with fascination and curiosity that evolved into passion and advocacy as my awareness of the experiences of autistic people grew.

As she shared both her own experiences and reposted what resonated from other accounts, I was able to learn from multiple first-hand experiences rather than the academic, removed, sterile, one-dimensional, and objective-sounding textbooks I had learned from in my psychology classes in college. And I say objective *sounding* because, importantly, textbooks and professors all carry biases. They rarely explicitly acknowledge them, which makes their words come across as objective even though they are anything but. By learning from someone's lived experiences, I learned how problematic textbooks and self-proclaimed experts can be as well as the importance of the slogan and movement "Nothing about us without us."

The more varied perspectives we're able to see, the more we also realize the monolith of "normal" we've been peddled does not truly exist. Regardless of what we're going through, people just like us are experiencing the same things, and unfortunately, our experiences are often quite "normal" indeed. It's been invaluable in helping me to process the shame and stigma I've felt around body image, being a woman, my own neurodivergence, and my place in capitalism. Whatever I'm feeling and experiencing, I've come to learn I'm never alone.

Paying attention to anything outside of our own experiences and the traditional narratives handed to us by socialization, media, and news outlets helps us to gain a fuller, more nuanced awareness of the world, which helps us expand our consciousness and break free of conventional dogma and ingrained mindsets. Gaining this broader perspective requires us to set aside what we "know" and be willing to open our hearts and minds to other perspectives. This gives us a beautiful opportunity to learn about others' experiences and explore other ways of being that exist outside of traditional power structures.

I'm thrilled more women are sharing their experiences of womanhood online. Not only has it made me less self-conscious as I realize I'm never alone, but it's also brought to light so many of the double binds we face as women.

The term "double bind" describes a dilemma in which an individual or group receives reciprocally conflicting messages that are inherently impossible to fulfill (Bateson et al. 1956). This creates a super distressing situation in which successful compliance with one set of expectations results in noncompliance with the other, such that the person faced with the decision will automatically be perceived as wrong, no matter how they act or respond. Such double binds are used as a form of social control without the use of open coercion. In a double bind, the person can neither resolve the dilemma nor opt out—judgment will be levied against them regardless.

Consider some of the gendered double binds prevalent today: Women are expected to be nurturing and compassionate. When we comply, we are told we are too "soft" and "don't have what it takes" to be promoted into leadership. When we instead lead with assertive directness, we're labeled "bitchy," "bossy," or "aggressive," deeming us similarly unfit. There's no winning.

So, what are we to do?

Consider again the idea of the "Republican Motherhood"—the paradoxical ideology that valued women's contributions while simultaneously determining they were unfit to lead. This paradox supported women in realizing they were pawns in a patriarchal existence, which in turn led to the organization of suffragettes and abolitionists. The double bind ideologies were both supremely antifeminist and gave rise to and created space for feminist movements.

Paradoxes and double binds, while often infuriating, can be keys to new ways of thinking and being. They ignite our curiosity and become a fertile ground for creative brainstorming and problem solving. They make us think.

The realization we're faced with a double bind or paradox is an invitation for a major breakthrough. Newly aware there's no winning, we are compelled to find another way.

Sometimes, this means finding a middle option, a Third Way, in which we integrate the strengths of both options to create an entirely new option. Other times, it can mean helping to educate people about the impossible criteria they're asking us to live up to and negotiating other expectations.

Other times still, it means recognizing the unwinnable game we're playing and opting out of the game entirely.

As we learned in our discussion of socialization, we're all playing different games with different rules. Some people are playing the "success is defined by the amount of money you make" game, while others are playing the "I work to live, I don't live to work" game. Language, like "I have to" and "I can't" reveals the unspoken rules that shape our lives without our consent. Unacknowledged, they shape our beliefs and confine our behavior. With awareness and intentionality, we can break free from their constraints.

When everyone around us is operating from the same system, playing the same game, running on the same hamster wheel, and peering through the same window of understanding, we have no reason to even consider another system, game, wheel, or window might even exist. We see "our" way as "the" way. When we believe there is one "right" way to be, we have no motivation to question it until that belief is challenged.

When we're cornered between two conflicting sets of game rules, on the other hand, we either succumb to the feeling of "wrongness" no matter what we do—and often seek self-help to teach us how to be "right"—or recognize the impossibility of the rules we're playing by and transcend these rules by opting out and choosing our own rules. This is the practice of turning something we are "subject" to into an "object" we can manipulate and be in choice about.

In common psychological parlance, we've reached maturity when we can deal with our experiences and meet developmental expectations for our age level. While we may expect people to "mature" by a certain age and to become wiser with time, wisdom is, in fact, a totally optional endeavor. It is not biologically dependent. Instead, it's a process wherein we become increasingly more self- and other-aware and develop an independent sense of self, one not defined by other people or relationships. For example, there's a good chance a twentysomething who has rejected the opinions of their family and chosen to follow their dreams according to their personal values is more psychologically mature than a seventysomething who does whatever their favorite politician tells them to do.

There are dozens of theories on adult development. This is just a taster, and I encourage you to check out others. They've all got their critiques, and despite how they're presented and how *I* am presenting this one here, there's certainly no rigid, universal, one-size-fits-all, predictable, linear, hierarchical path to human development. I encourage you to think about the path as less of a defined, straight line, and more of a fluid spiral, where we move between the stages that are available to us. As a general framework, models like this can be used to reveal trends and give us ways to make sense of ourselves and our world. They should not be used to insinuate anyone is more worthy or better than anyone else.

According to one of the most prevalent and influential theories of adult development, Dr. Robert Kegan's Constructive Development Theory, adults go through stages of development, just like children do (Kegan 1982). Over time, as we come into contact with new ideas, we are transformed by them. The way we understand and operate in the world shifts as emotions and beliefs that lived in our subconscious become conscious, and therefore, workable, controllable, and manageable. Ideas move from being this hidden, elusive thing we are subjected to, to being like an object, something we can turn around in our hands and inspect. This is known as the subject-object shift. During subject-object shifts, we transform ourselves from being subject to an idea (it controls me) to making the belief object (something we can hold, examine, and be in choice, and therefore control, about) (Pruyn 2010; Mallel 2017a; Kegan 1982).

For example: I am not my feelings; I have feelings. I am not my religion; I have a religion. I am not my job; I have a job.

I like to think of subject and object like a shadow. When we're too close to a wall, we can't see our shadow at all. Only when we back away from the wall are we able to see it. Similarly, if we hold a belief too closely, we cannot see that we are subject to it. It's not until we hold it out at arm's length that we recognize it as a distinct and separate object from ourselves.

As young kids, we begin so close to the wall, we can't see any of it. Kegan calls this the "impulsive" mind. Our impulses "have" us. We are subject to them, whether we're putting random things we find into our mouths or pulling the cat's tail. Most of us mature out of this phase by adolescence (Pruyn 2010; Kegan 1982).

As we step back from the wall, another way of experiencing life opens up to us. We see life through a second perspective, often called the "imperial" or "instrumental" mind. We are still hell-bent on getting our way but have learned about consequences. We respond to sticks (consequences) and carrots (incentives) when we think we'll be caught but don't yet take other people's wants and needs into consideration. Sometimes, we don't even realize they exist. We may act manipulatively and use people and relationships transactionally, just as a way of getting what we want. By the time we're eighteen, most—but not all—adults have matured past this stage (Pruyn 2010; Mallel 2017a; Kegan 1982).

Some of us get to this stage very early and move on to the next stage quickly. Most of us experience it during adolescence and grow out of it. Some adults, though, never leave this stage. Research estimates about 6 percent of the adult population is still operating from this mindset (Mallel 2017a). The literature, steeped in normative psychology, capitalism, and ableism, often describes folks who never mature past this second phase as the "prisoners, substance abusers, the unemployed or unemployable," unable to function in society because they can't comprehend balancing their needs with the needs of society (Eriksen 2007, 174–182). I think that's a wild oversimplification. I can think of politicians who govern this way and addicts who are clearly in later stages of development. I'm sure you can think of adults who operate similarly, acting from an unwavering, unexamined pursuit of what they want at all costs (and the self-help books that endorse this).

Once a few more windows of understanding open, we realize there are other people in the world who have legitimate wants and needs also worthy of respect. We transition into the "socialized mind." From this third vantage point, we're able to hold our personal needs, desires, wants, and interests object as we recognize there's a larger world out there that we are a part of. We recognize people will think of us a certain way if we don't abide by cultural norms. We care about others' opinions and the way their opinions impact our relationships with them (Pruyn 2010; Mallel 2017a; Kegan 1982).

In this stage, we care a lot about what the people around us think and use our newfound control of our own wants, desires, and needs to conform to the beliefs of those around us. In short, we accept the beliefs of our religious institutions, buy into what pop culture tells us is cool, and are desperately afraid of disappointing the people whose opinions matter to us. This is a deeply powerful evolutionary trait—to be ostracized in prehistoric society meant death.

Often, we end up adopting other people's belief systems and "rules" wholesale and think they are our own—we don't yet recognize beliefs and opinions are things we can examine and choose. We see this in folks with unquestioned religious beliefs, adherence to strict, gendered guidelines about the "right" way to be a man or a woman, and conformity to a shared culture and consciousness, whether via capitalism, consumerism, conservatism, liberalism, or any belief system. We have allowed our beliefs to be authored by someone else. We have been socialized.

The majority of adults are operating from this stage, and never transcend it. This includes people we typically look to for guidance—our parents, priests, politicians, teachers, and therapists. Most of us take it all the way to our deathbeds. We operate from within the mindset of the culture we are in without questioning it, and we truly believe we have chosen the beliefs we hold for ourselves (Pruyn 2010; Mallel 2017a; Kegan 1982).

Even though it's quick and easy to balk at the idea of being subject to the culture we are in, I'm sure you can identify a time within the last week when you've worried about what someone else has thought about you, spent energy worrying about letting someone down, or sought affirmation for a presentation, an outfit, or a social media post. It's an indication we are, from time to time, still operating from a "socialized" mind, subject to relationships and external validation. When we fear what "they" will think, we're subject to their opinions, which impacts our beliefs and behaviors.

I find the people who quickly dismiss this stage often live here, just in denial. "That's not me," they say, "I live for myself! I don't care what people think!" They're unable to recognize the ways society impacts them in covert ways. Folks who are moving into latter stages see themselves in it. "Oh yeah, I definitely recognize that tendency," they say. Or, "I don't do that regularly anymore, but I certainly do that when I'm home for the holidays and when I'm stressed."

In my experience, this is where most people look to self-help. And it makes sense. We know we're not living up to expectations in some way, so we look for someone to guide us, unintentionally replacing the rules we've learned about life with… someone else's rules. Unless someone in this stage finds uniquely liberatory self-help, or a mentor who encourages them to think deeply about their circumstances, it's not likely to fully change their perspective. Self-help can be extremely useful for navigating this stage, but it can also create stagnancy when the author is equally mired in socializing forces. It is typically through mindfulness, reflecting on paradoxes and personal experience, and seeing life through others' windows that I see folks move from operating within the limits of their socialization into self-determination.

During the fourth stage, "self-authoring" mind, we have stepped far enough from the wall to recognize we are our own person with beliefs and values that differ from those of the people and cultures around us. This stage typically involves examining our beliefs and behaviors consciously for the very first time. We work to determine our own understanding of the world outside of the forces that shaped our early lives and beliefs. In this phase, we question everything. We deconstruct. We interrogate expectations, establish our own values, and, released from the expectations of others and their value systems, must learn to negotiate our limits and boundaries with others anew. We explore our inner worlds with curiosity and take responsibility for ourselves in new ways. We recognize we are constantly changing. We become the authors of our own narratives (Mallel 2017b; Pruyn 2010; Kegan 1982).

Self-help aimed at this stage of adult development often encourages us to lean into our own values, separate from the values of those around us. Titles like this include *The Artist's Way* by Julia Cameron (2002), *Untamed* by Glennon Doyle (2020), and *The Desire Map* by Danielle LaPorte (2014). We experiment with reidentification and "being ourselves." I've often seen this present as a sort of midlife crisis. We feel a bit untethered as we let go of the way we've always done things in pursuit of a new paradigm not yet defined. We try to find the new rules by which to live life and reevaluate our priorities.

It is estimated only 35 percent of adults ever reach this stage, and it can be at any point in life (Mallel 2017a). Some folks, like most of my clients, hit this point astonishingly early, making them feel tremendously alone and misunderstood. Other people get there far later in life, when a major life event provokes reflection, such as retirement, a close loved one's death, or their own personal illness (Pruyn 2010; Kegan 1982).

These moments, too, reveal windows of understanding. They tend to pop open when we least expect them. After sitting in the depths of despair, or burnout. After being crushed by what feels like a massive failure. While being fired from the job you've given everything to. Losing a parent or child. Experiencing cancer. Infidelity. The options are endless.

These windows of understanding present themselves when something triggers an awareness, an understanding, and a level of consciousness we've never had access to before. And they can be jarring. Earth-shattering. They can rip us of the stranglehold we have on our identities and realities and leave us adrift. Untethered and trying to catch our breath, we search frantically for the safety of dry, familiar land.

Used to the comfort of feeling in control, we strain. We strain for something to hold on to until we're too tired to strain anymore. We tread water until our legs give out. Eventually, utterly depleted, we take a final sigh and let go. We give ourselves, exhausted and depleted, to the wild, chaotic ocean of existence. Grief washes over, and we sob from deep in our souls, unable to go on.

Only to find life has gone on. We're miles from a familiar shore. There's no land in any direction. There's no safety or hope in sight, but we haven't died. We float on. Sometimes for days. Sometimes for months. Sometimes for years.

We embrace the chaos and ride the waves.

And one day, we open our eyes to see we've washed ashore somewhere strange and new. We don't remember getting here. There was no defining moment, like there was when we were ripped from our familiar moorings, but we're here all the same.

For some of us, the transformation is immediate and all-encompassing. Others resist as long as we can until the information can no longer be ignored and must be integrated into our worldview. But eventually, we wash up on a new shore and find our feet planted in a new reality.

We may never have this experience. We may have it a dozen times. With enough mindfulness, reflection, and support, such experiences bring wisdom, perspective, and often, a recognition that we're all interconnected, all experiencing life differently, and that all our feelings and experiences are valid.

This is called the "interconnected" or "self-transforming" mind. In this proposed fifth and final stage, identity is object—it can be examined and reflected upon at a distance. Now, our sense of self is recognized as being constantly created, honed, and explored. We can hold multiple perspectives at any time, understand ourselves and the world through multiple lenses and vantage points, and adjust and evolve. Only 1 percent of adults ever reach this stage (Pruyn 2010; Kegan 1982; Mallel 2017a; Mallel 2020).

I see very few, if any, self-help books aimed at this stage, likely because by this point, both author and reader would realize self and reality as socially constructed and ever evolving. Self-help as we know it becomes all but obsolete. We no longer pursue knowledge as a means to fit in, we pursue knowledge simply for the sake of it, or for an artistic and emotional experience, or to expand our worldview.

The process of evolving our individual consciousness can be a tremendously challenging and confusing one. It's confusing for the people around us, too, who often don't realize we're going through a big transformation and are attached to us being who we've always been. In many circles, there's no framework for assisting us in this process. In fact, it's often seen as an existential threat to church doctrine, filial piety, and corporate authority. As a result, we often end up navigating the turbulent waters alone.

The communities we participate in really matter in this process. They are tremendously impactful to our overall maturation. They teach us how to learn, question, unlearn, and relearn, or they inhibit our growth by forcing compliance with specific belief systems through conditional acceptance.

As a result, our individual consciousness is pretty tightly linked with our collective consciousness, especially early on. Without a guide or windows of understanding to light our way, we're left searching for our own paths and vehicles to liberation. We search for liberation from intergenerational trauma, forces of oppression and socialization, and the myths of scarcity and insufficiency all on our own.

Self-help, in theory, could support us in our evolutions. Books that supported our development would help us to change how we see the nature of the problems we face and the ways we could go about solving them. They would present us with and encourage us to peer into windows of understanding that encourage an evolution in our individual consciousness and allow us to evaluate and find solutions to our problems in new ways.

In my experience, vehicles to liberation are rarely cut from the same cloth that created the problem. They do not require force. You should not need to pay for them.

Mine have been found in exploring ideas that live outside the bounds of "should." When my culture says I "shouldn't" take naps on a workday, I give it a go and see what happens. Actually taking afternoon naps was, of course, the only thing that helped me to irrefutably accept I not only work better when I am rested, but that my worth isn't bound up in my productivity whatsoever. After all, what better way to learn than to experience it for ourselves?

I found another vehicle to liberation in psychedelic experiences, which gave me glimpses into other ways of being, feeling, and existing, and embodiment and somatic practices that let me explore what my body was telling me, when those messages would typically be drowned out by "shoulds" flooding my psyche. As I reconnected to the sensations in my body, I wondered what my racing heart was trying to tell me in the same way I'd pay attention to my stomach telling me I was hungry. I need something right now—what is it?

I found vehicles to liberation in supportive partnerships and communities that held me when everything felt too heavy to carry alone. With the support of trusted friends, mentors, coaches, and therapists, I found liberation while floundering in the confusing, debilitating catch-22s that blinded me to the questions I should have been asking all along: Is their approval worth having? Do I even want to be the kind of person they approve of? Who do *I* want to be, anyway?

Each of these practices provided me with insights, worldviews, and windows of understanding that were wild, undomesticated, and uncivilized. They were the voices that hadn't been socialized into playing nice and being quiet, some from within, some from without, asking questions no one could answer but me.

SECTION III

ANALYSIS

CHAPTER 9

NAVIGATING OPPRESSION

Reuniting with our wildness can feel exhilarating; doing so in community can be transformational.

Gabriela, finally free to express decades of repressed anger, picked up the shards of the old dishes she smashed, and held them up to the camera so we could all see them.[2] The shiny white pieces contained scribbled fragments of blood-red words she'd never say out loud. "And when I was done with this..." She smiled, gleefully. "I took every single one of the dish towels from the office and shredded them. Ripped them into a million tiny pieces. Took a pair of scissors to the ones I couldn't rip with my hands."

Her proud, ear-to-ear grin was met with a chorus of whoops and woohoos and "Hell yes you did!"s and "Do the mugs next!"

---

2 Gabriela's name has been changed, and this story has been included with permission.

"Yes, the mugs are next! I fucking hate those mugs! Why do we need so many fucking mugs anyway? They're gone!"

Another round of cheering.

"I just can't tell you how good it feels to break things. To be angry. To feel angry and not feel bad about it. I swear to God, the only thing more cathartic than unapologetically crying into my ice cream in a bathtub is breaking shit. God *damn,* that felt good."

The rest of the Go Love Yourself community members nodded along from our Zoom windows. We could relate. Each of us could identify with feeling so down, so sad, that all we wanted to do was give in—to succumb to the sadness, to wallow a minute in self-pity and despair, and stuff our faces with junk food. Many of us wanted to be angry enough to break things but weren't there yet. Gabriela's brazen anger and release gave us hope.

For a few months, a group of us had been discussing just how shitty it is to be what sisters Emily and Amelia Nagoski describe in their book *Burnout* as "human givers" (2019). Human givers are women who are expected to "give everything, every moment of their lives, every drop of energy, to the care of others" who are allowed to just be human beings (read: men and sometimes children). We mourned the energy wasted on pretending to be happy, the hours of sleep and personal time lost to doing the laundry and house cleaning and childcare that wasn't shared by our partners, and the experiences we couldn't enjoy because we were so focused on making them perfect—for others.

The experience made us all feel seen. We shared our stories, listened to the stories of others, lamented the unfairness of the expectations and the awful, awful reasons they existed in the first place. We were vulnerable, and angry, and sad, and resentful, and remorseful, and empathetic in turn. We raged at, and then wept for our mothers and grandmothers for perpetuating unrealistic expectations and shaming us into following suit. We were incredulous and then compassionate toward the authors of the self-help books that told us all we had to do was manage our time more effectively, think positive thoughts, exercise more willpower, and we'd be the superwomen everyone needed us to be.

We learned in chapter 2 that as children, we pay close attention to what the adults are telling us is the "right" way to be. We learn *how* to be, but we also learn *who* it's "good" to be. We learn which identities are overvalued and which are undervalued in our society. This creates a ranking system that values humans differently based on social memberships (Nieto and Boyer 2006).

Social memberships such as race, gender, age, and sexuality are socially constructed groups. They are ways of oversimplifying complex identities to quickly make sense of another person or group of people. Once we have been able to describe a person based on a social membership, we're able to make quick predictions of how we expect they'll behave. In other words, it allows us to stereotype. Because of their social construction, these stereotypes are reflective of social conditions and beliefs rather than of any natural, existing order. This also means they change over time.

Each social category has over- and under-valued characteristics that contribute to social "ranks." For example, within the category "class," individuals from higher social classes are often presumed to possess superior qualities, leading to stereotypes of harder work ethics and better upbringings. Research shows that we are more likely to assume someone is competent if they appear to be wealthy than if they appear to be poor (Oh, Shafir, and Todorov 2020). I revealed my own insidious class biases when I assumed Mark's family would inherently be better than me—I internalized negative stereotypes about myself as a poor person. Assumptions and stereotypes like these can lead to biased hiring practices, resulting in discrimination against individuals from a perceived lower rank, including people from a lower economic class, those with a disability, and those perceived to be too young or old.

People who have desired characteristics and identities are what Dr. Leticia Nieto and Margot Boyer refer to as agents (2006). *Agents* experience *agency* around a particular characteristic or identity. For example, individuals in the so-called "prime" of their lives like Gabriela and me (midthirties) are significantly more likely to get a call back for a job than older candidates (Carlsson and Eriksson 2019). Our age gives us agency.

Those who do not have the desired characteristics or identities are targets (Nieto and Boyer 2006). Targets' characteristics are a liability in a society that does not value that characteristic. Folks who are older will experience their age as a liability when applying for jobs. In fact, callback rates drop by 5 percent for every ten years of aging, and folks close to retirement have a callback rate of under 3 percent (Carlsson and Eriksson 2019).

When we hold a privileged identity, we often internalize the positive feelings afforded to us via our rank, and hold unfavorable views of those who don't share our rank. I may, for instance, roll my eyes at "kids these days," and a moment later toss an "Okay, Boomer," to the old farts who roll their eyes at me.

Mass marketing preys on this hierarchical desirability, suggesting we should control what we can so we don't *become* a target. And if the characteristics are beyond our control, we should at least control the *image* we are portraying. This is apparent in beauty ads aimed at older women. There is an assumption that as women age, we'll want to mitigate the effects and liabilities associated with aging by filling fine lines and wrinkles and dying our graying hair.

Self-help operates similarly, "helping" us to control what we can so we don't become a target, or "helping" us to control our image as a target. By controlling how we show up, it suggests that if we at least try to be a "good" target, we might avoid further pain and scrutiny.

Remember the choices I thought I had? To be a femme fatale or a brazen careerist? These were the two archetypes I had of a "good" target—one who wouldn't be put at a further disadvantage due to her womanhood. In my mind, as long as a woman played her character well, she wouldn't be targeted for additional humiliation, just the regular run-of-the-mill harassment.

If, as women, we recognize we will be targets simply by virtue of being women, we can turn to self-help, which grants us two options:

1. We can try to be more like the agents (men) in this social rank (gender) by approximating their agency. This would mean moving, thinking, talking, and "acting like a man." Some self-help examples include Frankel's *Nice Girls Don't Get the Corner Office* and Harvey's *Act Like a Lady, Think Like a Man.*

2. We can be the epitome of the positive characteristics associated with our target identity's stereotype. This means conforming to sexist norms and gender role

expectations about what it means to "act like a woman." Examples include Hollis's *Girl, Wash Your Face*, Sandberg's *Lean In,* Doyle's *The Surrendered Wife,* and Gray's *Men Are from Mars, Women Are from Venus.*

Self-help books, by and large, are written by middle-aged middle- and upper-middle class cisgender straight white men and women. Authors born into unexamined agent status and privilege routinely fail to address folks who aren't just like them. Instead, they aim to help readers navigate just one identity at a time. But none of us are affected by one single identity. This is what American scholar, author, and civil rights advocate Professor Kimberlé Crenshaw refers to as "intersectionality" (1989). Each of us has a number of intersecting identities, leaving us impacted by multiple social justice issues. As a result, the way we experience life as a young straight wealthy Black woman or an old poor white queer woman changes our experience of being a woman.

Our intersecting identities can make us both agents and targets of discrimination. As I listened to Gabriela's story, I shared her experience as a woman conforming to the expectations of womanhood as a target. We were both in our thirties and experienced the shared relative privilege associated with being an agent. As a queer Latina woman, though, Gabriela faced discrimination and expectations not being shared by all of us in the mixed-age, mixed-sexuality, mixed-ethnicity Zoom group. Together, we navigated our experiences as women by reading books that addressed our womanhood, but fewer books were able to speak to her experience as a queer woman, and fewer still were able to speak to her experience as a queer Latina.

Gabriela chose to embody the "ideal" form of a woman to try and avoid scrutiny as a target but, as a queer woman, sought proximity to the group with power, the agents, who were straight. She hid her identity from family and colleagues, fearful of the shaming and ostracization she thought were inevitable.

Gabriela and the rest of us felt like we had two choices as women: we could either buck the expectations we were supposed to be superwomen or conform to them. Most of us had chosen to conform to them and read self-help books helping us to do so. We allowed ourselves to be made to feel fat and ugly and then dieted and made ourselves as small and attractive as possible. We allowed ourselves to feel insufficient and read up on how to be the perfect moms, wives, and employees. We studied how to be in tune with our emotions without being emotional, how to be assertive without being a bitch, and how to get what we want without being direct or demanding. We did everything we could to be the ideal version of a woman.

This false choice is what Nieto and Boyer refer to as "survival" mode, the first in a five-part, nonlinear experience of empowerment (2006). In survival, we are primarily focused on safety. We strive to conform to society's expectations, which often require constant shapeshifting. We may be completely unaware we're doing so or recognize our shapeshifting while ignoring and denying the -isms (racism, ageism, sexism) underlying our motivations (Nieto and Boyer 2006). When I read *Why Men Love Bitches* I wanted love and, in survival mode, did what I thought I had to do to get it. The larger sexist pressures shaping my decisions never crossed my mind.

Other times, the *survival* aspect of "survival mode" is much more literal. As a child, I conformed to who I was told a "good child" was—seen and not heard. I was silent for my protection and safety since there were very real physical consequences for noncompliance. The threat of violence is even more severe for identities that are marginalized and oppressed in our society when noncompliance can mean injury and death.

While in survival mode, we buy into these power dynamics. We reinforce them by criticizing ourselves and others for not meeting social expectations. Negative self-talk comes from internalizing society's shaming messages; this is internalized oppression (David and Derthick 2013; Asare 2022). This may also manifest in horizontal or lateral oppression, that is, the cruel treatment of others for not meeting expectations *we* feel compelled to meet. This looks like skinny women criticizing fat women or femme women calling other women manly. This looks like slut-shaming, othering, gossiping, bullying, and shunning (Armstrong et al. 2014).

At some point during this process, many of us start to suspect something being amiss. Perhaps we recognize just how exhausting it is to try and achieve unrealistic beauty standards. Or we finally recognize we shouldn't have to literally starve ourselves to gain acceptance. Or we realize people are, in fact, treated differently in this world based on factors both totally arbitrary and entirely outside of our control. This part of us whispers, "I shouldn't have to..." and "This isn't right..." and asks, "What's going on?" and "Is this as good as it gets?"

For Gabriela, it meant realizing she had a long history of conforming to sexist standards of womanhood when she felt unsafe or unloved. It meant realizing she was conforming to being a "good" woman by shrinking herself in the middle seat on planes while the men had no qualms about dominating the armrests, and in her seat at the office where men had no issue taking her ideas and using them as their own. It also meant realizing she was hypersexualizing herself in a way that didn't feel good in the hopes she would win the approval of random men by conforming to the image of a "good" Latina. It meant shoving down her anger about all of it. She began letting herself feel uncomfortable with how things had been going.

This second stage in Nieto and Boyer's framework is quite appropriately described as "confusion." It is the time when we both continue to conform and question the expectations we are conforming to. We doubt our own evidence that something's amiss as we question and contradict ourselves. During this time, we continue to perpetuate expectations, oppression, and judgment onto others. We are unable to untangle the individual struggles and shame we feel from our own actions and shortcomings. We cannot yet see these manifestations as symptomatic of systemic issues (Nieto and Boyer 2006).

The questions we ask in confusion lead us to the sort of "waking up" I shared with you in section 1. We begin to discuss what we're seeing and feeling with others in the stage known as "empowerment." During this stage, it's important to have access to an empowered, target-only space in which one can continue to talk and learn about everything, and stay engaged in order to stay "awake."

By engaging in a conversation with the rest of us, Gabriela could check her experiences against ours. She was able to realize she wasn't alone in feeling unworthy just by being a woman, and realize there was no winning—for any of us—by continuing to play this game. As a collective, we were able to point to the way sexism shows up in our lives from the youngest of ages to show us our place in the hierarchy and to remind us of our second-class citizenship in our own bodies, psyches, families, and communities. When any one of us would begin to get down on ourselves for not measuring up, another would chime in to remind us it wasn't our own personal failing and that the expectations were unrealistic on purpose. We then held space for the frustration at ourselves and at the systems that continued to keep us feeling inadequate.

This continued learning and community building allows for two things to happen. First, it enables the person to recognize the historic roots of the targeting and the social conditions that contribute to the oppression. Secondly, the group often creates a safe space for anger that may be activated and mobilized in solidarity with other targets to create change.

Gabriela was angry and finally allowed herself to express it.

As we become increasingly aware, we also become increasingly discerning in our use of energy. The fourth stage is called "strategy" because we strategically choose our battles. We choose when to collaborate with other targets, when to confront agents, when to make demands of our institutions, and when to not act at all. We conserve our energy to maximize our effectiveness. In this stage, we recognize self-care is important, for when we practice self-care, we experience increased energy, which supports us in making more effective and strategic choices (Nieto and Boyer 2006).

During this stage, we may not be able to discern liberating values, norms, and beliefs from the oppressive, dehumanizing ones we're accustomed to without help. In this stage, we begin to align our values more closely with the empowering values of our target group and become freer to make the choices that support ourselves and our group (Nieto and Boyer 2006).

Sound familiar? It beautifully parallels the process of evolving through the stages of adult development we discussed in chapter 8.

Together, we chose to create and embody our own values. In our community, we created a space where there were no expectations for how we showed up, so when Gabriela chose to show up tipsy, sans bra and makeup, proud of her expressed anger, she was welcomed and celebrated. When Gabriela shared stories of the way she shrank herself and played the role of the meek, hypersexualized Latina woman to avoid an altercation at the bar, we understood and supported her ability to recognize what she was doing and why. And when Gabriela fretted over the best way to shut down her mother's fat-shaming insults, we rallied around her and formulated a plan.

As we continue to collaborate with other targets and allied agents, we make increasingly adaptive and congruent choices. We acknowledge the impact of systemic oppression and use our understanding of these systems to change them in humanized, streamlined ways and move into leadership positions in our social change work. This is the process of "recentering" (Nieto and Boyer 2006).

Gabriela explored ways to move from a mentality of fat-shaming into fat-positivity and finally body-neutrality. She held conversations in her male-dominated workplace about the best ways to distribute work and pay equitably and joined the board of her field's professional society to continue the work at scale. She helped to create her industry's first set of standards for equitable treatment of individuals of all genders.

During this final phase of empowerment, targets access their internal, intrinsic power and utilize it. This power is not one reliant on permission, rank, status, or any socially constructed hierarchy, rather from one's ability to be their authentic self, grounded and compassionate, and supportive of oneself and others (Nieto and Boyer 2006).

It is important to note these stages do not function as linearly as Gabriela's journey seems to indicate. In other words, we do not progress cleanly from one stage to another and live in that stage until we move to the next. Instead, similar to adult development, as we move into a new phase, we unlock and gain new skills that enable us to engage in new ways. They function more like nested dolls in that as we grow, we transcend and include previous stages (Nieto and Boyer 2006). With each new skillset, we retain access to those gained in previous stages, granting us greater choice, possibility, and action.

Similar to other skills, or where we are in our adult maturity, the higher level the skill and the more recent the acquisition, the less practice we have with it and the more energy its use demands. When we are low on energy or high on stress, we fall back on our more familiar, less demanding, "automatic" skills. Someone in the self-authoring stage of development, when faced with acute stress like the loss of a job or a traumatic breakup, might revert back to earlier stages of thinking, such as wanting revenge at any cost or worrying about what others will think of them. This is what happened when Gabriela hypersexualized herself for her own safety—the stressful situation meant she turned to her more automatic skills of fawning to avoid pain and conflict.

Most self-help I see on store shelves helps us to answer the questions, "What should I do to be successful?" and, "How do I be a better version of myself, as narrowly defined by our culture?" As a result, the vast majority of these books teach us the survival skills of how to fit in and hustle for acceptance and belonging. They give us strategies to change ourselves in order to conform to the expectations someone else has for us. They rely heavily on comparison tactics we use to shame and coerce ourselves into being different.

While the number of books helping us to access and navigate further stages of empowerment are certainly increasing (check out our favorites at www.itsnotallyourfault.com), the fact is the self-help industry relies on us being in survival mode for its own survival. Like a bully needs someone to bully, publishers have no incentive to escort us out of survival mode and into more empowered ways of living and being. To take us out of the shame cycle would mean to take us out of their sales cycle, which would be detrimental to their billion-dollar business.

Reading books that invite us into further stages of development and empowerment in a liberating community allows us to have brave conversations with those we trust deeply, which allows us to move from survival, through confusion, and into empowerment, as Gabriela and the rest of us did. By connecting with other women about our similar experiences, we were able to recognize our common humanity and open windows of understanding into our collective suffering. We recognized our suffering and anger were not individual moral failings, which both allowed us to reduce the immediate experience of shame and uncover the shared, collective, external, and social sources.

While an infinite number of books seek to "help" us navigate our experiences as women, far fewer books aim to help individuals navigate the complexity of intersectional identities. While a few books aimed to empower Gabriela to become more comfortable with her sexuality, she lamented finding no books that helped her to process coming to terms with her desire to hide her sexuality from the people she loved. In our search together, we found no books that helped her feel fully seen as a queer woman in the Latinx community. Instead, she turned to memoirs and fiction.

Any book or strategy that seeks to help us to conform without questioning the belief systems behind the expectation simply helps us to mitigate our experiences of our oppression rather than to help us break the cycle of the oppression we are facing. They keep us confined to survival mode, navigating oppression rather than questioning, deconstructing, and finally, overcoming it.

CHAPTER 10

SELF-HELP IS A CAPITALIST RELIGION

My introduction to yoga came as an unwelcome surprise. It was during a softball team warm-up in high school. Our coach informed us that in addition to our typical stretches, we'd be trying this new yoga thing. We did what teenage girls are wont to do and scanned the room to see how we should feel.

I remember a mixture of skeptic brows and contorted, confused faces that said, "What the fuck does yoga have to do with crushing our competition?" Our coach shrugged and in addition to having us do our typical stretches had us do some… other stretches. I vaguely remember a tree pose as the coach mumbled something about the importance of flexibility and balance.

We never did yoga again.

I didn't touch the stuff for another decade or so until a teacher friend invited me along to a session at our gym. I was exhausted and couldn't fathom mustering up the energy required for spin-class levels of exertion after a long, shitty day in front of a classroom. Despite my reluctance, I agreed.

The instructor introduced herself as a DC lawyer by day and yoga instructor by night. Yoga helped her to loosen up and let go of the day before she went home.

Perfect, I thought, *I could use some of that.*

I was pleased to be met with ten minutes of the softball-style warm-ups I was accustomed to. We touched our toes. We got on the floor and touched our toes. We crossed one leg over the other and rotated our spines. It was familiar. It was comfortable. I let myself loosen up.

I made it through that session, appreciating that some bends and stretches could count as my exercise for the day and that I didn't have to be on the other side of the mirrored wall, where dumbbells and barbells hit the ground in a cacophony of clinks, clashes, and exaggerated grunts. I loved that I could check the box labeled "work out" without subjecting my battered nervous system to any more chaos, loud noises, or exertion. I could escape that world for a gently lit alternative that played soothing nature sounds to mask the obvious war happening outside.

Each gym I've belonged to in the ten years since my reintroduction has also offered yoga classes. Most offer a generic class labeled "Yoga." Others differentiate between hatha, flow, and "power" yoga. They have, with nearly no exceptions, been taught by American-educated, slim white women who reminded us this was what they did to calm down, relax, and get some gentle movement after their stressful, busy days in their prestigious, traditionally successful jobs.

Without a doubt, some incredible mental and physical benefits of yoga have been thoroughly documented. I've benefited from them personally. I'm also aware, however, that my participation is part of a larger pattern; yoga is just one of the many Eastern practices adopted by the West for profit and personal gain, devoid of context and without respect for its origins or original purpose. For those of us who practice yoga, or other Eastern practices, or want to, it's important to recognize the role our participation plays and to strive to honor and uplift the communities and cultures from which they come. As I share what I've learned, I am doing so from the perspective of someone who deeply respects the practices and wants their origins and purposes to be honored rather than appropriated, commercialized, or diluted.

As I understand it, yoga, in its current and most common iteration in the United States, is virtually unrecognizable from its original form. In its Western application, it is a pared-down, secularized, gym-studio version of what it once was, focusing on the benefits to the body and mind. Commonly advertised benefits in the West include feel-good, altered states of consciousness such as calm, relaxation, self-love, peace, and bliss for the purposes of feeling better and reducing stress levels.

This stands in contrast to many yoga practices of the East. While they vary in terms of philosophies and practices, most forms reject an identification with the self and reject acting in one's own self-interest. Rather than inviting spikes in contentment, Hindu-based yoga practices for attaining liberation call for the prevention and cessation of such mental fluctuations altogether. It is believed that by preventing altered states of consciousness, we are better able to distinguish between the true self, which is pure, transcendent consciousness, and the body and thoughts we've falsely come to see as our "self" (Carrette and King 2004).

As practitioners sought to popularize yoga, they adapted the practices to please a Western palate. Beginning in the 1930s with B.K.S. Iyengar, yoga became increasingly detached from its South Asian context and heritage and personalized to the wants of new practitioners. It was meant to be universalized and accessible, but its cultural neutrality gave way to strong Western interpretations through the lens of Western values (Carrette and King 2004).

As a Western collective, we took a curious side-eye toward the new-to-us, exotic practices and asked if it could help us to be more attractive and successful. We decided, "OHMygod, yes!" and dove in, extracting that which fit our Western values. We took the practices of an Eastern religion with a clear connection to society and mission to transform the world, one that critiques the idea of an all-important self, removed its social, ethical, religious, and ascetic dimensions, and rebranded it as an individual physical exercise regime that could help us to reduce the stressors of our lives without ever having to question or challenge them.

And yoga is far from the only casualty of the secularization and individualization of religious practices. Similar to yoga, Buddhist practices such as meditation have been appropriated and commercialized by the Western wellness sphere to meet the ego-driven goals of individuals. In Buddhism, many of the practices are individual in method and nature but not in goal or outcome. For example, a practitioner of Zen Buddhism may meditate individually with the intention of supporting the collective. Tonglen meditation practices, for instance, liberate practitioners from selfishness and awaken compassion by breathing in the pain and suffering of the world and exhaling peace to support the collective (Chodron 2023). Meditation supports individuals by recognizing that we, as individual humans, are a stream of constant change—conditioned, temporal entities in a web of causal processes. It helps us in overcoming the misconceptions we have about the nature of an ego-driven, all-important self.

The mental and physical techniques associated with many meditation practices support the individual in rejecting self-indulgent cravings thought to be the cause of all suffering. In rejecting and overcoming any notion of a separate self, we attain liberation. This liberation from suffering, called nirvana, breaks the chain of rebirths binding us all to worldly suffering. In Buddhism, to change the self is to recognize there is no all-important self and change society (Carrette and King 2004).

In Buddhism, the self is the problem to overcome. The process of enlightenment is *expected and assumed to take lifetimes.*

This is, of course, in direct contrast and opposition to our Western values associated with individualism, hedonism, materialism, and instant gratification.

Buddhism and other Eastern traditions saw a surge in popularity in the 1960s due to the tumult of the civil rights movement, war, financial rifts, increased interest in altered forms of consciousness, and an influx of Tibetan refugees in the sixties and Vietnamese, Laotian, and Cambodian refugees in the seventies. It promised a more methodical road to happiness than Christianity, and a way out of the spiritual bankruptcy and complexity of modern life (Carrette and King 2004).

Unlike other religions that require tons of research, self-reflection, community building, and commitment to be accepted as a part of the community, American Buddhism does not require any formal conversion practices. Practitioners are often encouraged to incorporate Dharma practices into their existing lives and traditions.

As a convert religion, it has appealed mainly to white, middle- and upper-middle class, left-leaning urbanites searching for peace, enlightenment, and transcendence. While "convert Buddhism" sects like Zen and Vipassana have gained traction, many Western Buddhists are nondenominational and influence/are influenced by the New Age movement, which has resulted in the mass acceptance and promotion of meditation (Carrette and King 2004).

Like Yoga, meditation was extracted from its original context by affluent white Westerners. It has been promoted as a way to escape the stressors of daily life, give respite to our troubled minds, and give us a way of coping with the realities of our individual existences in highly oppressive systems. A practice of transcending worldly suffering was reduced to a mild sedative.

These two Eastern practices and philosophies that decentered the self were co-opted for the optimization and placation of the self. Critiques of individualism from collectivist societies, wisdoms, religions, and cultures were repurposed to promote the transformation and development of the self for the sake of the self. Strong ethical and revolutionary social stances were removed almost entirely. We ignored the lessons about *inter*dependence so we could experience transcendence *independently*.

We've taken practices that could have supported us in challenging the stressors as a collective and desecrated them. We've taken rich, complex traditions, and leaned on the authority and wisdom Ancient Asian traditions imbue while neutering and fragmenting them, extracting what was privately useful for the individual before selectively repackaging them for commodification and purchase. Priceless messages of universal compassion, social responsibility, and revolution are translated into quick fixes we can learn in the span of one expensive weekend retreat for the sake of a calmer, happier self.

Individual practices such as yoga and meditation are lumped by wellness advocates into lists of practices aimed at calming the angst of modern living. They offer a means of transcending the vapid, meaningless world we live in typically reserved for religion with none of the communal or ethical requirements or responsibilities. This allows Westerners comfortable with the Christian trinity to seek spirituality and transcendence associated with the body-mind-soul without needing to join a traditional institution.

In the past few decades, spirituality, which once meant a relationship with the divine or God, has transformed into a concept that can only be defined by the one who claims it. In this way, spirituality itself has been able to transcend religious tradition, ritual, and institution, and in doing so, also separate itself from the baggage of these associations. It has been able to divorce itself from any occult, or "other-worldly" connections and connotations and be translated for use in the "this-worldly" here and now. This makes spirituality more appealing to folks on a quest for meaning, who would rather not be associated with organized religion or anything supernatural.

This utilitarianism and privatization of spirituality has become a perfect match for the seekers of the self-help world who are looking for values, hope, connectedness, and answers for how to deal without sacrificing any independence or having to examine their individual morals or ethics while on the hunt for the good life.

As interest in spirituality for personal development has grown, it has also become exploited as a trend and appropriated by businesses as a way to maximize the use of humans as company resources and turn workplaces into entities of cultlike devotion, in turn maximizing both loyalty and profits

(Crispin 2020). Workplace spirituality is big business. Consultants, specialists, and designers promise everything from deepening of Zoom practices and supporting the grieving of failed projects to bringing people some of the meaning they used to derive from places of worship (Bowles 2020).

Providers and the companies that pay for them are not only further commodifying and secularizing these religious practices but also using them to make individuals more resilient to work-induced stress purely for the sake of profit. While the ability to bounce back from periods of hardship is useful, more often than not, it is used to demand employees grin and bear toxic environments, overwhelming demands, and structural issues (Fosslien and Duffy 2022). This practice creates a pacified, accepting, flexible, and compliant workforce.

Spirituality has the benefit of being vague and ambiguous enough in intent and ideology to be marketed neutrally and secularly as a way to increase focus, optimism, happiness, and productivity. As a result, this "feel good" spirituality is both appropriate for the workplace and resistant to any attempts to criticize political, economic, and social injustices in those same workplaces. By directing individuals to cope with overwork and injustice rather than seek change, blanket "feel-good" spirituality becomes fully accommodating to and complicit in the perpetuation of capitalism and consumerism.

In *Selling Spirituality*, authors Jeremy Carrette and Richard King describe four ways religions can relate to capitalism. Religions that reject the pursuit of profit as a goal and have "this-worldly" commitment to social justice are Revolutionary or Anti-Capitalist religions. Those that see profit as a legitimate goal but seek to do so ethically are known as Business Ethics or Reformist religions. Prosperity religions, such as those that pick and choose practices based on an interpretation of what would lead to the most success, are Individualist or Consumerist religions. Those that exploit religious themes and practice for profit are Capitalist religions (2004).

In case it needs stating, religion isn't inherently good or bad. Neither is spirituality. They aren't inherently self-serving or other-serving. Religions are simply systems of faith and worship. Systems interpreted and put into practice by humans, some of which are self-serving, and some of which believe in other-serving.

Religions give us something larger than ourselves to connect with. They give us structures, guidelines to live by, and rituals for dealing with difficult situations. In times of hardship and uncertainty, people often look to religion for clear and absolute frameworks for how to live and to find reassurance for their own decisions with an external endorsement. It's important to know if the religions we adhere to are revolutionary/anti-capitalist, ethical, individualist/consumerist, or explicitly pro-capitalist.

Some religious groups, such as the Quakers, played a key role in abolition and women's rights movements in the United States (Murphy 2017). Many Quaker Friends became conscientious objectors during World Wars I and II (Mascari 2006). Christians who believe Jesus preached brotherly cooperation over competition have played major roles in socialist movements worldwide (Williams 2016). Many original religious texts, including the Bible and the Quran, preach equality for all. There are infinite ways to be a religious person and fight for equity, support your communities, and dismantle the harmful systems holding us captive.

Other groups will read the exact same texts and cherry-pick practices for the sake of this-worldly personal gain, and to use religious ideologies to reinforce the status quo. From the Bible, opportunists have found what they need to justify slavery (Rae 2018), Manifest Destiny (McSloy 2018), and the subjugation of women (Ruether 2014). The Protestant Work Ethic, or the idea that salvation comes through the frugal use of the gifts God has given us and service to others was bastardized as a justification for capitalism (Bucholz 1983). Prosperity theologies come from the ideas that God wants us to be healthy and material wealth is a sign of divine favor. They have been used to justify exploitation and supreme inequality, much to the Pope's dismay (Bergoglio 2016).

Manifest Destiny, Prosperity Theology, and the American Dream share similar threads—the belief in exceptionalism, capitalism, and support for exploitation of humans and resources at the behest of a higher power that wants you, in particular, to be wealthy. This version of biblical reductionism centers the well-being of the believer and turns God into someone who grants wishes (Bergoglio 2016). This is where we see a transformation from humans as servants of God to God as servant of humans. He becomes a power at our service and turns religion into a utilitarian and nearly secular phenomenon.

One of the most well-known self-help books, *The 7 Habits of Highly Effective People,* was written by the modern master of self-help, Steven Covey (2004). The book is a secular sequel to an earlier book, *The Divine Center,* in which he advises fellow Mormons to teach gospel principles using the vocabularies of non-Mormons (Waldrep 1998). While the book reads like any other secular self-help book, Covey notes in his personal note on the last page that God, the Creator, is the true source of correct principles, and that the degree to which we align ourselves with God determines the degree of our divine endowments. Considering the book sold more than forty million copies worldwide and was named the most influential business book in the twentieth century, I'd say his gamble to secularize his message paid off (Covey 2004).

The idea that we could get whatever we want from God just by speaking it into existence came into prominence in the 1950s with New Thought and "positive confession" (Christian Publishing House 2022). Around this time, we also see the explosion in popularity of televangelists who recognized the power of mass media, and mixed marketing with ministry. Televangelists such as Kenneth Copeland, Norman Vincent Peale, Robert Tilton, and Pat Robertson blur the lines between spiritual mentors and evangelicals of the American Dream, penning and hawking religion-adjacent, economically rooted books that became best-sellers.

Titles like Tilton's *The Power to Create Wealth* and Robertson's *The Secret Kingdom: Your Path to Peace, Love, and Financial Security* are more subtle. Titles like Copeland's *The Laws of Prosperity*, and Peele's *The Power of Positive Thinking*, *You Can if You Think You Can*, and *A Guide to Confident Living* could be mistaken for faith-free self-help texts. God becomes another resource in their arsenal, and faith becomes just one more way of proving worthiness in the land of capitalist meritocracy.

Prosperity theologies do capitalism's bidding directly, exacerbating individualism and victim blaming. The rich get to feel good about themselves because they believe they are such good, devout believers that God has rewarded them with riches. This also allows them to renounce any social responsibility, reinforcing the belief that if only the poor worked harder and had more faith in God, they, too, could be rich. The belief has also been popular with the middle class who have no reason to be compassionate for the poor since it is, of course, their fault. The belief has been associated with support for laissez-faire capitalism and a disdain for social liberalism, social and political rights, and government support in the areas of healthcare, education, and climate.

It's also, unfortunately, popular with poor Americans who are hungry for personal and social advancement. Prosperity theology explains capitalism and promises security. It suggests rather than being a pawn in global capitalist systems, we take control of our reality. Unfortunately, this control often requires divine intervention from a supernatural power to achieve the dream. It means too many opt out of collective organizing and politics—something many of us feel too small to actually affect—and instead rely on a miracle-centered approach prioritizing faith over social and political responsibility to each other.

Over time, religion, economics, and self-help have become so enmeshed, it can be hard to fully discern which is which. Sometimes, that's on purpose.

We find religions exploiting capitalism and capitalism exploiting religion, and people struggling to find their way through the chaos. And then, there are the religions that explicitly and flagrantly leverage religious practices for profit.

Any religion that exploits religious traditions for economic gain is a capitalist religion. And because self-help does everything associated with capitalist spiritualities while exploiting religious themes such as transcendence and meaning for profit, it is a capitalist religion.

As I've noted before, neither self-help nor religion are inherently bad. However, leveraging either for the exploitation of people and for the purpose of worshiping and acquiring money is at best misinformed and, at worst, deceitful and immoral. If religions are systems of faith and worship, and entire swaths of self-help are devoted to faith in economic systems and the worshiping of work for the sake of money, then as former Labour MP Tony Benn has noted, "The most powerful religion of all... is the people who worship money" (Carrette and King 2004). In this way and as suggested by self-help books like *The Secret* by Rhonda Byrne (2006) and *Ask and It Is Given* by Esther and Jerry Hicks (2004), God and the Universe become "partner[s] in business" in the worship of money.

That self-help should function as a religion in an era in which we have so much suffering and so many unanswered questions about how to thrive doesn't surprise me. We are desperate for answers, and as we learned in chapter 6, that makes us vulnerable. Karl Marx referred to religion as the opium of the masses in its ability to reduce suffering and provide illusions that give us the strength to carry on (1844).

Self-help and the meditation and yogic practices we've extracted do exactly that—they provide us with ways to reduce suffering, albeit temporarily, and give us hope that things can be different, if only we choose to carry on, and keep trying.

The desire for meaning, purpose, and a connection to something larger than ourselves is an inherent part of being human. Throughout history, we have looked to religion for meaning and connection. When we realize this desire is being exploited by those in power for their own gain, we're able to make it conscious and therefore be in choice. Is work the place where we want to contribute and find meaning? Is this workplace, and this company in particular, the thing larger than ourselves we want to feel a sense of connection to? Are we okay with our workplaces acknowledging we're burnt out and bringing in spiritual practice, devoid of their original purposes, to serve as the antidote to the stressors they cause?

Religion prevents revolution the same way self-help does. We may feel so hopeless in our economic situation that we turn to prosperity televangelists or pray God will help us win the lottery, instead of organizing and taking action in our own communities. We turn our attention to ourselves and away from the collective issues of oppression and exploitation.

My hope is that even if we engage in practices like prayer, meditation, or yoga for individualist reasons at first, we still develop greater awareness, compassion, and curiosity that leads us to dive deeper into our practices and the traditions from which they came.

I hope they lead us to develop greater equanimity and that practices used as pacification begin to feel so inherently paradoxical we have no choice but to grapple with them. I hope through this grappling, we recognize the ways our desires for transcendence and community are being used against us by people with selfish economic desires, and we recognize our position as pawns in a capitalist system. I hope we rise up to challenge this system through collectivist movements, thereby creating an economic system that inherently works for all of us and rendering self-help utterly irrelevant.

My hope is that we can reengage with our search for meaning and purpose in a way that isn't clouded by capitalism. May we rediscover, reconnect with, re-relate to, or even evolve powerful, contemplative, connective spiritual practices and religious communities that embrace interconnectivity, faith, equality, and mystery.

CHAPTER 11

PRIVATIZING THE SELF

I have a degree in psychology with a concentration in cognitive psychology. When I received my anxiety diagnoses, you'd think it would've set off a chain of clicks, as all the puzzle pieces fell into place with a slew of ahas.

But, of course, that's not what happened.

I felt terrible. Ashamed. And somewhat hopeless. I knew there were medications for it—and my therapist was downright relieved when I finally considered that option—but other than confirming I was "abnormal" and providing a justification to share with friends and family, the diagnoses didn't actually *do* anything for me. It didn't help me at all.

My studies had required some coursework in developmental psychology but otherwise centered around abnormal psychology and cognitive psychology, the branches dedicated to psychological disorders such as anxiety and depression, and cognitive functions like perception, motivation, language, and learning, as well as the neurochemistry and neurosciences behind them.

That focus isn't atypical. Many psychology programs in the United States focus on the clinical and counseling sides of psychology because that's where the jobs are. As a result, we often get some exposure to other facets but predominantly study the causes, prevalence, and treatments of mental health disorders.

Like anxiety.

Despite this information, I was absolutely unprepared for my own diagnosis, how to handle the information, or what it meant for me. When I dove into the self-help literature, I found books suggesting I do everything from *Rewire* my brain, to *Untangle* it, to *Unf*ck* it. I must have missed class the days we learned our brains were jumbles of wires that could be rewired, untangled, and unfucked. Undeterred, I read up on all the ways my brain was working against me, with an overactive amygdala and unrestrained fear-center ruining my life. I learned about the drugs I could take to "fix" my brain chemistry and the practices I could use to get my brain in check and finally find peace.

I found some calm in breathing exercises, but otherwise, none of the books, their ideas, or their strategies resonated with me.

Was my brain really the problem? I've been anxious my whole life, fearful of authority figures and bullies, but was that really because I had a fucked brain? Could it be as simple as a broken brain backing me into a corner of debilitating overthinking I could get in check with a chemical correction?

Maybe.

But I wondered if I was overthinking or really just thinking. Over-worrying, or appropriately worrying. Who is to say? What, I wondered, would these books recommend I stop worrying about? The fact I couldn't make ends meet as a young working professional? The excessive pressure I was under at work that had me up toiling past midnight most nights? Or should I simply toss my fear of judgment in social situations—the one that had protected me from further abuse and ridicule for years?

In reality, the answer is likely yes, they'd suggest I stop worrying about all of that. But getting rid of the worry wouldn't help the problems go away.

I continued to wonder: Is all this really a me-brain thing? Is it really that I'm broken? Wouldn't anyone with a hundred thousand dollars in debt, untenable work expectations, and toxic relationship stress be entitled to experience some or perhaps even *a lot* of stress without being considered classifiable?

Wouldn't you be worried about someone in those conditions who *wasn't* just a little stressed? And wouldn't it be conceivable that someone who was facing all those things at once for years be stressed for years?

Unfortunately, our mental health and healthcare systems don't exercise that level of nuance or consideration. Therapy was financially inaccessible without insurance, which I needed a diagnosis to access. Most insurance companies and psychology practitioners operate through the medical model of psychology. Mental and emotional problems, they suggest, are like biological problems; they have detectable, specific, and physiological causes—such as genetic origins or imbalanced brain chemistry—and therefore respond to treatments that target that specific thing.

As a result, I was prescribed medication. The benzodiazepine I was prescribed increases a chemical messenger in your brain called GABA, which is responsible for slowing down your brain by blocking signals to your central nervous system (Cleveland Clinic 2022). It wasn't that I'd have less stress, it's that the stress signals wouldn't make it to my brain to be interpreted and *felt* as stress. In short, I was prescribed a tranquilizer.

Once it kicks in, the problems just don't seem so big anymore. The debt hasn't gone away, and the expectations and relationships haven't changed. The stressors are still there, but the stress is meant to dissipate.

How is that a solution?

But similar to the capitalist, corporate model of meditation, it's not meant to solve the cause of the stress. It's only meant to soothe your experience of it temporarily so you can keep going.

Capitalism will still be there. Our higher education system will still exploit students for years of salary. Our employers will still get to pay us less than what it costs to live. The people in our lives will still be able to treat us any kind of way and we won't be any better equipped to respond.

We're just expected to turn down the volume of the feelings and keep it moving.

And more and more of us are being encouraged to do so. Benzodiazepines are highly prevalent among US adults, with 30.6 million adults reporting use in 2015 and 2016. This number is increasing despite serious fears associated with misuse and growing adverse outcomes, including overdose and death (Maust, Lin, and Blow 2018). Between 2005 and 2016, 17.5 million adults were diagnosed with depression each year. About 58 percent of those diagnosed received treatment that included antidepressants (Almohammed et al. 2022).

Studies showed there was no significant difference in the physical or mental quality of life between patients who used antidepressants and those who did not. In fact, nominal improvements experienced by folks on antidepressants have even been chalked up to the placebo effect—the beneficial outcomes that come simply from anticipating an intervention will help (Almohammed et al. 2022). In fact, the use of antidepressant medications was actually associated with higher rates of relapse compared to placebos, meaning people were more likely to feel depressed again if they had taken antidepressants than if they hadn't. The conclusion of the study was that antidepressants alone are not sufficient for improving quality of life.

It seems so logical—if you simply give someone with a depressing life antidepressants and change nothing else, their quality of life won't actually change—but this information has caused quite a stir in the world of psychology and psychiatry.

Johann Hari dives into this topic beautifully in his book *Lost Connections* (2018). For years, he says, society has told us depression is caused by a chemical imbalance in the brain without actually stopping to ask us if we have something to be depressed about. In the last few decades, however, people have begun questioning this widely touted explanation. In 1998, a meta-analysis of depression studies showed antidepressants were no more effective than placebos (Kirsch and Sapirstein 1998). As a matter of fact, there has been very little evidence to support the idea that serotonin actually makes a difference at all. Instead, it was likely a simplistic explanation pushed by pharmaceutical companies to sell more drugs (Hari 2018).

While antidepressants might do enough to take someone off a ledge temporarily, some practitioners say they are best used as a stopgap—a reprieve from depression that allows you to deal with the underlying problems. Hari outlines nine common reasons for depression, most of which stem from life circumstances: Disconnection from meaningful work, disconnection from other people, disconnection from meaningful values, disconnection resulting from childhood trauma, disconnection from status and respect, disconnections from the natural world, disconnection from a hopeful and secure future, genes, and changes in the brain (2018).

If the cause of depression is lost connections, it makes sense the solution would be reconnection. Hari recommends a variety of social prescriptions meant to reconnect the depressed individual to whatever they were feeling disconnected from. This includes things like reconnection to people, work, meaningful values, joy, nature, oneself, and the future.

Depression isn't an indication the person *is* a problem. It's an indication the person *has* a problem. Often, multiple problems work in tandem to make life exponentially harder in every other way and contribute to increasing levels of stress that both obscure the entangled, foundational causes of our stress and make each individual challenge harder to address.

But again, that's the point. Our solutions to mental health issues have been built out of our systems, and the perspectives, biases, and values that permeate our systems. We can't talk about psychology's influence on the self-help industry without recognizing the incarnation we are experiencing is a system that grew out of the seeds of Western European and United Statesian colonialism, patriarchy, supremacy, and capitalism.

Whew.

Okay, let's do this.

"The history of psychology is almost exclusively the history of white men" (Harrogate 2019). While the interest in studying the psyche and the soul has been nearly universal, Western perspectives have come to dominate the field globally. Western researchers hellbent on "proving" things empirically take philosophical, unprovable ideas from the Middle East and East, interpret them through Western lenses, experiment using Western methodologies, and claim ownership via publication. A review of psychological studies conducted between 2003 and 2008 revealed the United States and Canada produced nearly 60 percent of all studies (Harrogate 2019).

Researchers then publish their findings with the assumption their findings are universal and generalizable—that what they find about their participants will be representative of any other population of humans. The problem is, researchers at universities often study the people they have access to—students. One influential article noted broad claims were being drawn from subpopulations who were, in fact, WEIRD: Western, Educated, Industrialized, Rich, and Democratic. Not only are results based on such a specific subsample *not* generalizable, they are particularly unusual when compared to the rest of the human species. Studies based on WEIRD participants and WEIRD societies were actually among the *least* representative and, therefore, least generalizable (Henrich, Heine, and Norenzayan 2010).

In short, it's nearly impossible to answer the big questions about human nature by drawing conclusions about this one, thin, unusual, WEIRD slice of humanity.

Maslow's hierarchy of needs is one of the most popular motivation theories in the world. You've probably seen it or at least heard about it. The pyramid depicts the five needs of humans: Physiological needs serve as the foundation at the bottom, including food, water, sleep, and warmth. After we have our physiological needs met, this suggests, we pursue security and safety. Once we've got those, we move one level up to the higher-level needs of love and belonging. With love and belonging acquired, we're free to pursue esteem and feelings of accomplishment and social status. At the very top of the hierarchy is self-expression, creativity, and self-actualization, or achieving one's potential (McLeod 2018).

Maslow based his studies on an even weirder subpopulation than the WEIRD subset: *his friends,* famous figures like Thomas Jefferson and Walt Whitman (or, more accurately, what he *thought* they would say—he never asked them), individuals he hand-picked, and male university students (Maslow 1954; Maslow 1962). Prioritizing sex over love and self-actualization sounds like what I would expect from college boys. He fully admits the framework was never empirically validated (Maslow 1954). It ignores important cultural, contextual, and situational factors: Some cultures prioritize social cohesion over individual needs, for example, or spiritual well-being over material well-being. Folks with pets experiencing homelessness have overlapping needs—needing shelter doesn't preclude anyone from needing love and connection, so it wouldn't make sense to abandon a beloved pet because we require a home first. Maslow himself later updated the theory when he realized there were untold exceptions and additional needs (Maslow 1967; Maslow 1954; Maslow 1962).

It is completely unsubstantiated as a generalizable, universal theory of human motivation.

That doesn't stop it from being used as such.

We can't ignore that the majority of psychology studies and findings that exist are being conducted in individualist societies. They study individualist participants and are interpreted by professors and researchers with individualist lenses. It's no surprise we are handed answers suggesting our problems are individual in both cause and solution.

And it's not just individualism that sneaks in. In fact, psychology has a long, troubled, racist and sexist past that often goes unacknowledged, especially by proponents of popular psychology. One of the earliest "fields" of psychology was phrenology, the pseudo study of skull shapes and bumps as an indicator of mental traits, aptitude, and ability. Researchers could come up with a hypothesis about mental ability and then find the bumps, sizes, and shapes to "prove" it (Ktitowsky 2017).

The pseudoscience uncoincidentally took off in the US after the 1830s, as the US was struggling to find a justification for slavery in the face of growing abolitionist movements and conflicts with native peoples. They found their justification in the research of someone who just so happened to also support racism and genocide and contributed to the belief that people of African descent were mentally inferior. This belief perpetuates racism until this day (Ktitowsky 2017).

Scientific racism is the practice of using the perceived objectivity of scientific knowledge to legitimize racial inequality. Researchers at Harvard used phrenology to "prove" white biological superiority, explain Black Americans' "predisposition to disease," and hypothesize a collective destiny—extinction (Harvard 2023). Psychiatrists in Nazi Germany touted the eugenics movement as a positive step in purifying the race while other psychologists "proved" the inferiority of the "Jewish race" through "biopsychological typology." During the Third Reich, *Mein Kampf* was literally named the textbook of German psychoanalysis (Vine 2009).

Even IQ tests have origins in eugenics movements. They were explicitly created to measure the perceived, inherent superiority of the ruling class and legitimize the existing social order (Reddy 2008). While we typically believe they are a measure of innate intelligence, they're not. They measure cultural capital, the information gained through one's schooling, and the ability to take tests. In other words, they test knowledge upper-class white people were expected to have in order to highlight "abnormalities" and "deficiencies" in anyone who didn't score highly, or "normally." It was utilized as a way of keeping kids who didn't go to their private high schools from going to their elite Ivy schools.

And racism isn't the only place supremacy shows up. The field is highly sexist. For centuries, women were excluded from academic training and practice altogether. That meant all of what was to be "known" about the psychology of women was determined by men and by their interpretation of studies. As a result, famed psychologists such as the "father of psychology," Sigmund Freud, had free rein to say and "prove" whatever they wanted about women.

Despite psychoanalysis as a whole being contested as a science and most of Freud's theories being disproven, the impacts linger. Freud believed women added nothing to society and that their lives were dominated by their reproductive functions. Many of us have likely heard of "penis envy," his belief that women were simply men without penises, who were, therefore, both inferior and envious of men forevermore. When critics noted it made sense as a metaphor for the social prestige men experience, Freud doubled down and insisted it was literal (Yadav 2018). He staunchly opposed social change as a means of attaining happiness and health and saw it as a deluded pursuit (Menand 2017). It wasn't that society was unequal, you see! It was because women wanted penii!

Most of us have also heard of the "Oedipus complex," his belief that young children experienced a desire for their opposite-sex parent. What we don't always realize is this stemmed from his stance that young female patients were making up stories of rape at the hands of their fathers—many of whom were his friends. To protect the men, he blamed the girls' wild, perverse imaginations, framing accusations of rape as a deluded fantasy and singlehandedly set the study of child abuse back by a century. The girls were stigmatized and traumatized (Yadav 2018). As a result of his work, many victims of rape continue to be blamed for imagining, inviting, wanting, or deserving abuse today.

Victim blaming occurs when the victim of a crime or wrongful act is held either entirely or partially at fault for what happened to them (SACE 2023). It's also a perversely comforting self-preservation technique in which we find a reason the victim brought the act unto themselves so we can give ourselves the false assurance that the bad thing that happened to them won't happen to us. It creates distance. It suggests we can learn how to control our lives and avoid such pain in the midst of an otherwise chaotic existence. It also shifts focus from holding the perpetrator accountable. And it's a prominent part of Western culture, psychology, and self-help literature.

And it's not just these "findings" and theories that are problematic. While more and more blatantly racist and sexist "findings" are being discredited, the patriarchal, supremacist, and individualist mindsets behind them often remain. They continue to be perpetrated by researchers, professors, providers, and practitioners who haven't done their own inner work to uncover and process biases. Instead, we see folks pushing the status quo because, as we learned in chapter 8, most practitioners, like most of us, are operating from a place of socialization and belief there is one correct answer and one right way to be.

We also see superiority manifest in paternalism prevalent in the industry. Paternalism is the use of authority to restrict freedoms in areas typically left up to personal choice and personal conscience. Practitioners in a few fields, including psychology, are prone to making decisions on behalf of patients in their supposed "best interest" under the guise they know better than their patients. We see this in the governmental prohibition of psychedelics, supposedly for our own safety, despite the fact some psychedelics, like MDMA, have been shown to reduce PTSD and anxiety (Alcohol and Drug Foundation 2021). We see this in facilities wherein patients are hospitalized against their will for attempting suicide. And we see this in researchers and practitioners prioritizing "findings" over patients' lived experiences.

Similarly, we see this air of superiority through the lens of condescending, patronizing treatment plans and self-help books suggesting that if we could just "think happy thoughts" our depression and anxiety would magically go away. Authors of self-help who don't struggle with the issues they write about boil solutions into easy steps that, if indeed were so easy, probably would have been tried already. We also see this in the world of life coaching, wherein brand new, unaccredited coaches believe that with just a hint of positivity, we can do anything we set our minds to, regardless of the actual obstacles in the way.

Perhaps worst of all are the impacts of pathology in the psychology industry. To be pathologizing is to treat someone or something as psychologically abnormal or unhealthy. As in my case, where completely justifiable stress was diagnosed and considered abnormal, the field is full of practitioners diagnosing, labeling, and treating that which is presumed to be "abnormal." The problem is, we don't actually know what "normal" is.

People typically define normal as the typical, average state of things.

If 63 percent of US workers are ready to quit their job to avoid work-related stress, though, does that mean work stress is normal or that we've normalized the stress in the midst of a mental health epidemic (Milenkovic 2019)? Is it, then, normal to be stressed or normal to not be stressed? In this case, is it better to aspire for normality?

As the saying goes, "It's no measure of health to be well-adjusted to a profoundly sick society."

Yet that's exactly what we expect of humans—to simply adjust. We assume anything but happiness is due to a personal failing, ailment, or issue. Defiance, even in response to oppression, is diagnosed and pathologized in psychology.

To over-pathologize, as we do in Western psychology, is both to patronizingly and paternalistically assume to know what is "normal" and to presume anything that is different is "abnormal." These labels allow us to categorize people into hierarchical classes of humans. In practice, this functions as sanctioned ableism.

And the stigma associated with being pathologized is real. Stigmas may come from family members, potential employers, and even mental health professionals and mean that folks have to not only deal with the often-devastating effects of having a mental illness but also the prejudices and discrimination that come with them—often from mental health professionals directly (Lockett 2022; Knaak, Mantler, and Szeto 2017). Folks facing mental illness often internalize the stigma, too, believing what they are told about themselves, and experience reduced self-esteem and self-efficacy, which, of course, limits their prospects for recovery.

Unfortunately, due to the pathologizing system mental health professionals are trained in, mental health professionals often display even stronger negative beliefs and attitudes toward patients with mental illness than the general population (Nordt, Rossler, and Lauber 2006). In my four years of studies in a highly regarded university psychology program, I had just one class in which we connected directly with people who experienced the disorders we were discussing. Disabilities are discussed and treatment plans are evaluated from a distance, without ever interacting with someone impacted by the conditions. As a result, students and practitioners often create a sort of unidimensional stereotyped caricature of persons who have been diagnosed.

It's easy to dehumanize people we neither know, nor understand, nor respect. Destigmatization is difficult but not impossible. Being in close contact with and caring about someone who suffers from mental illness is one of the most effective ways of reducing the stigma. While opportunities to connect with folks aren't as readily apparent as we might like (I never wore a sticker that said, "Hello! I'm Sharon! I've got social anxiety!"), the reality is about 50 percent of people within our society experience a mental illness during their lifetime that requires treatment, meaning it's pretty likely we meet someone every single day who has struggled, is struggling, or will someday struggle with mental illness (Rossler 2016). The opportunities are more common than we think.

It's also a major reason we need to include folks directly in all stages of support—from research study design and interpretation through diagnosis, treatment development, and administration. The slogan "Nothing about us without us" describes the principle in disability activism that no policies or treatments should be decided without the full and direct participation of folks affected by the policy and treatment (Charlton 2000).

Unfortunately, too, what's normal and what's pathologized changes all the time. In the era of phrenology, having a certain shaped head was all it took to be considered deficient. In Freud's era, being a woman was once all it took to be considered inferior. What counts as social and sexual deviance changes as soon as the culture changes. It is an absolute reflection of the zeitgeist rather than any stable, reliable, or universal measure. Because our reality is changing all the time and how we interact with our world is changing all the time, new models, explanations, and corrections are a constant in psychology and typically backed by "*the latest neuroscience!*" for extra credibility.

Even though we are constantly changing, psychology tries to nail down what it means to be human as one would try to nail down what it means to be, say, a sapphire. Because geology has the whole rock-composition thing on lock and biology has the whole human body composition thing cornered, what psychology aims to capture is what it means to be a human *right now,* in this incarnation, in this particular moment in time, space, evolution, and chaos. As a result, psychologists are internal trend catchers who capture the zeitgeist as internalized by individuals in individualistic societies. Psychology is the study of the manifestations of individualism.

Western psychology isn't just the history of white men, it's the study of Western white men who practice individualism and ride the waves of culture. When the vast majority of our studies center the experiences of WEIRD people—again that's Western, Educated, Industrialized, Rich, and Democratic—and approximately 60 percent come from the US and Canada, we have to acknowledge we're predominantly studying humans in individualist societies and the impacts of that lifestyle on our psyches (Henrich, Heine, and Norenzayan 2010).

Outside of Western conceptualization, the study of a private "self" makes little sense. Elsewhere, the self is acknowledged to be socially constructed, fluid, and based either on social group or on the divine (Carrette and King 2004). While in Western cultures, we categorize and define issues in order to isolate and treat on an internal and individual basis, other cultures see humans and processes in relationship. In this far more holistic view, the body and the spirit are in relationship with one another and with other humans. This holistic view emphasizes both complexity and context. Instead of looking to an individual to see what's wrong and to blame them for any issues or misdeeds, there's often an emphasis on looking to the whole group, and often the family, to determine causal factors.

An interesting story highlights the difference in blame via internal and external attribution between Eastern and Western cultures. In 1991, a Chinese Physics student named Gang Lu at the University of Iowa shot several faculty members and students before shooting himself. The incident was reported in both American and Chinese newspapers. American newspapers focused on the individual, noting he was a dark, disturbed man with a temper who drove himself to both success and destruction and believed guns were a means of addressing grievances. Chinese newspapers, on the other hand, noted the strained relationship he had with his advisor, the rivalry that existed between students, the pressures he faced, and the availability of guns in the US (Nisbett 2004).

Westerners look to the person. Easterners look to the contexts influencing the person.

It's why Westerners blame individuals for their troubles. It's why we point to "one bad apple" in the police force, for example, instead of looking to the system that creates, embraces, immunizes, and protects bad apples. It's why we blame ourselves instead of looking to larger forces and systems contributing to the issues. We're myopic.

And this is music to capitalism's ears. Capitalism requires individualism in order for each person to pursue wealth, and prioritize personal success and "the good life" over the success of the whole and "the good society." Capitalism benefits both from the categorization and assigned superiority of people who are fit to work, and the pathologization and assigned inferiority of people who aren't. Capitalism benefits from labeling those who conform and function within its economy and the inequity it creates as "normal" and blaming everyone else for their own suffering. Capitalism benefits by requiring individuals to cope with the deep, collective inequity it creates and then selling them the solution. And the main beneficiaries of capitalism are rich white men.

When we are each individually responsible for living "happy," "normal" lives, we become the largest force of socialization and status quo perpetuation there is. We take it upon ourselves to shoulder the manifestations of individualism and capitalism, internalizing our pain and shaming ourselves for not being "normal" and happy-go-lucky despite the hellscape we live in. We accept palliative recommendations that reduce immediate symptoms and give us ways to calm the fuck down without ever questioning why we should need to.

Social nonresponsibility is not new, but the expectation we should thrive despite it is. When our social systems don't provide us with the solutions we need, we do our best to take control into our own hands. We recognize no one is coming to help us, and we find ways to help ourselves.

We try to support our own mental health and well-being. Thanks to our profit-seeking medical model, most mental health support is reactive, financially inaccessible, and low on high-quality, caring, approachable, and patient-focused education. Recognizing the need, enterprising folks in our capitalist society devise and deliver solutions, even when they are not the most effective, fulfilling, or justice-creating ones there could be. We are bombarded with ways to take our lives and well-being into our own hands because it's clear they are the only means we have. And, of course, because it makes people money.

We now commonly associate "self-help" with books about wellness, mental health, and psychology—areas where we have both insufficient resources to support our people and a tendency to blame the individual. Recognizing the issue, practitioners are even *prescribing* self-help (Price 2013). Regardless of how well-intentioned this strategy might be, we need to recognize the ways that individualizing both problems and solutions unintentionally supports the status quo and perpetuates both our socialization and the systems keeping us sick and stressed.

The practices of individualizing, pathologizing, and treating issues medically are the results of both confirmation bias and the Law of the Instrument that suggests when all you have is a hammer, everything looks like a nail (Kaplan 1998). In other words, when all you've been trained to do is recognize symptoms, diagnose, and prescribe medication, that's what you do. When all you've been trained to do is look at the individual, you provide solutions at the individual level. With limited tools, we use what we have at our disposal to solve our problems.

Individualizing the field of psychology makes things cleaner and simpler. We "prove" causation by isolating a particular variable and experimenting. In doing so, though, we completely strip the human of the contexts that created them and continue to impact and shape them. By categorizing thoughts and behaviors in relation to the individual, we operate as if each human functions as a "closed" system, one not open to influence by the outside world.

But we know that's not how it works. We know stress contributes to anxiety, and disconnection contributes to depression. We must have a model that accounts for the social dimensions of existence.

To be fully adjusted to an abnormal society is a testament to how powerfully we can adapt to any situation. The people who most worry me are not the depressed and the anxious—we are the canaries in the coal mine. I am far more worried about those of us who have adapted completely—those of us who were silenced early or are so detached from our own feelings we don't notice anything wrong. To be fully human is to feel it all, including how inhumane our systems are.

For years, our mental health model has felt a bit like my old coat—a bit too small and a bit too restrictive. Recently, I've come to terms with it and accepted it. It's just not a system that works for me. But the reality is, the process of responding to mental health crises with the same thinking that likely created the crises is not a system that works for most of us. And we're seeing greater and greater discontent with the system as we recognize the difference between a high-quality life and a high-functioning life.

We no longer want to be highly functioning. We demand a high-quality life.

CHAPTER 12

FAULT OBSCURES RESPONSIBILITY

I knew when I created Go Love Yourself that community would be a primary focus. While I originally conceptualized it as an extra-large book club, the group took on a life of its own, evolving into something better than I ever could have planned. With each author who visited us, and each community member who left her mark on our collective, we transformed into a community far more powerful than anything I could have created alone.

As we discussed our books, our conversations naturally turned to the places where the concepts showed up in each of our lives. We shared our perspectives and our strategies for dealing with them individually and, over time, began to have the kinds of breakthroughs and experiences we read about in chapter 9.

How did that happen?

The more time we spent together, and the stronger our community agreements, the safer we felt and the more we shared. The deeper we got to know each other, the more we realized the other women in the group weren't crazy or lazy or any other awful thing society liked to insinuate we were. And the more alike we realized we were, the more we recognized we, personally, were not any of those terrible things either. The ways we were engaging in the world were absolutely valid responses to our circumstances.

Brené Brown says shame needs three things to survive: secrecy, silence, and judgment (Brown 2012). Our community was open, authentic, and compassionate. Shame couldn't thrive in such a supportive environment.

Being together in a safe space with clear guidelines and agreements around confidentiality, acceptance, and respect allowed us to explore our shame, stories, and experiences together. We had a space that was just ours, where we could vent and validate each other while learning more about the systemic issues affecting us. It became a place where we could practice being vulnerable, owning our stories, and realigning our values and narratives with empowering, liberating ones. In other words, we explored Nieto and Boyer's phase of "empowerment" together (2006).

As we learned earlier, guilt is the idea we've done something bad. This self-reflective feeling of remorse comes as a result from having broken your own personal values or moral code (Gillette 2022). It's fundamentally pro-social because it promotes responsibility, resolution, and repair. Guilt encourages us to right our wrongs.

Shame is the idea we *are* bad, and there's no real coming back from that. Unlike guilt, it's not productive. It erodes our sense of self as a person and tends to lead us to destructive behaviors and feelings. Many violent behaviors and family dysfunctions come as the result of shame (VanScoy 2016). Whether we "act out" with anger or violence against others, or "act in" through isolation and self-hatred, we feed into a cycle of shame that keeps us trapped.

Shame is inherently alienating and lonely. Disconnected from people, status, respect, and a hopeful future, depression sets in. When we're busy coping and mitigating our individual symptoms, we're missing a big opportunity—one that could help to not only improve our individual experiences by reconnecting us to ourselves, each other, and our purpose in the world but also create lasting change that prevents others from feeling that way in the future.

Any time you experience shame, you've found the bounds of what our rigid, slow-moving, noninclusive systems approve of. You've found the places where our families, communities, churches, and societies haven't yet found a way to do right by you. You've found the place, where, as children being hurt by our caregivers, we faced the impossible decision of assuming our caregivers were good, kind people who didn't mean to hurt us—and it was, therefore, all our fault—or acknowledging the pain they caused and strike out on our own.

Except we have much more agency than we had as children. We have the ability to acknowledge our hurt and shame and to choose to not identify with it. We get to let go of the shame embedded in fault and embrace the responsibility of choosing a different way forward.

When we are bombarded with the message that our suffering is our fault and are mired in the shame it causes, we miss the distinction between fault and responsibility. Where we are now is not *all* our fault. The historical contexts that led us here, the intersecting systems of oppression that impact our daily lives in complex ways, and the ways these factors have impacted our psyche and made us desperate for help—these things are not our fault.

But our choices? Our concrete, day-to-day actions that perpetuate stagnancy or create change? That's our responsibility.

Focusing exclusively on fault obscures the conversation. It doesn't absolve us of the need for resolution or the responsibility of making things better. Just because I suspect the neighbor's kid of TPing my house doesn't get rid of my need to un-TP my house. And just because I suspect I inherited some emotional issues from my family doesn't mean I shouldn't examine my own behavior and try to stop the cycle.

Many people who turn to self-help are trying to take responsibility for their lives. But self-help rarely reveals who our responsibility is to: both ourselves *and* each other.

Society influences our behaviors implicitly, through culture and conditioning, and explicitly, through laws, commandments, and other regulations. But we influence our societies, too—directly as politicians, clergy, parents, and community leaders and indirectly, through voting, our tax money, and the social systems we implement. This is just as true at the macro levels of federal governments and international religious bodies as it is of the micro levels of one-on-one relationships and everywhere in between.

Individual humans and our human-built and human-propagated societies are inextricably connected. Everything affects everything. We are all responsible for what we contribute to the collective and what we allow to be done on our behalf. I am responsible for what my taxes fund and where I choose to spend my money. I am also responsible for the violence or healing I contribute to the world, the kindness or cruelty. We are in constant, cosmic cocreation with each other at every step.

When I blame myself for everything going wrong, I create more individualism in my world, my community, and my society. When I find the ways my issue is connected to others' issues, I promote awareness and interconnectivity and start seeing opportunities for cocreating a society that supports all of us.

Once we accept we're all interconnected, we can help others in our community see how everything is interconnected, and together, we can work to make the world a better place for everyone, *including me.*

Self-help and social justice should not be mutually exclusive.

Booksellers keep self-help and social justice on different shelves as if they were totally irrelevant to each other. To do the most good in the world, however, we really need to be working on both at the same time. To transform ourselves, we need to transform our societies, and to transform our societies meaningfully, we need to transform ourselves. To integrate the two means we use self-help to heal, to self-actualize, and to examine our beliefs and behaviors, and to bring to social justice a self that is self-aware, self-regulated, and self-reflective.

We'll never eliminate the need for social justice through self-help. We might, though, be able to significantly reduce our reliance on self-help through social justice.

Across the millennia, humans have been curious about the self and motivated to self-actualize. That won't stop. Traumatic natural disasters will continue to happen, and we'll need trauma care and healing. The helping professions have always been here and always will be. But if we're able to create an equitable collective that takes responsibility for itself, its systems, and its impacts on people, we will decrease our dependence on DIY solutions.

I devoted the first decade of my career to supporting schools in historically oppressed and systemically under-resourced neighborhoods. I believed education had saved me, and it could save the students in the neighborhoods I worked in, too. Two problems with that: none of us need to be "saved," and great schools aren't enough.

Even when schools are high-quality safe havens for kids, an entire world and culture outside affects their ability to thrive. We still need high-quality health care, a safe and supportive environment to go home to, and so much more. Folks who work in education know this thoroughly—teachers often talk about the need for supportive home environments and the importance of parental involvement. And the impact of trickle-down stress is larger than most of us think: 91 percent of children know when their parents are stressed and a third end up feeling their own stress in the form of belly aches and trouble sleeping as a result (DFW Child Editors 2022).

Knowing it takes a village, educators like Geoffrey Canada have created an education-centered village through comprehensive community support. Through his program, Harlem Children's Zone, students receive not just the traditional daily academic support that's expected of school systems but also a neighborhood-wide net of social, health, and developmental supports. Similar programs, like President Barack Obama's "Promise Neighborhoods," aim to offer "cradle to career" services (Promise Neighborhoods Institute 2010). Entire countries that prioritize well-being, like Finland and Bhutan, consistently rank as the happiest countries in the world; they know communities either facilitate or thwart our abilities to thrive (Miller 2016; Morton 2022; Leaver 2018).

While ideally, we'd all live in communities and nations that prioritized our well-being from cradle to grave, we're not there yet. Rather than wasting time looking for utopia, social psychologist and author Dr. Devon Price says we need to create the communities we want, relationship by relationship (2022). This is great news. Instead of needing to fix everything everywhere all at once, we get to dream about the ways each relationship, family, workplace, and community could be more conducive and invite each one into a new way of being with us.

When each of us invite our relationships and communities to expand who is accepted and supported, we create spaces of belonging and thriving that work for more people. The more people we have in our communities of liberation, the more likely it is we will cocreate a world that works for more of us. We learned in chapter 10 the importance of the slogan, "Nothing about us without us," and that applies here, too. When communities and societies are created without the input of all the people they affect, they cannot take into account the wants and needs of all of the people within.

So, what does this really look like?

Sometimes, this means allowing conflict to enable greater connection and calling in a friend who has said something hurtful. It means regularly having conversations with our partners about expectations and gender roles and negotiating a relationship that works for all involved. For many of us, it means setting boundaries about what we will and won't tolerate at family holidays.

Through Go Love Yourself, this meant creating an inclusive environment where everyone was welcomed and supported. We chose to acknowledge our many lines of difference and honor, respect, and appreciate them. We regularly had important conversations around group agreements, norms, boundaries, and confidentiality.

At The Center for Conscious Leadership, the professional development firm I founded, it means we intentionally support the individuals within each organization and the organization as a whole at the same time. We provide one-on-one executive leadership coaching, team coaching, collective workshops, and communities of practice so we intentionally evolve together, cocreating a new and more beautiful future for all involved. It means bringing to the table a diverse slate of coaches and facilitators so the future we're creating isn't done through the lens of the dominant culture.

For you, this might mean starting with getting to know your neighbors—we can't create strong, supportive communities if we don't know who is in the community already—and finding out what the village needs. It might mean creating inclusive and accessible spaces and events if they don't already exist. It could mean door-knocking for progressive candidates or establishing a culture of mutual support and aid where people look out for one another. It might mean joining your neighborhood Buy Nothing group or establishing a bartering network to trade skills, tools, or services in lieu of money to make sure everyone is getting what they need, regardless of ability to pay. It might mean patronizing your local library and businesses instead of hopping on Amazon. It could mean creating an employee resource group at work or a Gay-Straight Alliance at your school or church. When we are conditioned to think of ourselves as separate from others, it can be difficult to feel a sense of village or to find community in the abstract sense. But when we find a cause we care about and get involved, we find and create community all around us.

The best community leaders recognize they don't just create and lead the community, they, too, are the community. They are a voice for and in their community, building and rallying and organizing collective power toward a shared purpose in a way that honors both the individuals in the community and the community itself.

Frederick Douglass was deeply committed to both self-improvement *and* social change. Born into slavery, Douglass once overheard his enslaver say learning to read would give enslaved people the tools to fight for their freedom. He taught himself to read and, after escaping to freedom, became one of the most influential voices of the Abolitionist Movement. His autobiographies, especially *Narrative of the Life of Frederick Douglass, an American Slave* and *My Bondage and My Freedom* furthered the movement significantly.

Even though folks point to Frederick Douglass as a self-made man, he, too, recognized the importance of community and being community made. In his 1872 speech, "Self-Made Men," he acknowledged the title was a bit of a solecism—that is, a bit grammatically incorrect. "Properly speaking," Douglass says, "there are in the world no such men as self-made men. That term implies an individual independence of the past and present which can never exist." In the learning of language, in the building of ideas, and in the avenue of discovery, "we have reaped where others have sown, and that which others have strewn, we have gathered." Even self-improvement, therefore, relies on others (Douglass 1872).

Douglass knew it was not a popular idea with the folks in his audience: "It must in truth be said, though it may not accord well with self-conscious individuality and self-conceit, that no possible native force of character, and no depth of wealth and originality, can lift a man into absolute independence of his fellowmen, and no generation of men can be independent of the preceding generation. The brotherhood and interdependence of mankind are guarded and defended at all points. I believe in individuality, but individuals are, to the mass, like waves to the ocean" (Douglass 1872).

Frederick Douglass spoke of each individual's responsibility to do what they could with what they had. To take our uniquely human gifts of reason, language, and aspiration and to use them to our utmost advantage to develop ourselves. This, he argued, was the most profoundly amazing feature of the United States and her Constitution, which he referred to as a "glorious liberty document"—it protected the rights of each and every individual to develop themselves (1852). And, in developing themselves, each human would come into the most fully developed and realized version of themselves, which in turn would lead us all to a shared understanding of the importance of individual development and of our common humanity. With an understanding of common humanity, Douglass proposed, we would go on to support the protection of the rights of each and every individual within the collective, creating a beautiful, virtuous circle (1852).

To create a society that creates the conditions for all its members to thrive is to take responsibility for the society, its collective and individual impacts, and each other. It starts with acknowledging we haven't done right by everyone, including ourselves.

To create the world Frederick Douglass spoke of, the one that makes it easier for all of us to belong and to achieve our potential in this world, we'll need to both protect individuals' rights to develop themselves and work together to create structures that respect our common humanity. Women, immigrants, people of color, folks with disabilities, working class and poor citizens, native peoples, and members of the LGBTQ+ community know the power of community and have been banding together to create change since time immemorial. In fact, the United States' history of community organizing is just as long as its history itself.

We see what happens when we individualize everything from health to happiness. We've tried it this way for a long time, and we are witnessing, in real time, the effects of this way of existing. It's time to shift the collective belief systems we hold around individual fault. It's time to see what happens when we take collective responsibility for one another.

This isn't about taking on the burdens of the world, or running yourself ragged trying to fix everything at once. It's about finding a new way to move forward individually and collectively. It's about replacing, "If you don't like it here, leave," with, "What's not working for you? How can we help?"

With great power comes great responsibility, but with great responsibility also comes great power. Accepting responsibility gives us the power to make changes and improve our lives in ways that transform our current landscape.

It's not my fault I am highly sensitive and hypervigilant. I accept responsibility for my healing so I don't perpetuate its negative effects onto others. We did not create the extraordinary wealth inequality in the world or any of the systems of oppression that exist. Will you share with me the responsibility of creating a more equal society for the next generation?

Our circumstances are not our fault, but the effects are our responsibility. By taking responsibility, we have the ability to fulfill our purposes on this planet: to create the effect on the world we were meant to have while ensuring our futures are conducive to all of us. We'll talk more specifically about what it looks like to do all of this in the next few chapters.

Until then, know we don't have a choice to make: self-help or community care. We need both, all the time.

SECTION IV

ACTION

CHAPTER 13

RETHINKING ACTION

The more we try to control life, the more it ends up controlling us. For years, I believed if I did things just right, I would be able to control the anatomical systems of my body, the thoughts and actions of people in my life, and how my life would ultimately play out. I spent nearly all of my energy trying to control what people thought of me. In the end, my attempts to control controlled me.

During the Go Love Yourself era, I deployed all the lessons I'd learned in education about planning, preparation, and control. No matter how many times I set goals around membership or profit, I never met them. Not once. Lo and behold, I could not control strangers on the internet. I could not control the size we would grow to or who would spontaneously feature us (thanks, *Good Morning America* and *Oprah!*). I could not control what profit we would bring in at the end of the year. Despite having left education behind, I brought the mindsets, actions, and strategies that made me both effective and miserable into my brave new world.

Most of the leaders I coach come to our first conversation with remarkable visions for their lives and ambitious, detailed plans for how they'll get there. We rarely get beyond the second session before we realize it's just not going to work as planned. Learning happens on its own timeline. Healing happens on its own timeline. Growth happens on its own timeline. None of it can be forced. Not if it is to be transformative. Transformation takes its time and requires different tools. As Marshall Goldsmith is famous for saying, "What got you here won't get you there" (Goldsmith and Reiter 2007).

We're in the action section of the book, and I want to start by reframing what action can look like. If you're used to self-help books promising a clear path to your intended outcome, with concrete, specific steps to follow for and by yourself, I encourage you to keep an open mind. Notice pulls and yearnings you have toward predictability, big promises of quick fixes and fantastical futures, strategies for doing-it-yourself, and immediate gratification. Observe the deeply conditioned want for the kind of motivation that spurs shame and fuels willpower. Acknowledge the urge to discount strategies when they don't look the way we're used to. Try on comfort with a new way of thinking about action—one that's patient, iterative, emergent, and dare I say, easeful and joyful.

The actions it takes to liberate a consciousness or create a new future are neither linear nor predictable. We can't demand wisdom or compel liberation. Those are the tools of oppression. That's not how liberation works.

For those of us used to forcing things, evolution can end up feeling rather happenstance. We try to choreograph it, and it doesn't work the way we think it will. Maybe we keep trying. Maybe we let go and let God. One day, life is different. We try to point to exactly what led to our result, but the truth is often hard to pin down. Was it the journaling every day for years? The therapy? The community? All of it? Who's to say?

People will ask us, and we'll want to be helpful, so we'll name something, and they'll nod and think, *I'll try that.*

When we experience evolution in this way, we're actually experiencing emergence.

Emergence is the understanding that the future comes into being as a result of infinite simple interactions (brown 2017). These simple interactions create patterns that produce complex systems with unplanned results. We've all experienced and are the result of it, even if we don't realize it. Our DNA is shaped by what our great-grandparents ate; our breaths are the result of pre-Cambrian evolution; we are made of stardust. Our very existence is the result of simple interactions across space inconceivable and time immemorial.

Because most of us don't recognize the world works this way, and we struggle to grasp the immense complexity of it all, we artificially oversimplify. We reduce generations of genetic mutations to a three-step system for losing weight, call our internalization of centuries of structural sexism and racism "imposter syndrome," and offer you a meditation to restore the confidence the system destroyed in you. In this process, we give someone a strategy—a narrowly defined path toward a narrow goal. As *Emergent Strategy* author adrienne maree brown notes, this is the process of reducing our wild, wonderful world into a thing we can manipulate and control (2017).

The tragedy, brown notes, is that creative, compelling, and visionary ideas are often reduced to a plan of action that is anything but exciting and compelling. Resulting strategies rarely account for the complexity of our emergent realities. In social justice work, this reductionism often leaves out crucial segments of our communities. In politics, we end up knowing what we're fighting *against* and losing sight of what we're fighting *for.* In self-help, it means we reduce the magic of living into a set of steps to follow.

While directed, focused work is still important, it's equally important to recognize and honor what brown calls our "chaotic fertile reality." Rather than continuously narrowing down strategies and goals while doubling down on willpower and control, future cocreation through emergent strategy invites us to be present to what is—all of what is—and engage both with what *is* and what *can be* through experimentation, the shaping of conditions, intentional adaptation, and the riding of nonlinear, iterative waves of change.

This is not to suggest all action must be adaptive and emergent. Sometimes we have easy goals with easy solutions. But a deep understanding of the types of challenges we face and the variety of solutions available helps us to choose the next right step.

Technical and transformational challenges are different and require different solutions. Technical problems are defined, finite problems that can be solved using existing know-how and problem-solving techniques (Heifetz and Laurie 1997; Heifetz and Linsky 2002). They involve using knowledge and/or skills that are directly knowable and wieldable to solve understood problems. Technical growth is usually represented as growth along a horizontal axis; it is casting a wider net until we know everything there is to know about a particular topic. Technical solutions use technical knowledge to solve technical problems.

If I am out of coffee, I get more coffee. Problem solved.

Transformational challenges, or what the leadership world calls adaptive challenges, are often nebulous in nature. They may be difficult to define or not even universally recognized as a problem. Transformational solutions often require the person or institution to experiment with new ways of being, thinking, and problem solving in complex situations without easy answers. This often involves interrupting cycles, adjusting beliefs and actions, and lots of experimentation to find what works. The process routinely requires changing the thing that is the problem from the inside out, not only solving the problem but reworking it entirely. Transformational growth is often represented on a vertical axis and allows for an entire transformation of a thing from a previous way of being (not necessarily "broken") to a new way of being (not necessarily "fixed"). It is an evolution.

It's tempting to apply technical fixes to transformational challenges the way self-help does. Applying concrete skills and know-how is a place of comfort for most of us. It implies things are controllable, predictable, and understandable. It also has short-term appeal: we feel good about *doing* something, even if it doesn't create the intended effect. It feels good in the short term as we experience hopefulness but often leads to disappointing results as we apply technical fixes to complex, multidimensional challenges.

Technical fixes imply the thing we're fixing is broken and repairable. Humans are not broken machines. Our bodies are working as designed—we get tired when we work too hard, and our bellies grumble when we're hungry—we just don't always like the impacts of these messengers. Our systems, too, are not broken. They are working as designed; we rightfully don't like their effects.

We won't be able to improve our systems by making technical tweaks, especially when our technical solutions are born of the same beliefs that created the current ones. As writer, radical feminist, and civil rights activist Audre Lorde asked, "What does it mean when the tools of a racist patriarchy are used to examine the fruits of that same patriarchy? It means that only the most narrow perimeters of change are possible and allowable" (Lorde 2007). To create real change requires creating a new system not using the same tools and thinking that created the old one. "The master's tools," she writes, "will never dismantle the master's house" (2007).

This is where transformation via "nonreformist reform" comes in. According to social philosopher André Gorz, the term nonreformist reform describes changes that require a reworking of the problem from the inside out. It suggests anything else is just a fine-tuning of the status quo—one that might actually prevent large-scale change by making life bearable rather than better (Engler and Engler 2021).

Forgiving student debt, for example, alleviates immediate pain, but won't create the meaningful change that will help future generations to avoid this pain. It won't undermine predatory lending systems, and it won't solve underlying issues of affordability and accessibility in higher education. Instead, taxpayer money will reward these institutions for keeping prices astronomically high by paying the bills for them rather than reforming them.

Appeasing the public through stimulus checks provides immediate lifesaving support, but won't prevent corporations from raising prices and profits in tandem while stagnating worker wages. In fact, such short-term relief often thwarts the revolution that could transform work and capitalism as we know it forevermore.

Rather than assuming we have two options—the way it is or amelioration—transformation encourages us to consider both what *is* and what *could be.*

Superficial fixes won't transform a system that doesn't work for everyone into one that does. True reform comes from undermining it, deconstructing it, and building something anew. This action can feel like slowing down, moving backward, and starting over. But that's kind of the point.

Transformation feels different because it is different. It is born of a generative, creative, inclusive, and expansive energy. It is exciting and idealistic and visionary. Transformational solutions cannot be reductive, controlling, or isolated. They cannot require a lone hero; in fact, any solution born of a single hero contains all the assumptions and biases the hero carries, unchallenged by the many perspectives that come out in a collective conversation.

Transformational actions come from a fundamentally transformational energy. Most of us require a mindset shift to consider the change we most need to create is not a change in what we're *doing* at all, but in who we are *being.*

Our culture glorifies and affirms doers. We love to see the man with the plan, the mom hustling to make it all happen. This recognition of *doing* implies *doing* is the morally superior and more effective route. But is it?

Our *doing* is deeply rooted in our *being.* When we are stressed, we make decisions grounded in the beliefs that made us stressed in the first place. When I'm overwhelmed by my calendar, I micromanage myself even further, planning out in fifteen-minute increments the tasks I will accomplish. This technical, superficial fix leads to even more stress, hurried email responses, and solutions that prioritize efficiency over effectiveness. This is not what I want to do, or who I want to be, but is a reflection of what I believe about the world right now: if I can work harder, longer, and faster, it can all happen, and things will get better.

For the last fifteen years I operated this way; it never got better.

By reflecting on our *beingness*, we can bring attention and awareness to what's causing the overwhelm in the first place and try to eliminate the cause. Instead of micromanaging my day, I could examine the beliefs I have around hustling, commit to fewer priorities, or prioritize streamlining systems.

As we learned in chapter 8, trauma, unexpected stressors, new life phases, and new perspectives can all affect how we see the world and how we choose to act in it. Starting a new job, moving to a new town, or taking a long leave of absence to embark on our own version of *Wild* or *Eat, Pray, Love* may feel terrifying but may also open the door for a change in being. We step out to step back in differently. And lest we think it's all or nothing, we can also create the conditions for shifts to emerge organically through smaller pauses and reflections, including meditation, journaling, and conversations with people who challenge us to think and be differently.

Rooted in *beingness*, we tune in to our bodily experiences and, rather than reacting based on socialization, respond in a way that pulls us into the future. *Being* encourages us to trust the evolutionary pull within each of us that compels action in each moment.

Our highest, wisest selves are our uncultured, nonconforming, feeling bodies. Their wisdom is the immutable message of a feeling self. It's something we cannot force. We all have and experience intuition—the seemingly divine guidance that works with emergence to pull us into an unknown future. It is the result of our infinite bodily intelligences making sense of the complexity of reality to arrive at a decision our technical problem-solving, sense-making, and data-weighing systems may be otherwise unequipped to handle.

In a culture that values scientific ways of knowing and the written word of external authorities over wise, feeling bodies, we're chastised for using our intuition. There's some legitimacy in the challenge, but we also miss out on a lot of wisdom because we're undervaluing this knowledge system in favor of rationality. Rational does not mean correct; it's ecological—that is, environmentally dependent—not universal.

Research on intuition is finding it can lead to more effective decision-making than analysis (Marcus 2015; Julmi 2019). Under pressure and without time to debate, people make near-instantaneous evaluations that have proven to be lifesaving (Hodgkinson, Langan-Fox, and Sadler-Smith 2008). Science shows practice can make intuition-based decision-making more confident and accurate (Lufityanto, Donkin, and Pearson 2016). Friends and clients who report listening to their instincts often start getting stronger signals, clearer messages, and outcomes that may have been better than ones they'd have chosen on their own. They might pass up a good opportunity for no apparent reason, thereby making space for a great one, or leave the decent-enough partner on the faith there's an exceptional one, trusting the future that wants to emerge rather than resigning to the predictability of the hamster wheel.

Imagine how easeful life could be if we trusted ourselves to make decisions and to be at peace with the outcome, regardless of what that outcome was. What would that take? What could that lead to?

Regardless of whether we lean on intuition or analysis when we make decisions, it's important to be careful of the biases and beliefs we hold that impact both. It's a classic case of "both/and": It's *both* important to understand the signals your body is sending *and* get curious about where these feelings came from; It's *both* important to use available science *and* understand science is always evolving and sometimes biased.

This complex approach allows us to honor our beingness *and* create transformational change from an informed and curious place.

An integral part of this process is experimentation. As we discussed earlier, we experiment as children to see how to get our needs met. So, too, will we need to experiment to find what works for us as adults.

Experimentation is part of daily life as a child. Unattached to being right or smart, our curiosity and beginner's minds reign supreme. We put this in our mouths and stick our fingers in that. We cuddle and plead and tantrum to see what will help us get what we want and need. We stumble over our new language and speak our truths without fear. We learn a lot, and we learn it fast.

Along the way, and typically through formalized schooling, we lose our sense of experimentation. We learn it's good to be right and it's bad to be wrong. We are taught to control our bodies and use our brains. We're taught to prioritize the future—what they *will* think of you, how you *will* be successful—and to control it as much as possible. Learning slows.

As adults, we like to think we already understand the causal relationships that govern our world. Despite our best efforts, we draw incorrect causal relationships all the time. Self-help regularly draws faulty causality and recommends bizarre and futile next steps. People encourage us, for example, to dress like Barack Obama or Steve Jobs to get what we want—as if the clothing was what contributed to their success and not the mindsets undergirding their clothing choices (Bloem 2018) or the greater circumstances that contributed to their success. What happens if you dress like Steve Jobs? You look like Steve Jobs. As Theranos founder, Steve Jobs dress-alike, and convicted felon Elizabeth Holmes can attest—even if you dress like him and act like him, it does not necessarily make you successful.

As we learned in Psychology 101, correlation is not causation. Just because ice cream consumption and shark attacks tend to increase together doesn't mean one triggers the other. Similarly, just because a self-help book has millions of sales doesn't indicate the solution in the book works. The cause of high sales numbers is high purchase numbers. The fact that a book is a best-seller only reveals that people want something badly enough to buy it.

When we don't have the fullest picture of cause and effect, it means we don't have an easy problem with an easy solution on our hands. Most of us have never experienced the more beautiful, peaceful, equitable, and just world we know is possible. The path there will require some experimentation to find.

During my time as a subscription box business owner, I tried everything the "experts" told me would help me grow my business. Few of them worked as promised. I felt like an utter failure. Again, if they were the "experts," I figured the problem must have been me. Noticing I was being crushed under the pressure, my biz bestie Renee Powers of Feminist Book Club offered me the idea that "everything is an experiment." This phrase changed everything for me. Suddenly, the plans I was holding so tightly became less do-or-die. Failure became useful feedback and information about an approach rather than a personal failure. It empowered me to try things on smaller scales before risking my entire business for any one particular tactic.

Experimentation as a form of action is deliciously juicy. Under its guise, we have the ability to be imaginative, creative, and try wild new things with much lower stakes. We can try out strategies other people use and ones we have hunches about. We bring curiosity, awareness, and an openness to new ideas, new ways of thinking, and new ways of knowing to the experience. And then we wait. We watch what happens. We gather massive amounts of data just by tuning in to what's happening, free from the pressures of needing the experiment to "go right." In the process, we learn.

Clients often come to coaching with a tickle of "what if" they can't let go of. Their intuition won't let them forget they love to sing, or they might be with the wrong person, or life is meant to be more beautiful than this. They have to somehow know they can make a full income singing before they jump, know there's a better partner out there waiting for them, or have proof life really can be more beautiful. The prerequisite of certainty gets in the way of actually finding out.

By embracing experimentation, they get to conduct tiny experiments to find out. They observe what emerges when they take baby steps: Singing at a friend's wedding and getting their first referral; taking a solo trip and realizing they had simply been missing the feeling of independence; spending time in nature and remembering life is already beautiful and realizing that their workplace is an unnatural hellscape.

Similarly, I didn't quit my job in education to become a writer. I quit because I couldn't quiet the voice telling me to run. I had no idea where I was going, only that I needed to go. I didn't set out to publish a book, I followed my curiosity when my friend Coonoor Behal published her book, *I Quit!*, and I was desperate to hear all about it (2021). Trusting where my body wanted to play next and engaging with experiments has transformed everything in my world without having to know exactly where I was heading from the start. Rather than beginning with the end in mind, I pursued the means because the means were worth pursuing. By following my deepest, scariest wants, an unclear future and unclear end built itself without my conscious planning, scheming, or forcing. I have stumbled my way into my more beautiful world.

When we're open to experimentation and emergence, we get to read the room, sense what wants to emerge, and give it a place to grow and thrive. The act of creating a new future will mean living differently, beyond the bounds of what is reasonable and, often, socially acceptable. It means creating new social realities and categories in which humans can assign meaning. The more transformational it feels, and the more ecologically irrational it is, the more we likely need it.

Imagine if, instead of forcing willpower for the sake of "health," we experimented with rest and allowed healing to emerge, thereby resolving whatever prevented us from living healthfully in the first place. Imagine if, instead of negotiating a raise just for you or fighting for marginally better conditions in the workplace, we banded together to create co-ops that had those conditions in place for everyone from the beginning. Imagine if, instead of fighting to be who we are in adulthood, we raised our children to recognize the forces of socialization and be in choice from the beginning.

I imagine what it would be like to be the imperturbable bad bitch on a mission I've always wanted to be. When I close my eyes and feel into it, I recognize all I really want is to be in control of how I feel. I want to be unruffled by other people's opinions. I want to be able to speak without fear of judgment and abandonment. To be unfuckwithable. So I experiment with being steady. Breathing. Creating communities I feel safe in. Staying calm in the face of disagreement and disapproval. It hurts, but after surviving a few rounds, it hurts less. I practice speaking my mind, though my hands shake. I survive that, too. I am emboldened and encouraged. I am awarded with the courage to experiment with new ways of being and doing and experiencing my world.

I imagine a world that doesn't require coercion or shame for progress, and one that doesn't require conformity for acceptance and belonging. I dream of a world that doesn't need self-help because we've got community-care in spades. I believe societies can exist in which we all belong and contribute because we all recognize our interdependence and have respect for one another's perspective, gifts, and talents.

In that way, the future isn't so much the product of passing time as it is the result of today's decisions and actions.

What is the world you want to live in? What's the world that doesn't feel plausible but the one you know is possible? What's the world that is downright provocative in how preposterously, improbably possible it is? That's the one I want for you.

How can you create that world right now? What is your intuition guiding you to try? What will you commit to experimenting with? Who might you invite to join you?

By conducting experiments and learning along the way, we learn to hold things lightly while embodying presence and the beginner's mind. We also gather more data that allows us to begin asking better questions.

If you're wondering where to begin, here are a few strategies to try.

- **Identify a future you want but think is impossible. Take the smallest step in that direction.** If you dream of being an artist, buy an adult coloring book. If you want more equitable relationships, have conversations with loved ones about the future that wants to exist and what you might do to create the conditions for it today.

Not sure where to begin? Have a conversation with a child to get inspiration—they won't be limited by the same educated incapacity adults have.

- **Find the opportunities for nonreformist reform.** If you crave a world without a police force, contribute to building what will replace it. If you yearn for a healthy planet, make your city, or backyard, or balcony, or local park into a regenerative ecosystem. If you know a future can exist on the other side of consumerism, practice minimalism, use public transportation, advocate for commerce-free, advertising-free zones, and experiment with alternative economic models, such as the gift economy or sharing economy.

- **Get curious about your beliefs and fears. See if they are true.** If you fear you'll only be accepted if you look and act a certain way, test it. If you know you can only be successful if you work twice as hard as everyone else on your team, try doing less. If you fear you will die public speaking, join Toastmasters. Will your family really disown you if you speak up for yourself? Will you be fired if you speak up at work? How can you find out for sure?

- **Identify patterns in what you've been *doing*. Try the opposite. See what happens.** If you're used to leaving when things get hard, try staying and making things better where you are. If you're used to staying and trying to make things better where you are, try leaving. If you're used to doing things alone, recruit helpers. If you're used to things being hard and requiring willpower, try letting it be easy.

- **Experiment with your *being*.** If you've always considered yourself Type A, see what happens if you commit to "good enough" for a while. If you've considered yourself an introvert, see what happens when you're surrounded by your very favorite people in the world. If you're absolutely sure there's something wrong with you, entertain the idea that you make sense, exactly as you are.

- **Consider the past an experiment conducted.** What learning opportunities presented themselves? Which have you glossed over that it's time to unpack? What lesson can you be grateful for? What lessons are you still learning?

Once you have data, you get to decide what to do with it. How will you measure the results? What learning can you distill? How will you apply what you have learned? What experiment does it beg you to conduct next?

We often learn hard truths along the way: No, dieting doesn't work for everyone, and many of us gain more weight the harder we try. Yes, my acceptance in this relationship/family/job is conditional, and I get to decide what that means for me.

Through the lens of experimentation, we get to play with the unknown and the emergent. We get to release the stranglehold that being "right" has on us. And through the process, we often learn that not only is there not one "right" answer, there may be many right answers or no right answer at all.

Perfectionists, procrastinators, and self-help enthusiasts like to wait until they know enough to begin. That works well with technical fixes, but it won't work here. Living well is not a defined, well-understood problem. There's no need to wait until you feel like you have enough knowledge to start experimenting in your own life and in places where you have influence. We may never know all the variables impacting us, and we may never have a complete picture.

Changing how we approach life and the challenges in it can be hard. *Can be.* Change is hard when we've decided it's hard and when we're more comfortable with the known status quo than evolving into an unknown future. Change is hard when our identities are bound up with being perceived a certain way. But change is also a part of life. It is the experience of being in process, in evolution.

Beneficial action will likely look less and less like the ones we're accustomed to seeing in self-help: independent, concrete, specific, and absolutely certain. It will require accepting that the world is volatile, uncertain, complex, and ambiguous, and that control is both ineffective and antithetical to where we want to go. It will require embracing change and experimentation. It requires stepping into the big unknown and figuring it out as we go, working together, and with the Universe already in motion.

That's going to make many of us very uncomfortable. Life is going to be uncomfortable either way. Which flavor of discomfort will you choose? Let experimentation help you decide.

CHAPTER 14

SPIRALING UP

By ten, I was an expert at dissociation. I remember sitting in the dentist's chair, getting a cavity filled without Novocaine. Every once in a while, the drill would hit a nerve, and a ripple of searing, electric pain would grip my entire body.

I stared at the ugly, drop ceiling tiles repeating over and over in my head, *Mind over matter, mind over matter, mind over matter.* I practiced controlling my pain levels. I dropped into my body, felt the pain, and took the elevator back up to safety. Pain. No pain. Pain. No pain.

As I grew older, I found new uses for this strategy and new ways to detach from my body, my identity, and my reality. As a teenager, I told myself I didn't care what anyone thought until I just about believed it. I watched conversations "from the balcony," where it was safer. Eventually, I was old enough to dissociate like a real adult, and I drank.

I mastered social drinking over high school bonfires and German schnitzels. By the time I went to college, it was no longer recreational drinking, it was a tool: a shot of amaretto to coat the throat, a shot or two of Bacardi 151 to coat the nerves, and I was ready to pregame with the girls. When college ended, I learned the joys of overwork to get me out of awkward, dreaded social encounters. Happy hour? Sorry, I've got too much lesson planning and grading to catch up on. By the time I was twenty-two, I'd mastered the trifecta of what would become the armor of my womanhood: perfectionism, busyness, and booze.

Common knowledge says when you dissociate, overwork, or drink such that it interferes with life, you should seek medical help. When you feel numb, have trouble sleeping, overeat, or experience anxiety, they say, talk to your doctor. By this measure, two-thirds of the globe would be seeking medical attention for sleep issues alone (Philips 2019), including 75 percent of high school students (Wheaton et al. 2015). According to the American Institute of Stress, 77 percent of individuals studied experience stress that has impacted their physical health (2022). According to these studies, the vast majority of us should be seeking medical treatment.

But for what? So we can be told we're too stressed? We know this. So we can be prescribed a new medication that helps us power through our days and nights? We're already doing this. That's why it hurts.

Or so we can be told we're not alone? We're simply being overworked by a system not designed for us to thrive in? So we can be supported through the process of reducing those things we've been tolerating that are superbly intolerable?

Right. Good luck.

We are, as humans, all trying to cope with a world not designed for all of us to thrive. In a world with more humanity, one in which we are well-rested and well-resourced, we could deal with stress as it comes, rather than shouldering ongoing stress until we shatter. We'd cope with the stress, solve the problem, and move on.

But our problems rarely seem to fully dissipate, even with professional help. I have turned to many helpers over the years as I tried to manage my overwhelming levels of stress and anxiety. They never asked if I had anything to be stressed about. They never asked if I felt safe at home. They never asked if I was drinking myself into a coma. But they did prescribe me medication while looking me up and down and asking if I was overeating.

In my world, leaving my body meant leaving my environmental stressors, if only temporarily. It wasn't just a problem; it was a solution. Under no circumstances did I want those sources of relief to go away—I wanted to mentally check out. I felt like I needed to drink to make my world an acceptable place to inhabit. Overwork was my respectable excuse for both staying on the edges of workplace drama and avoiding the other stressors in my life. It also granted me the financial freedom to escape crippling student debt and finally leave my toxic employer.

In short, my coping mechanisms have each given me a way to survive. I credit all my coping mechanisms with collectively getting me through and to where I am today.

I would never recommend dissociation, alcohol, or overwork as a solution for anyone. I fully understand in many cases, emotion-focused coping mechanisms become more problematic than useful. I also know they were the best solutions I had at my disposal during major, stressful periods of my life, and to eliminate them without eliminating their causes and replacing them with more effective coping mechanisms would have been short-sighted and possibly dangerous.

As the saying goes, we must be gentle with ourselves for what we did while in survival mode.

Each time I sought support from a professional, I was diagnosed. Each "solution" I've been offered focused on me, the person, as the problem, rather than the circumstances I was trying to cope with. In our shitty medical models, we're always the problem. The problem is the one who eats. It's the overworker, the alcoholic, the addicted, the pleaser, the performer, the perfectionist, the one who doesn't sleep, the one who sleeps around. We point to the person rather than recognizing the environmental effects of working in stressful jobs, living in stressful neighborhoods, or navigating stressful financial situations. In other words, our allostatic loads.

Our allostatic loads are the cumulative burden of our chronic stress and life events (Guidi et al. 2021). Known as the "wear and tear" on the body, they are the result of living in and experiencing stress (Rodriguez et al. 2019). When the stress in our lives exceeds our ability to cope with them in healthful ways, an allostatic overload ensues. Proactive bodily responses meant to protect the body against stress, like the release of cortisol, result in secondary outcomes such as increased blood pressure. Over time, our systems adapt to living at chronically elevated stress levels, and we begin to experience issues like chronic hypertension. Similar to chronic shame, chronic stress can lead to a downward spiral.

We head to the doctor, they diagnose our high blood pressure and tell us to lose weight, or drink less, and prescribe medications that artificially lower our blood pressure by relaxing our veins and arteries so our readings normalize without ever examining the underlying cause of stress, weight gain, or alcohol use. We stay stressed while trying to reduce specific manifestations of the stress on the body. Without resolving the root causes, we may manage our hypertension, for instance, while watching other chronic diseases pop up, such as cardiovascular disease, diabetes, and depression.

Biomarkers like obesity and hypertension tell us how the body is doing but don't tell us why it's that way. Social causes such as lack of sociopolitical power and resources, and ethnic, class, and racial discrimination are some of the greatest determinants of health worldwide (Williams, Priest, and Anderson 2016). Despite this knowledge being widely available, treatment responses from traditional practitioners rarely address these factors. There are a lot of reasons for this—from restrictive insurance systems and the limited time they have with patients to the desire to do something right now to help. As a result, many patients never get to the bottom of their symptoms, or worse, receive treatments that create additional issues, like side effects that actually *add* to the wear-and-tear on the body.

Surface-level solutions prioritize profit, pathologize the person and the symptoms, and leave the underlying causes untreated. Surface-level solutions mask what's really going on, which routinely leads to things getting worse. Just like the self-help and dieting industries, the medical and pharmaceutical industries don't benefit from us escaping their cycles, even if individuals *in* the system want to do their best for their patients. As has been noted elsewhere, we don't have a health-care system, we have a disease-care system, and it's profitable (Weil 2013).

So how do we exit the spirals of coping, shame, mental, and chronic illness? Generally speaking, we walk the same path we walk in this book: create awareness, learn more, take action, and work with others to usher in a better way.

While we're reacting unconsciously, the actions we take spring from our socialization or in response to a stimulus. We do what we've learned. We're likely to drink if our parents did. We're likely to stress eat if our parents did. Many of us learn this suffering is simply part of life. Rather than reworking gender roles and demanding the societal supports that would provide moms with some relief, for example, we joke about how much wine moms drink, buy them cutesy "mom juice!" wine glasses for Mother's Day, and let them keep suffering. While on autopilot, we prioritize comfort with the status quo and internalize our pain rather than demanding change that would alleviate our pain and reduce our need to cope.

When we start to pay attention, we start to pick up on our tells—the early signs the stressors and pressures of life are getting to us. I bite my nails, crave crunchy things, and retreat socially. Unheeded, the tension and stress build and turn into a downward spiral, a negative, painful, self-reinforcing cycle of physical and emotional distress. While the stress may not be easily resolvable, listening to the signs of my body can tell me what I need to cope effectively and interrupt the downward spiral.

Early recognition enables mutual support. When we are able to pick up on signs of trouble early, we can support one another in coping effectively and healthfully with both the emotions and the problems we're facing and, in turn, reduce our stressors. When my friends, partner, or colleagues see me retreating, they venture into what we have lovingly titled the safety of my "turtle shell" and see how I'm doing. They try to help me be okay. We joke, commiserate, and laugh. They help me to get some perspective. From a well-resourced and well-rested place, and aware of both the stressors and coping mechanisms, they help me to be in choice about how I want to move forward; I can take the action that makes sense while being supported and held accountable by folks who love me. Together, we get me spiraling back up.

When I'm downright overwhelmed, and we aren't able to restore a sense of equilibrium, we eat, we drink, we cry, and we find other ways to make life tolerable.

And this happens to all of us, no matter how enlightened and practiced and well-versed we think we are in meditation or breathing or whatever productive, healthy coping strategies we've got in our toolkit. Sometimes, our systems are just overwhelmed, and we resort to the tools we have available. If all we have time and energy for are diagnoses and medications, that's what we use. If what we've been taught is to use alcohol or shopping or scrolling or Netflix or dislodging our own pain onto others, that's what we use. We know these will only relieve our pain temporarily or distract us long enough it won't hurt for a while, but none of these will ultimately solve the problem. That doesn't make them inherently bad, and it doesn't make anyone bad for doing them. It just makes them ineffective in the long term.

The difficulty is, when we're prioritizing meeting the deadlines and tending to obligations all day long, we rarely have time to consider *how* we're going about meeting the deadlines and doing the tending. To gain awareness, learn from the suffering, and turn our downward spirals into upward spirals, we need to stop ignoring the messengers. Our bodily messengers exist for a reason, even when the reason is inconvenient. The path from ineffective to effective coping mechanisms requires we be honest about our suffering, develop a nonjudgmental relationship to the suffering, and work with and through the suffering (williams, Owens, and Syedullah 2016). Unfortunately, most of us are unimaginably estranged from our bodies, and for unfortunate reasons.

I remember hearing the threats from a young age: "If you don't quit crying, I'll give you something to cry about." The suffering adults in our lives are so dissociated from their own experiences and so unable to cope with ours, they threaten us with violence. It's the only way they know to deal. We learn to suppress feelings that make others uncomfortable. Later, unpracticed in coping with our own big feelings, we eventually suppress them in ourselves as well.

Our softness, our sadness, and our pain are deeply uncomfortable reminders to others of the unexpressed softness, sadness, and pain in their own lives. The reaction of the adults in our lives had everything to do with the adults and nothing to do with who we were as children. It is the direct manifestation of white supremacy's hold on us: shoot or gaslight the messenger to maintain total control. It trains us against speaking up about injustices and punishes speaking truth to power early (Cullors 2022). It keeps us individually coping rather than effectively transforming our world to be less distressing.

The problem is, we cannot selectively block emotions. When we suppress our pain, we inadvertently block the feelings needed to resist oppression and reduce our capacity for joy. We can't change the circumstances creating suffering if we refuse to see and feel the suffering. This is why toxic positivity doesn't work—ignoring pain doesn't make it go away. Liberation comes from accepting things exactly as they are so we can process them and move forward with choice and agency.

We'll talk more about what acceptance looks like in chapter 17, but it bears introducing now: we need to make peace with the things we are—animals with full-fledged biological systems that are going to kick in whether we want them to or not. Our bodily responses aren't meant to be vilified and shut down, they're meant to be honored for the messengers they are and offered compassion, ease, support, and safety. It's what we need as living creatures.

Permission to feel is a permission to make decisions from a place that honors our feelings, needs, and wants as well as those of the community around us (Cullors 2022). It is a radical departure from our internalized oppression. It is compassionate and kind. Acceptance facilitates recovery. When we acknowledge our feelings, we get to fully process them in healthful ways and express what we want and need from others. Honored feelings create relationships, organizations, and societies that respect our humanity.

Imagine if, instead of judging ourselves and each other for how we coped, we recognized our best efforts at making it through. What if we affirmed how proud we are of our ability to survive another day? What would it mean if you knew you were doing the very best you could do and that *you* didn't need fixing?

The way I see it, our bodily sensations tell us what's ours to do in the world. It is the way the Universe works and evolves through living, feeling bodies. When we are hungry, we need to eat. When we are thirsty, we need to drink. And when we feel our heart beating in our throats, we need to speak up. But to do so, we have to acknowledge our hurts and hungers are valid and be willing to honor our feelings rather than stuff them away. Which, we know, is far easier in a community that won't threaten you with judgment, ostracization, or violence just for speaking up.

Action here might look like finding what helps you to feel safe enough to feel what you feel. And then feeling what you have the capacity and bandwidth to feel. Action might look like respecting and honoring your wants and needs and limits, voicing them, and taking a nap. Action could look like acknowledging all the ways life is hard and that the hardships aren't necessarily your fault but might be within your power to change. Action may require deep curiosity about your suffering and your feelings, your intuition, and your daydreams; after all, they just may be the greatest indicators of what will provide the deepest, truest, longest lasting results for you, and be the way to your—and my—liberation.

And lest I introduce another either/or binary, let's recognize we have more choices than to mindlessly cope, or intentionally feel what's ours to feel and act on it every time. There's always a third way, and often a fourth and a fifth.

The goal of this chapter is not to eliminate coping mechanisms so you can feel everything all the time. Unfortunately, most of us still have bills to pay, and it's not fun to be swept up by the Big Sad all the time. Instead, I invite us to cope *and* feel our feelings to the extent we're able. Cope *and* build awareness of the coping strategies we use so we can recognize when our coping mechanisms are no longer serving us. Cope *and* get curious. Cope *and* be present to our coping mechanisms to know when they are being used effectively and when they are becoming dysfunctional (Hübl and Avritt 2020).

I used alcohol as my coping mechanism of choice for more than a decade. I had no intention of quitting. In fact, I only read Annie Grace's *This Naked Mind* (again, at a bar, beer in hand) because I was downright incredulous that a single book could have such a profound effect on someone that they'd immediately go sober (2015). The book helped me to understand my beliefs around alcohol, the effects it was having on my brain and body, and revealed, in no uncertain terms, that alcohol was making everything significantly worse. It took another three weekends hugging the porcelain throne for it to sink in. I drank to be okay... but it was making everything worse. The awareness interrupted my downward spiral long enough to see how ineffective it was. It wasn't the hangovers or the relationships I'd ruined that interrupted my spiral, it was knowing that it was exacerbating all of my issues.

Let me be super clear here. I do not mean to suggest it should be this easy for everyone. There are no one-size-fits-all solutions to complex challenges like addiction and mental health struggles. I also do not disagree with the advice to get professional support. In fact, I think everyone should have a village of supportive experts to turn to. What I find to be tremendously important, however, is to be extremely discerning in whose support to seek and whose advice to take. Get curious about their biases and beliefs; be aware of how much fault, blame, and responsibility they are suggesting you take on as an individual versus how much responsibility they attribute to environmental stressors. It's okay to acknowledge the reality of interconnection and long-term structural change while still pursuing the immediate support we need.

Unfortunately, as we get support, heal, and feel what's ours to feel, we're still out in the world, living and commuting and going to family reunions. We will still encounter stress, and we'll still need to tap into resilience. As we level up our awareness and our coping mechanisms, it becomes important to recognize what we're asking ourselves to tolerate. Our lives should not require us to live in a permanent state of coping and resilience. It's important to know when we've outgrown the coat.

Humans are inherently resilient. We wouldn't have lasted through the eons if we weren't. Our current environments, however, are asking us to be resilient in ways no other humans have had to be resilient. We're being pushed past the threshold of what we can and should be asked to rebound from on a daily basis. Resilience should be the practice of rebounding from temporary hardship, preferably from a foundation of being rested and resourced and ready, and not a permanent way of existing in the world.

Companies use our resilience against us, demanding we rebound from injustices we shouldn't have to rebound from. Women who have experienced sexual assault at the hands of coworkers are asked to return to work with their assailants is if nothing happened. People of color are asked to ignore microaggressions daily. We've seen companies weaponize resilience and self-regulation as a way to pacify workers and encourage workers to tolerate the intolerable.

When a company asks me to do a presentation on resilience, I now ask them what conditions they are creating that require their employees to be resilient.

We've got to entertain the idea of a life and a world and a way of working that doesn't require us to be resilient all the time. The more we dream about what that world could look like and come to expect the peace that exists in that world, the less willing we are to tolerate anything less in our realities. Without guilt or shame, we can accept we are tired—tired of our own coping mechanisms, tired of being strong, and tired of accepting the unacceptable. We can instead seek the help we need to create the change in our lives that removes the cause of suffering or helps us to navigate the cause of suffering more effectively.

Interestingly, I find the clients who are best able to do this are the ones who are just too damn tired to be resilient. They are the moms with a child on their hip during Zoom meetings who don't have the energy to care about your professionalism standards anymore. They are the heartbroken who can't muster the energy to perform happiness. They are the social justice workers who have given everything to their cause, and have no strength left to play nice.

Rather than holding on to hope that a tweak to the system will finally make it right, they're the ones so tired of coping and suffering that they're ready to burn it all down. In response to the idea that social justice takes time, Fannie Lou Hamer said at some point you get "sick and tired of being sick and tired," stop ignoring the facts and hypocrisy, and demand change (1964). Demanding change is a form of problem-focused coping (Lazarus and Folkman 1984). It requires us to recognize we aren't the problem; we have a problem. Once we create that distance between ourselves and the problem, we can engage in action from a place of discernment.

Discernment is wisdom. It's knowing what you are willing to accept and why. It's being willing to establish boundaries and hold them. It's knowing what's worth your energy, presence, life, and resilience. It's about being in choice about when you will cope and how.

The best coping mechanisms often involve the support of other people—you don't need to carry what you're carrying alone. Having a supportive community and a refuge can be tremendously beneficial to both problem-focused and emotion-focused coping.

Around the time I started seeing my third therapist, I was turning to self-help books to help me understand everything—myself, my coping strategies, and why I just couldn't figure out the whole adulting thing. Caring but unempathetic friends recommended shame-inducing technical fixes like *Skinny Bitch: A No-Nonsense, Tough-Love Guide for Savvy Girls Who Want to Stop Eating Crap and Start Looking Fabulous!* (Freedman and Barnouin). Caring and compassionate friends handed me *The Impossible Will Take a Little While* (Loeb),

The Body Keeps the Score (van der Kolk), and *Rising Strong* (Brown). Through their suggestions and support, I was able to see more clearly who was aiding and abetting my self-shaming and who was providing me with badly needed refuge.

A refuge is a safe space where we can be sheltered from danger. It is not coddling, and it is not enabling. Rather than be expected to "get over it," a refuge is a place where we are safe to be with our pain so it can move through us as it needs to. Rather than avoiding the discomfort, we build our capacity to be with it. Refuge provides safety and support as we rest, recover, and gather the resources and strength to cultivate the long-term care and prevention we also deserve.

My husband is my very favorite refuge. He is the safest space for me to work through my every insecurity and trauma. He doesn't shield me from my feelings or save me from what hurts but provides the spaciousness I need to feel understood, to feel everything that's mine to feel, and to find my most conducive way forward. His unconditional support has shown me what love can look like and feel like, and quite honestly, it's raised the bar for every relationship in my life. It's reminded me that I'm deserving of time, attention, care, rest, and love, and has meant I'm less willing to accept anything less from the close relationships in my life.

Experiencing his unconditional compassion means I'm acutely aware of when others attempt to shame me. The sense of belonging we've created together means I immediately recognize when others expect me to change to be accepted. Our sense of team means I feel extra aware when others operate from combative, competitive mindsets, or weaponize my pain and sensitivity.

It's also helped me to realize not all people and places are for me and, through the guidance of *Radical Dharma* and

Nina Simone's song "You've Got to Learn," empowered me to leave the table when love's not being served without embarrassment. I've learned that leaving a hostile environment is not a bad reflection on me; it doesn't mean I wasn't good enough. It simply means I am responding with agency when they weren't willing to create a space where I felt comfortable. I see my departure as a stress-reducing act of personal power and no longer slink away in shame. It's just another way of coping. Having a supportive place to land and a refuge to process has helped me to choose my people extra carefully. I don't need just anybody in my life, and I don't need to hold on to family for the sake of holding on to family. I've created my own, and it's good.

Along the way, I've developed an intolerance for everything and everyone that's not equally as safe and healing. Rather than living with pain and shame and finding ways to cope with my feelings alone, I now head back to my refuge. I sit with my people and emote: *I am so sad! I just want a goddamn plate of nachos! And a venti java chip frappuccino! And people to not suck so bad! Is this really so much to ask?* And they offer to take me out for the night and, often, the offer is enough. They hear me, validate my feelings, and let me know they'd feel that way too. Maybe we go out and I drown my sadness in guac, or maybe we don't. Either way, I'm reminded I'm loved and supported. Over time, "Wanna get nachos?" becomes "Wanna go for a walk?" or "Call me. Let's talk about it," and together, we trade in unhelpful coping mechanisms for more productive, collaborative, and empowering ones.

My refuge has also helped me to land in my own fullness and wholeness without relying on others' approval. For me, that's been an extra boon; I've found living in your wholeness both requires and brings about the courage to be disliked. As Glennon Doyle says, "Every time you're given a choice between disappointing someone else and disappointing yourself, your duty is to disappoint that someone else. Your job, throughout your entire life, is to disappoint as many people as it takes to avoid disappointing yourself" (2020). Choosing to proactively reduce stress means I'm frequently disappointing others and cultivating new relationships that don't require me to disappoint myself or cope to make it through.

Reflecting on my coping behaviors now, I see that at each turn, I was doing my very best to get through my days, and these strategies were the best I could do. That's easy to say in reflection. At the time, though, it didn't feel like it. I felt like an outcast who couldn't figure out how to thrive in the world like everyone else. I felt alone. I felt helpless. I felt like a failure, and my doctors by and large seemed to agree with me.

The goal isn't to never use coping strategies, it's to stop vilifying our current ones and lean into more healthful and liberating ones as we're able. It's to interrupt downward spirals wherever we can and reverse course. Do what we can. Offer ourselves compassion along the way. Find ever more effective strategies for dealing with both the original source of stress and our response to that stress.

There's more to life than making it through.

CHAPTER 15

WRITING A NEW STORY

The most powerful coaching conversation I've ever experienced lasted thirty seconds. I was participating in a round of speed-coaching during my coach training. I had just ten seconds to present my dilemma to my coach: I don't feel comfortable being myself around other people. I find it impossible to open myself up to that level of vulnerability and, therefore, judgment.

She asked a simple question in return: "What if everyone were safe?"

Such a simple, absurd question. My body's visceral "no chance" shiver revealed my own story: No one is safe.

Around that time I first met Renee Powers, who would go on to launch the Feminist Book Club. She was curious about launching a subscription box and wanted to hear about my experience. As we chatted, she mentioned something about cooperation over competition. I was just learning about feminist business practices, and I wanted her to like me, so I went with it. "Sure! Yeah! Cooperation, absolutely," I agreed. Cooperation doesn't exactly jive with my "the world is not safe" belief, but being aware of my belief system meant I could try on hers for a while to see what would happen. So I shared everything I knew about starting a subscription box. I told her all my hard-won lessons and secrets. Miraculously, she didn't take them and run. The relationship didn't become extractionary at all. Instead, it became the foundation of trust for a years-long friendship and planted the seed that perfect strangers could be safe.

Months later, an acquaintance I'd known for years also requested insider knowledge about the subscription box industry. Emboldened by my experience with Renee, I gladly shared with her everything I knew. When I reached out a few weeks later to ask her for some support in helping me to understand *her* industry, she gave me her hourly rate and suggested I book some time with her through her assistant if I wanted to learn more.

As Anaïs Nin says, "We don't see things as they are, we see them as we are" (1961). The world is neither inherently safe nor inherently unsafe. People are neither all safe nor all unsafe. How we treat other people is based on how *we* see the world and has very little to do with them. Our beliefs and stories become the lens through which we interpret and take action in the world. Sometimes, we will be met with people who wear similar lenses, and sometimes we'll be met with radically different lenses. There is no correct lens, and there is no best lens.

Our lenses have tremendous impacts on our lives. When I operate in the world as if everyone is unsafe, I find myself being more guarded and look for evidence that bolsters my belief. Thanks to confirmation bias, I find it. I find myself feeling paranoid and looking for all the ways the people in my life are secretly judging me. Maybe they are, maybe they aren't, but my lens determines how I'll interact with them and whether I shut down or stay open. Our lenses define what we see before we've seen it. Our beliefs become the foundations for our actions.

Our individual belief systems don't come out of nowhere, they come from our socialization. My belief that the world is not safe was grounded in ample evidence. It came from emotional, psychological, and physical abuse handed down my patrilineal line. It came from a family culture that protected bullies and punished vulnerability and truth-telling on my matrilineal line. It came from a deep awareness of economic inequality as a child and knowing I was a member of the "have-nots" while other people in my family were the "haves." It came from having friends equally impacted by unprocessed trauma. It came from learning at a young age the police could come at any time to take me away from my mother. It came from growing up in a school that threatened to keep track of every misdeed on some everlasting "permanent record" and a church that terrorized us with an omniscient being who would record all our unseen misdeeds and send us to the depths of hell for transgressions. I believed the world wasn't safe because *my* world wasn't safe, and I saw no difference between *my* world and *the* world.

Before we understand there is a difference between how we perceive the world to be and how the world is, we are subject to our beliefs; we believe there is one truth, one set of rules, and one reality, and it dictates what we see as possible. The number of possible futures is hamstrung only by our relationship to what our current belief systems tell us is possible.

Until I am able to operate from a new belief system, my future will be beholden to the beliefs and actions of my past. In *Healing Collective Trauma,* author and spiritual teacher Thomas Hübl notes that our futures are reverberations of our pasts until we come to terms with our past in the present.

Unacknowledged and unintegrated, our past shapes our future as we act out of habit, driven by unconscious forces (Hübl and Avritt 2020).

For our futures to change, we have to process our pasts, be conscious of our beliefs and actions in the present, and intentionally cocreate the future.

According to Hübl, the world as we currently experience it is a manifestation of millennia of collective, unresolved traumas (Hübl and Avritt 2020). We know individual trauma lives in our individual bodies (van der Kolk 2015). Collective traumas, such as genocide, war, famine, poverty, COVID, and the climate crisis, Hübl suggests, live in our collective bodies (Hübl and Avritt 2020). They become part of our shared experiences, shared histories, and shared belief systems. They are felt and live on in the bodies and brains of individuals who go on to create our tangible political, economic, and social systems.

These collective traumas are rooted in what author Charles Eisenstein calls the myth of separation (2013). The myth of separation is the view we are separate from each other and separate from nature. It serves as the foundation for othering, exploitation, and conquest. It justifies appalling and unconscionable treatment of people and the planet. We see the manifestations of the myth of separation, interpret them as evidence the belief system is true, universal, and irrefutable, and that's that. We see ourselves as logical, rational beings whose beliefs are grounded in reality and never stop to ask how such a reality came to be.

In the same way that our individual beliefs and actions are reflective of our individual journeys, adult development, and maturity, so too are our collective beliefs and actions reflective of our collective journey, societal development, and maturity. According to the model of Spiral Dynamics, individuals, organizations, and societies evolve along a predictable pattern of development that both mirrors and incorporates the trajectory of adult development theory (Beck and Cowan 2005).

Societies' values and worldviews emerge as a result of environmental conditions and humans' capacity to deal with them. The systems and structures created by a society reflect the lens of the collective stage they inhabit. As with individual development, this collective development is a constant response to the problems and problem-solving frameworks of the previous level. As we encounter new experiences and new problems that reflect the increasing complexity of our world, our societies must adapt by developing more complex perspectives and problem-solving skills. In other words, the evolution of our societies is a reflection of the complexity of our societies, the problems that emerge, and our ability to cope with and resolve those problems. Our collective evolution is an emergent process.

Spiral Dynamics explains how we collectively evolve to meet environmental demands but goes beyond adult development theory by highlighting how environments shape our ability to imagine and create new worlds. It demonstrates how shifts in collective consciousness emerge from previous ways of being and thinking.

We can also use Spiral Dynamics to predict where our personal and collective belief systems are headed in the future. If we're fighting each other ruthlessly over a lack of resources, we can predict an emergence of order to get that behavior in check. If we're seeing an obsession with wealth for some damaging the health of all, it makes sense we respond to the inequality with a push for civil rights and equity. What emerges is a perpetual iteration of consciousness that enables us to deal with our current environment.

Unfortunately, different forces can keep us locked into certain ways of operating individually and collectively. Education systems that are bureaucratically locked into a value system of order and discipline will punish those who try to exist outside of that way of being. Our economic system currently values and rewards competition and individualism and vilifies models that value cooperation. It makes sense that we would have a hard time transcending these ways of being and even considering what other ways could exist.

Similar to when individuals are taxed beyond their ability to cope, when our systems are taxed beyond *their* ability to cope, we risk collectively regressing to a less evolved and mature way of existing. Instead of breaking new ground in living cooperatively, for instance, we might fall back on extreme tribalism.

Because the truth is, we are not exclusively competitive or cooperative. We've been these things off and on since the dawn of time in response to our circumstances. We just happen to be trending toward cooperation, evolving alongside all of nature.

So how do we transcend our current collective systems? How do we create the more just, kind, loving world we know is possible?

Well, we update our beliefs, our values, our behaviors, our environments, and our socializing forces to match the world we want to see. And we do it kind of the same way we evolve individually—incrementally and kind of experimentally or a bit traumatically with a sudden breakthrough. A family can proactively choose to embody values of togetherness or wait until a tragic death brings everyone together. A nation can institute proactive reforms or wait until revolution demands it. When we're conscious and enough of our collective is conscious, we get to pick.

For organizational and systemic change to take hold, we need to transform ourselves and our belief systems together (Anderson 2021). As long as corporate interests dominate the media and dictate government policy, business leaders will control the predominant narratives and continue to push their interests and belief systems around consumerism, capitalism, and individualism, having us believe it's the only way.

Gandhi's quote isn't just a cliched truism; we do need to *be the change we wish to see* in our communities, organizations, and in the world. As we personally evolve in our consciousness and ability to tackle ever more complex problems, so too do the organizations and communities we lead. Our fates and our evolution are interdependent.

Our collective systems cannot transcend the level of developmental maturity and consciousness of its leadership. Our leaders must evolve for our systems to evolve, and until they do, the beliefs and development of the people within the system are limited. Only when enough of the population has evolved beyond the system and is also willing to exert pressure on the leaders of the system will the system itself change. Only then is an evolutionary leap possible.

Studies show 85 percent of change efforts in organizations fail (Wheatley 2006). The majority of change management efforts focus on making outer behavioral changes without supporting us in making the prerequisite inner change. As a result, we're expected to adapt and solve ever more challenging dilemmas without evolving our beliefs, decision-making strategies, or the identities we have bound up in them.

In 2015, The United Nations General Assembly identified seventeen Sustainable Development Goals meant to serve as "a shared blueprint for peace and prosperity for people and the planet, now and into the future." They are meant to demonstrate the interconnectivity of our people, planet, and the economy. Neglecting for a moment they are heavily influenced by Western beliefs about development and sustainability, the goals advocate for research and action focused on areas of synergy—increasing health, for instance, by eliminating poverty and hunger, supporting gender equality, and providing quality education, clean water, and sanitation.

While the goals seem to point to actions that lead us toward a future of interdependence and interconnection, it overlooks the abilities, skills, and qualities needed to address these challenges. As a result, the Inner Development Goals were born—a framework of twenty-three skills and qualities fundamental to reaching the UN's Sustainable Development Goals. These twenty-three transformational skills fall into five Dimensions: Being/Relationship to Self, Thinking/Cognitive Skills, Relating/Caring for Others and the World, Collaborating/Social Skills, and Acting/Driving Change (Inner Development Goals 2021).

Based on what I know to be true about self-help readers, many of us are off to a good start. We have a learning mindset, spend time cultivating our self-awareness, and sustain optimism and perseverance in the face of challenges. We are poised to be able to facilitate the shift from independence to interdependence and from competition to cooperation. We are able to lean on the self-awareness we've cultivated from all of our self-analysis and use it toward our ability to analyze our systems and take courageous action toward change.

I see self-help evolving toward inner-compass work, empathy, compassion, inclusivity, courage, and being here and now without judgment—all of which happen to be Inner Development Goals. The same beliefs and qualities that support us in escaping the self-help cycle will support us in replacing the story of separation with the story of interbeing and working together for the sake of peace and well-being for people and planet.

The creation of our more beautiful world requires us to consider the beliefs we hold about who we are and what's possible for us and the world, *and* to consciously cultivate the skills and qualities that help us to bring that world into existence.

So where do we begin?

The creation of the future can sometimes feel a little like a question of chicken or egg; which comes first, belief or action? Causality can feel wonky, here, too. Are we creating the future, or is it creating us? We don't actually know. Either way, there are some ways we can play with the evolution process. For me, evolution came through a process of learning to be present with myself, healing my relationship with myself and my past, and responding to my personal evolutionary pulls, which meant experimenting with new ways of being and making a living. As such, that's the general order I'll discuss them in. As with all things, though, you know where your future is pulling you. Trust it.

Present awareness is a beautiful way to create the conditions that allow a new future to emerge. Within mindfulness, we're able to create the space in which to separate ourselves from our thoughts and feelings. In practices like meditation or journalling, we're able to allow our thoughts and feelings to come and go and recognize we are not our thoughts and feelings but that we *have* thoughts and feelings. The process makes them object. The spaciousness and distance we create allows us to process our old stories and reflect on them through the lens of our personal ethics and chosen values. We're able to metabolize our pain and trauma and work through our pasts, opening up the opportunity for new futures to emerge.

Healing our relationships with our pasts can only happen if we're willing to acknowledge them. We can't heal traumas we won't acknowledge, individually or collectively. Our refusal to reflect, collectively, on the traumas we're currently creating through our systems means we stay loyal to our unexamined beliefs and the systems they have manifest. Without distance between ourselves and our beliefs, we identify with them, and a criticism on either our beliefs or the systems they have created feels like a direct attack on our person. When losing a belief system feels like a direct threat to my safety, I'll cling to it, especially when that's what my belief system tells me to do—fight like hell.

Integrating presence, healing, and nonattachment return us to the present to metabolize what exists in the moment and create the space to tune in to the future that wants to emerge. From a place of healing and feeling, we are able to sense the pull of the Universe and our individual calling to contribute to our collective evolution. Following our calling, we rarely seek fame or fortune or the American Dream. Instead, we feel that familiar pull we've always felt—the whisper that pulls us toward advocacy, or artistry, or community. It's the quiet pull that transcends the fads of consumerist desires, external pressures, and societal conformity.

You know the one.

Pursuing your whisper often feels terrifying. Like my dream of writing, confessed only under the cover of liquid courage, the future that wants to be created through us can feel downright foolish when examined under the light of our current belief systems. Examining the beliefs that lead us to our conclusions can be even more challenging. As we get curious, interrogate, and deconstruct then reconstruct our belief systems, we lose the sense of control we once thought we had. It's destabilizing to lose the footing that got you where you are. We often feel as though we are swimming against the powerful current of collective belief; it's because we are. The current pushes against us all the time, our cultural environment threatening to imprison us in the collective worldview. Developing and holding on to new beliefs is tough, and we truly benefit from having friends and collectives that support us in our process, in effect changing the immediate environment around us to create a more conducive ecosystem for the seeds of our new beliefs and identities to germinate and grow.

Within our new, supportive environments and collectives, we get to practice creating the world we know can exist. Whether through a trusted professional who has been there herself, through a recovery group, or a new community, we get to experience life on the other side of our beliefs. For individuals with targeted identities, such as women, people of color, and any folks who have been marginalized and mistreated, this is especially important as we challenge the beliefs that have been given to us about who we are. We get to examine and discard the social constructs we inherited and internalized and be more discerning about the beliefs we choose to take on in the future.

And then, we get to create our future.

Earlier, we explored experimentation with beliefs and actions to see which held true after testing. Here's another invitation to play: Consider what belief you want to have and what evidence you could seek that supports that belief. Envision the world you want to exist in, and seek the evidence that shows its existence today. Find the tendrils the future has sent back to evidence it is starting to exist or wants to exist. Write a letter to your future self, laying out your hopes and dreams for your future. Ask a few questions. Another day, from another chair or pen or perspective, respond from the perspective of your future self. Don't overthink it, just write. See what the next iteration of you already knows.

If there isn't a ton of evidence the future you want is on its way, how can you become the evidence? I believe the cities of the future can and will be regenerative and life-centered. I believe they'll be more walkable, green, and community-driven. Mark and I are evidence this wants to exist simply because *we* want it to exist. We create the demand simply by being the demand. We commute by walking, biking, and taking public transit whenever possible. We become statistical data for our city that transit is a desired resource, and in turn, they create more transit options, helping us to cocreate the walkable, accessible, community-driven sharing economy we wish to see.

Beliefs can also be disrupted through nonexamples. We know when people try to change our minds on a topic, we often double down on our beliefs. When we personally experience something that challenges our prevailing narrative, on the other hand, we often find a way to update our schema. As kids, our friends have parents or caregivers, who, by default, were child-rearing adults. Most of us grow up with depictions of nuclear families in the media and are taught that's the way it is supposed to be. Uniquely, Mark and I each grew up with an aunt and an uncle who remained child-free. It shattered the illusion there was no other way and made the choice a conscious one for us. We were able to evaluate our desire for a family against our desire to retire early and make environmentally friendly choices. We have chosen to remain intentionally child-free and, in doing so, have helped to shatter the illusion for other folks while being a safe space for the questions and fears that accompany such a decision. Our belief in the possibility of being happy without children has made it possible for others to see themselves in that lifestyle, too.

Rather than fighting against the prevailing system and world order directly, systems theorist, philosopher, and futurist Buckminster Fuller encouraged change by rendering the old model useless (Fuller 1981). He is routinely quoted as saying, "You never change things by fighting the existing reality. To change something, build a new model that makes the existing model obsolete." We might *believe* something to be necessary until we simply find ourselves living in a better way, never having had to confront or challenge our beliefs directly. We are living in a wave of obsolescence, wherein we can see the antiquation of cash, paper, cords, and keys before our very eyes. It's hard to tell people to just let things go, but as soon as we have better options, they're gone.

Identify something you'd like to see change, but struggle to envision. What would render it obsolete?

If you desire a world on the other side of capitalism, how can you create it and make it worth living in, today? What values and beliefs would need to exist? For the first few years we lived in our condo, we did our own renovations. One of my very favorite services in my neighborhood quickly became the Tool Library. Like a traditional library, our Tool Library is based on the sharing economy; folks in the community can join and check out any tool in the library—from miter saws to cider presses. It saved us hundreds in tool rental fees from traditional hardware stores, thousands from not having to purchase unrentable items, and the environment from having to digest rarely used, disposed-of tools in a few decades. Gift economies like Buy Nothing groups, free little libraries, and volunteer fire companies value community and relationships over the market value of and legal relationship to property. If you believe abundance can be shared, value is created in connection, and communities are sources of strength within themselves, then you believe life can exist on the other side of capitalism, and can start creating it today.

Do you believe a racially just society can exist? In 1935, W.E.B. Du Bois discussed the concept of an abolition democracy to describe what would be needed to create a racially just society—not one simply free of chattel slavery but truly racially just. Du Bois recognized that to truly live as equal members of society, radical, community-powered institutions could supplant the oppressive social structures, creating new institutions, practices, and social relations that would afford free Black persons economic, political, and social capital. Without such a reconstruction of society, slavery would technically be abolished, but a criminal justice system that enforced racial segregation, discrimination, and peonage would live on. And it did. Despite law changes, many discriminatory beliefs stayed the same, incapacitating post-Civil War Reconstruction attempts. That criminal justice system is still in place today and is increasingly militarized, especially in communities of color, with no detectable public safety benefit (Mummolo 2018; Du Bois 1935).

Policing does not prevent crime. It responds to crime, and poorly, often aggravating the situation. Police are ill-equipped to support victims, investigate crime, and prevent reoccurrence. They do not prevent mental health distress, domestic violence, or sexual assault but are often the ones called when it happens, thanks to a lack of other options. We have a hard time envisioning another way.

What would it look like to render policing obsolete? Hint: it's not body cameras or more training, and it's not increasing the diversity of the police force. All these initiatives have failed (Defund the Police 2023); we need nonreformist reform. Through an array of well-resourced, community-based social services, many believe abolition is an attainable reality (Kaba 2021). Strong communities make cops obsolete (Maher 2021).

Real-world alternatives to policing abound (Sherman 2020). Imagine if we could supplant police as first responders through an array of pro-health professionals, EMTs, or firemen. People trust their fire departments. As Snoop Dogg said, "Nobody ever made a song called f*ck the fire department" (Mendez 2020).

Currently, when individuals experience mental distress and call 911, they are met with multiple armed, uniformed police officers. Mental health disorders are a factor in as many as 50 percent of fatal law enforcement encounters (Fuller et al. 2015). Imagine if, instead of being confronted with armed guards while under distress, a team of social workers or a mental-health crisis intervention response team trained in de-escalation and treatment came to support you. Decriminalizing drugs and providing health-focused social services for those suffering from addiction, such as harm-reducing needle exchanges and overdose-reversing naloxone would also reduce the demand for policing (Pearl and Perez 2018). A world with healthcare and homes for everyone, compassion and connection, community-based restorative justice and crisis intervention response teams would render police obsolete while helping us to feel—and be—safer.

What does your desired future entail? What stories and beliefs and systems would make it possible? What is your irresistible alternative?

Envision a future that is peaceful, equitable, and just. What is the most beautiful world you know is possible? Write down your manifesto. Describe it in exhaustive detail—what it looks like, sounds like, and smells like; imagine the minute-by-minute play-by-play of your day, what it feels like, who is there, and what you do together. Close your eyes and visualize it so deeply it feels like you're in it. Feel what it feels like to exist in that world. Envision it so vividly and compellingly that the present feels inconceivable. What does this tell you about your core desired feelings? What values and beliefs do you see manifest? What would it take for all of us to exist in that reality?

And then find ways to create that life here and now. Tap into those feelings in your current life, whatever that looks like. Bring it to life in whatever medium and through whatever power you have available; if you're an artist, paint it. If you're a writer, write it. If you're a parent or teacher, make it the only reality your kids tolerate. If you're an organizational leader, embed it in your values and embody it in your leadership; create the conditions for a more just and peaceful world to exist at work.

To move forward in our liberation, we need to make our dreams, mindsets, and beliefs conscious in order to evaluate them, deconstruct them, and reconstruct them differently. Awareness and analysis of where our beliefs come from can help us to be accountable to ourselves and each other about the actions we take as a result.

As Hübl notes, our collective social structures are the pathways through which our energies are channeled, like water through a pipe, to become the architecture through which we live our lives (Hübl and Avritt 2020). When we choose to see the shortcomings of the systems created by our current collective consciousness, we can begin to challenge the ideas individually (in ourselves), in community (in our relationships, families, workplaces), and collectively (in our systems and structures). We can dream of new ways of existing in these places, and each time we act on it, individually, in community, and collectively, we create a future not beholden to the past.

The future is emerging every day. We get to decide if the future we are creating will be a reverberation of the past, or if we will harness the disruption and emerging values and commit to pulling the provocative vision we have of the future closer.

CHAPTER 16

CREATING JUSTICE

I've been writing this book for two years now. About a year ago, Mark and I started fighting more than usual, escalating into, "What are we even doing here?" questions and potentially relationship-ending answers. At the time, he chalked it up to the stress of writing a book and managing a business. I chalked it up to an evolution in recognizing what I needed and a new willingness to make demands of the relationship I made up half of. Today, as I sit down to rewrite this chapter for the third time, the story I'm telling myself is that we had to go through that experience for me to understand the deep and inextricable connection between love and justice.

We met when we were twenty-five years old. We've both changed since then. We've evolved. What we believe about love and the world has evolved. What we need in our relationship has evolved. But in many ways, our habits, patterns, and actions hadn't evolved with the rest of us. I was feeling dismissed and disrespected by some of his behaviors—behaviors that had existed since we started dating—but also, newly, unloved. I hadn't recognized that feeling before.

I started to recognize traditional and stereotypical gender-role behaviors popping up. I was nagging, and he was dismissive. He'd make executive decisions, and I'd begrudgingly accept them for the sake of harmony. He made ball-and-chain jokes that weren't true, that he didn't even believe, that shocked both of us. Despite our intentions to create a love and relationship of our own, we were at risk of becoming tropes. After months of fighting and failed negotiations, I realized we weren't fighting each other; we were fighting our socializations. He still loved me and wanted me to be happy. I still loved him and wanted him to be happy. But riding out the waves of our socialization was not allowing us to be happy together. I could not be happy in a marriage that embodied the inequality and injustice of the marriage tropes we were handed.

Love and injustice could not coexist.

If he was committed to loving me, it meant committing to loving me the way I needed to be loved—respectfully, equitably, compassionately. Choosing love meant unpacking everything in the way of justice in our relationship—every belief, every habit, every defense mechanism, and every conditioned response that got in the way.

Love is a universal experience and motivation. It manifests in extraordinarily different ways thanks to cultural influences, but as far as we know, it has existed in every human culture and in every time period. Love is the great connector and is, therefore, the greatest danger to the story of separation. When I love you, I cannot dehumanize you, and I cannot stand by while others dehumanize you. When you love me, you cannot dehumanize me, and you cannot stand by while others dehumanize me.

For eons, folks in power have sought to privatize and make love abstract, thereby controlling it. Love, as a privately held, felt sense between two people, is relegated to experiences behind closed doors. It is made to be ephemeral, theoretical, pleasurable, and a little taboo—kept out of the public eye. By relegating it to the private sphere of romance, we're able to limit its effects and rob ourselves of the publicly felt, concretely experienced love otherwise known as justice.

This is by design. American sociologist William J. Goode noted that because love often serves as a basis and prelude to marriage—a binding contract that affects the inheritance of property and power—it must be controlled (1959). Within stratified societies, elders of the upper strata wield great power over their children to ensure they marry into other powerful families and consolidate, rather than share, their resources. A union grounded in sameness—similar social strata, similar belief systems, similar resource access—ensures the status quo of the systems and power hierarchies, and therefore their family's safety atop those structures of inequality as aligned parents pass beliefs and resources on to their children.

Random mating, in which spousal solidarity takes priority over clan solidarity and power consolidation, is a direct threat to existing social structures. Love is liberated from racial, religious, class, and other confines and extends humanity, in-grouping, and power to those who would have otherwise been excluded.

Love is a precursor to justice that does not require litigation for substantiation.

The same love that keeps people committed to one another when the going gets tough has the potential to serve as the source of justice within the relationship—the way forward that works for both partners. It is the same love that demands each person be treated fairly and justly. Liberated from behind closed doors, this love is no longer limited to romantic relationships; it is familial love, platonic love, and every other love that exists.

As Dr. Cornel West said, "Justice is what love looks like in public." Justice is love in action (2011).

When I love you, I have to stand up for you, both privately and publicly. I have to show up and step in. I have to create justice on your behalf. If I say I love you but stand by while others dehumanize you, I'm complicit in your dehumanization.

For years, the self-help and self-care industry has pushed intangible, ephemeral, felt-sense self-love that never felt authentic to me. No amount of affirmations, belly rubs, or bath bombs made me feel any more love for myself. And then I started fighting with Mark. I started standing up for myself, and demanding what I needed to be happy. I began creating boundaries and doing what I needed to do to feel safe and respected. I started leaving the table when love wasn't being served at home, with extended family, and in business proceedings. I now know what love for myself feels like—it feels like knowing I've got my own damn back.

Many of us turn to self-help because we want to create change in our lives. We want things to be better, so we exert power and create justice in the only place we know how—in ourselves. And it makes sense because of how we've come to understand power.

Most of us only know power in the institutional, hierarchical, consolidated, power-over form. It's a thing we've learned to exist within, allowing it to shape our lives while feeling powerless to shape it. And to be fair, we kind of are. In consolidated power structures, there's a limited supply of power and a limited number of people able to wield it. Unless we're granted institutional power by those who hoard it, there's not much we can do to shape it.

So, to avoid feeling like the powerless pawn in the chess game of life, controlled by forces and systems outside of our control, we control what we can. Self-help, returning to its original definition in law, is about using any lawful means to remedy wrongs. We know something's wrong, and we don't have many lawful ways of creating the justice we wish to see. As a matter of fact, according to the World Justice Project, the United States ranks 115th out of 140 countries on measures of accessibility and affordability regarding civil justice (World Justice Project 2022).

For all its faults, though, self-help does have the potential to reorient us to our intrinsic power. That is, when it's not suggesting we merely navigate being oppressed within it.

Power comes from the Latin *posse,* meaning to be able. Power is the ability to do. Power as *the ability to do* moves away from requiring external and institutional permission to act. It is to be in choice, agency, and ability, whether or not this power is institutionally or socially acknowledged (Casey 2021).

In classrooms, students are typically not allowed to get up and go to the bathroom whenever they want—it's not institutionally sanctioned—but children who are aware of their intrinsic power know they have the physical ability to stand up and leave the room anyway, and they do. In social situations, it's typically considered an uncouth breach of etiquette to point out where someone else is being offensive—it's not socially sanctioned—but those of us aware of our intrinsic power know we have the physical ability to speak up anyway, and we do.

Intrinsic power is the ability to act that comes from within. It is your ability to use your body, your voice, and everything you have at your disposal, with or without permission.

Combined with the intrinsic power of others, we create collective power. Collective interpersonal power is the ability to use collective agency, collective strength, and collective courage to act on collective values and beliefs.

Collective goals mean we don't require power over anyone else to achieve them. Because they are shared values and aims, we can work collaboratively to accomplish them. This means we can replace old structures of domination and hierarchy and the beliefs in meritocracy and supremacy that support them with new beliefs and structures that respect collaboration, interbeing, and the inherent value of all people and things. These replacements allow for entirely new cultures to emerge, ones that value justice, love, and equality.

A culture of justice encourages fairness, cooperative decision-making, a respect for diverse strategies and visions, and the implementation of regenerative practices, including regenerative cycles of power (Casey 2021). A commitment and respect for shared power means no systems of domination need to exist to justify its structure. Men would never need to subjugate women just to consolidate power in their own hands, and white folks wouldn't need to discriminate against people of color to hoard jobs, housing, or capital.

Mutual power is the recognition and respect for mutual existence, mutual equality, and mutual agency. It is the ability to rediscover our own humanity in relation to all others' humanity. It is a commitment to mutual consent and mutual accountability. It is the ability to leverage mutual power toward mutual goals. It is to accept a less-than-perfect mutual present, heal a shared, mutual past, and evolve together toward a better mutual future.

But accessing and reorienting to this power isn't easy. We must first interrupt our own internalized attachments to transactional relationships and hierarchical power, like Mark and I did when confronting our unconscious attachments to sexist gender-based power. This invitation has been extended from people of color to white folks for centuries and is seeing a resurgence in popularity and collective consciousness under the term anti-racism and especially, liberatory, anti-racist self-help.

Anti-racism, broadly speaking, describes ideas and actions that counter racism (Kendi 2019). Anti-racism creates racial equity by confronting racism wherever it shows up, including in our belief systems, in our systems and structures, and in the inequality and oppression they produce. No matter who we are within the system, we need to confront the unearned positive stereotypes unfairly awarded to those who are overvalued (agents; white people), and the unearned negative stereotypes unfairly awarded to those who are undervalued (targets; people of color). In other words, we need to challenge stereotypes we hold about both white people and people of color, regardless of our own skin color.

For white people in particular, this means considering all the benefits of being white in a racist society, whether we feel like we've personally benefited or not. It means exploring our attachments to, and our personal investments in, the system as-is and confronting our unconscious and conscious resistance to social change. New books and programs emerge regularly to support all of us in this process and are part of a wave of liberatory self-help I see hitting the market.

Thanks to Kimberlé Crenshaw's work on intersectionality, we know we are more than any one identity we hold. We hold multiple identities at once (1989). We also know overlapping systems of oppression and hierarchies are used to consolidate power based on those identities into even fewer hands, and that oppression can't be resolved by eliminating any one form of oppression. They are interlinked. As a result, to interrupt our attachments, we must divest from a multitude of conceived social hierarchies.

In other words, we may start with anti-racism work, but it can't end there. We must also confront our internalized sexism, ableism, classism, heterosexism, ageism, antisemitism, educationalism, transphobia, xenophobia, fatphobia, and every other -ism and -phobia preventing us from seeing each other as perfect equals.

This practice is again walking Dr. Love's path of building a liberatory consciousness by gaining awareness of injustice, analyzing its impact and causes, taking action to divest and interrupt, and committing to accountability and allyship as we build a better future (2013).

Many of us gain awareness, read the books and study up, and bail out somewhere around action. We decide learning and cognitive analysis count as action and stay in intellectual discourse and knowledge gaining, where it feels safe. As a result, too many of us end up knowing more while not doing much to interrupt inequality and discrimination in the real world.

It takes tremendous courage to sit down and list out the ways we benefit from discrimination toward others, especially if we haven't confronted our own desire to be better than and have more power and resources than other people—in other words, if we've bought into the myths of meritocracy and supremacy. It takes courage to confront our privileges, especially when we feel like targets ourselves, like we've had to work harder than others and cannot imagine where we might have benefitted or be invested in interlocking systems of oppression. It takes a lot of love, and a commitment to love in action, to do this work when we don't feel close to someone who is negatively affected by our privilege.

It takes courage to unpack all the ways we've all hustled for worthiness to gain power in a system that relies on just a few having it for its own existence. But to do so is to begin to embody love and create justice.

To create justice is to bring equality into existence. It is to make the world more fair and just in every action—internal and external, individually and collectively. It is to interrupt the ways you've supported the systems and the way the systems work in you and through you.

Bob Anderson is a thought leader in the field of consciousness and the creator of the Leadership Circle Profile—the consciousness-raising leadership assessment we use at The Center for Conscious Leadership. He reminds us that change occurs at the intersections of the internal-external continuum and the individual-collective continuum (Anderson 2018). For simplicity, I'll explore how we can create justice in the four quadrants these two continuums, overlapped perpendicularly, create: individual-internal, individual-external, collective-internal, and collective-external.

Creating justice at the intersection of the individual and the internal is what we do within ourselves to interrupt oppression and reorient to our intrinsic power. This might look like journaling, meditating, and practicing compassionate self-talk wherein you remind yourself of your innate goodness and worthiness as a living being. It is having the courage to confront internalized oppression when it shows up as negative self-talk, refusing to let it operate within you without your consent. It is creating an internal, felt sense of justice, creating the conditions for fairness and love within, and refusing to operate exploitatively toward yourself. It's a way of tending to ourselves, our bodies, and our innate sources of power—resting when we need to rest, honoring our passions and needs and wants, and living from the knowledge that we cannot pour from an empty cup. It is owning your story, your presence, and your past nonjudgmentally, recognizing the strength it took for you to make it through, and healing any lingering undesired effects it has on you. Therapy and coaching at the hands of trauma-informed, oppression-conscious, wise practitioners can support you in building justice here.

Individual external justice is how we show up for ourselves in context with others. This looks like setting boundaries, cultivating liberatory, mutually beneficial relationships, and using your intrinsic power to stand up for yourself. It might look like reaching out for help when you know you can't manage something alone or leaving the table when love's not being served without a peep. It might mean wearing what you've always wanted to wear and being exactly who you are, unashamed and unrestricted by social mores. It is both owning your personal truth and speaking truth to power in ways that allow you to exist the way you were meant to. It means using your talents and gifts to create justice in the world in the way only you can—like Amanda Gorman using poetry as power to inspire her nation.

Collective internal justice means supporting both ourselves and our collectives, whether they are families, chosen families, allied groups, friends, or coworkers in addressing the ways our culture has impacted our shared belief systems and rules. It means addressing our socialization. We might expose harmful rhetoric and propaganda when we hear it at the dinner table, correct damaging misconceptions or stereotypes when we hear them at work, and make a point to be welcoming to all, including people we may see as "other." It means interrupting the story of separation to cultivate a shared understanding of interdependence and connection and replacing individualist belief systems with one of mutuality. As Hübl notes in *Healing Collective Trauma*, "Collective wounds need a collective body to heal" (2020). Offering compassion, care, healing, truth, and kindness to all humans and all beings is one way of supporting the collective in our goal of healing.

Collective external justice means using our collective power to create justice; to create new systems, render the oppressive ones obsolete, and implement systemic reform in institutions we don't know how to replace yet. In *Radical Dharma*, Rev. angel Kyodo williams notes we're yearning to be engaged in collective action (2016). By finding fellowship through the friction, we can become one large entity defending ourselves against what she calls the "modern threats of mass disposability."

"Together," she says, "there are no individual selves to be defended. Together, self-defense is collective transformation." Collective external justice means working together to make sure everyone has not just their survival needs met, but also basic needs, including healthcare, housing, and ways to contribute meaningfully in society. It means finding and using power in community—like the gymnasts who worked together to bring down Larry Nassar (Orbey 2019), and the #MeToo movement, which resulted in nineteen states enacting sexual harassment protection for victims and more than two hundred powerful men losing their jobs (Carlsen et al. 2018). It looks like the UPS Workers' Strike of 1997 when 185,000 workers shut down delivery operations for fifteen days, President Clinton refused to use the Taft-Hartley Act to halt the strike 75 percent of Americans supported, and UPS was forced to surrender to every key demand (Levin 2017). It means joining together as unionized workforces to demand fair work for fair labor performed and value produced, not just fighting for the bare minimum it takes to live.

The proletarian think tank The Hampton Institute noted, "a ten-day General Strike would accomplish more for the working-class majority than a century's worth of elections. It would represent an immediate momentum shift by bringing the capitalist behemoth to its knees. Our true power is in our collective labor, not a voting booth" (Hampton Institute 2020). We have tremendous collective power in the form of strikes and protests, boycotts and rebellions, revolts and revolutions. External collective pressures have the power to create massive change in the systems that otherwise exert power over us as individuals.

There are far more ways to use our power than we've been conditioned to believe; we can do more than vote and protest. Activism isn't only protesting on Capitol Hill. As one activist shared, activism can also be everyday acts of kindness through which trust is nurtured. By cooking, making coffee, and serving elders, for instance, we build meaningful relationships that bring fulfillment and joy (Brady 2021). In *Pleasure Activism,* adrienne maree brown shares that folks experiencing oppression who embrace desire and pursue pleasure are acting in defiance, using their power to reclaim their whole, feeling selves (2019). Activism is liberating desire, embracing the natural abundance and joy that exists, and defying capitalist suggestions that we have to buy and earn rest, satisfaction, and happiness.

Activism is reconnecting to the land, respecting our inextricable connection to her as a relative and not a commodity, and creating change that allows us all to thrive. Soul Fire Farm in New York State creates anti-racism food system justice by shifting away from corporate-controlled food systems and toward food sovereignty. They reverse the damage of industrial agriculture by using regenerative farming practices rooted in African-Indigenous wisdom and create health by eliminating food apartheid—the system of injustice that provides an abundance of nutritious foods to the rich and denies access to others, resulting in health for the wealthy and chronic disease for everyone else. They foster joyful connection between land and community and mobilize efforts that support farm workers, rematriation of land for indigenous peoples, reparations for Black farmers, and regenerative ecosystems (Soul Fire Farm 2023).

If you're built for big feelings, big sensitivity, or big shame, use that. If you are pulled toward creating harmony, or creating art, or teaching, use that. Create justice wherever you're pulled. I can only imagine the harmony that could be created on the other side of today's justice-free peace, the art that could inspire visions of a new way of being, and the collective power that will be wielded by an entire generation of students who have been raised by liberatory teachers and elders.

I thought I'd be able to create justice in the historically oppressed communities where I taught and led. I might have created some justice, but I also inflicted pain and did harm as a result of my own unexamined beliefs around power and because my fragile, fractured nervous system couldn't handle the stress. Personally, I'd love to run for office or head up a huge, multinational organization creating change. But I need to be honest, here, too. My nervous system isn't ready for the pressure or the global criticism that would engender. The desire reveals what remains of my attachment to power and my desire to show I know better—not exactly the culture and belief system I want to create and propagate in this world.

Instead, I have chosen to first create justice within by healing my relationship with myself, owning my story, and speaking my own truth to power. My healing has sent ripples of healing throughout my community. My Big Shame and inexplicable pull toward writing became this book. It has become an act of personal liberation I hope results in collective liberation and an act of personal power I hope results in radical love, social justice, and collective power.

Instead of running for office or creating systems change on my own, I work with the most incredible, diverse, and liberatory facilitators, leadership coaches, and rebels-with-causes I know. Together, we support organizations and political candidates in walking their walk, creating justice, and doing so sustainably and with integrity. We are all invited to participate in the ways we're built for while also contributing the most good we can.

As American activist, author, organizer, and cofounder of the Black Lives Matter movement Patrisse Cullors notes, as you consider what's yours to do in this work, take into account what you're built for (2022). Notice what you're called to. Feel the anger and injustice you feel, and leverage that insight to create change. As Audre Lorde reminds us, it's not our responsibility to hide our anger to spare others guilt, hurt feelings, or the responsibility of answering our anger (Lorde 2018). Embrace your desires, and build the communities and systems that will allow you to experience the kind of pleasure, connection, and joy you seek.

Our businesses, our families, and our movements can all be incredible places of healing. They are spaces, opportunities, and communities in which we can move against racism, sexism, homophobia, ableism, and every form of injustice there is, every time we come upon them, day by day and action by action (Lorde 2018). Action is neither linear nor predictable—finding the best way forward for each of us will require experimentation. Consider it a form of praxis, creating change and justice in every step we take.

The way forward is uncertain, and what it will require of us is uncertain. Reflect anyway. Take action anyway. Then reflect again. We've moved beyond the good/bad dichotomy now, so experiment using the best information there is about successful movements in the past mixed with a dose of intuition, a sprinkle of calling, and a dash of play, and see what happens. Make your art. Write your book. Speak up. Create justice. Embrace pleasure. Keep going.

And if all of this feels overwhelming from the start, let me offer you a first step to start you on your path forward—one not meant to be prescriptive or restrictive or trite but one meant to guide you into reorienting toward your own regenerative power. Make it yours.

Breathe. So simple, so undervalued. Breathe.

Breathing exercises can be first steps on our path to justice creation through intrinsic power activation. By breathing intentionally, we calm our autonomic nervous system, which helps us to regulate unconscious bodily actions like heart rate and respiration—the ones that put us into fight or flight. By adding conscious intentionality, we access not only the intrinsic power found in our bodies but also mitigate and modulate the effect of the external, outside world on our internal condition. We are able to consciously choose how we will *be* in the world and exhibit choice and agency with what we *do*, how we respond, and how we use our personal power (Casey 2021).

Conscious regulation and choice mean we're able to create awareness of our unconscious responses, of the way the outside world impacts us, of our internal power, and the way our actions impact ourselves and the people around us, too. We begin to make external conditions object—something we are in choice about, rather than subject to and controlled by. Being in conscious choice around our agency and power means we're able to move from our core, acting from our personal values and beliefs and honoring our personal strength, resilience, and power when we're met with institutional and social resistance. Over time, we can join our personal power with others' to create collective, interpersonal power for the sake of mutual goals, mutual benefit, and mutual accountability.

You have the power to be and create the just future you wish to see in this world; to act from personal power with courage and conviction; to create the relationships, communities, and institutions that are just. Creating justice in the smallest of places and interactions is just as important as creating them in the largest, and may, in fact, be the only way to create the sweeping change we wish to see with integrity and mutuality.

SECTION V

ACCOUNTABILITY AND ALLYSHIP

CHAPTER 17

A MORE RADICAL ACCEPTANCE

Our activism is only as effective as our understanding of the problem.

When I went into education, I had a clear intention: to eliminate the achievement gap for students of color. I thought I could go into any classroom and change the long-term trajectory of my students' lives. Over time, I realized the achievement gap was the result of a variety of factors, including unequal access to resources and opportunities, systemic under-resourcing, underfunding, undervaluing, and so much more. My efforts were nothing compared to the lifetime of obstacles my students would face. I had a superficial understanding of the problem, and applied a superficial solution.

As Mark and I sought to create justice in our relationship, our next steps, too, were only as good as our shared understanding of the problem. If Mark believed justice already existed and I didn't, we had a hard time agreeing on the problem much less the solution. It dramatically affected what we were each willing to do next. If I was feeling undeserving of justice or he was stuck in an outdated belief about how he was showing up, we couldn't see things clearly enough to create change.

This final section of the book is about the action we take in concert with other people and the ways we use our interpersonal and collective power to make things better for all of us. Our collective efforts and activism, too, are only as effective as our collective understanding of our problems and our willingness to see our collective realities clearly.

We think we see things clearly—*more clearly* than the people who see things differently than we do. As we learned in chapter 15, our stories create our realities. In the 1980s, Republican political strategist Lee Atwater coined the phrase "perception is reality" to explain the phenomenon wherein people could participate in the same *collective* experience yet interpret it through the lens of their *personal* experiences, beliefs, and political views (Kelner 2014). It's been a defining political strategy since then on both sides of the aisle. If you could make people believe something, it was as good as fact. It didn't matter what the evidence showed.

The changes we make are in response to what we think the problem is. If we are unable or refuse to see life as it really is, we are also unable to see the most effective method for creating change.

So how do we create collective change when we don't even agree on what's happening?

As Rumi says, "The cure for the pain is in the pain" (2004).

Acceptance is, fundamentally, the process of receiving what *is* and allowing what *is* to *be*. It is the process of seeing what there is to see and feeling what there is to feel, nonjudgmentally, with compassionate awareness. This isn't an invitation into resignation but an acknowledgment that things exist, exactly as they do, in this moment without any of the stories or suffering. When we stop resisting what *is*, we move from denying, repressing, and resisting into conscious awareness of the present—how small the coat is, how bad the drinking is, how toxic the family is, how little the self-help is helping. We see our reality without resisting or sugar-coating it.

When we accept the present, we can be with the entirety of the feeling, the emotion, and the meaning-making, exactly as it is. Research suggests the physiological lifespan of an emotion is just 90 seconds (Chauncey 2017). When we are confronted with an experience, the sensations—the rush of adrenaline, the beating heart, the tummy rumbles—typically arise, peak, and dissipate on their own. They are the natural bodily response to the experience. The thing is, we rarely just let the sensations be sensations. Instead, we insatiably curious, signal-interpreting, meaning-making, story-generating beings seek to understand, to make connections, learn, and stay alive.

The famous adage says pain is inevitable, but suffering is optional. In Buddhism, the oft-told parable of the second arrow describes the relationship between the two: When we experience pain and suffering, they say, two arrows fly our way. The first arrow is the hardship that causes us pain. If we don't look up, see where the pain is coming from, and get out of the way, we'll be struck by the second. The second arrow is the suffering we tack onto the original pain through our *response* to that pain. It's the shame we levy, the stories we tell ourselves, and the way we add insult to injury. Suffering is an optional experience.

We often conflate first-arrow pain and second-arrow suffering, but there's an important difference, and knowing this difference reduces unnecessary suffering in our lives. When we grieve the loss of a loved one, we experience pain—heartbreak that physically hurts, a mourning so powerful days go by in a blur. Blaming oneself for not being over it fast enough is the avoidable second-arrow suffering.

With PTSD, we live through not only the original, painful experience of trauma but also the ripple effects in the present—like flashbacks, nightmares, or hypervigilance. They are painful. Internalizing messages about being a damaged human, however, or self-flagellating for the ways we cope creates second-arrow suffering. When we are let down—we didn't get the job, or the date, or our experiment fails—we may feel sadness, rejection, or disappointment. Tacking on resentment, shame, and self-doubt—the stories we tell ourselves about our pain—extend and transmute pain into suffering and get in the way of feeling what really hurts.

Our curiosity, story-telling, and interpretations have helped us tremendously over the millennia. We have continuously learned more about existence, inferring helpful things like, "My friend ate a berry from that bush. He died. I bet that berry made him die. I'm going to tell my friends not to eat berries from that bush." The reality is, it may have been the berry, it may have been cholera from the water he washed it down with, but we want to survive, so we do what we can.

We continue to infer things today, regardless of whether or not they are true. Because our societies have evolved to incorporate so much knowledge about the natural world, and because it's so readily available, most of the inferences we make now are primarily social in nature. We're no longer questioning whether or not the witch down the street sabotaged our crops; we're pretty sure it was the weeks-long drought combined with nutrient-depleted soil from decades of unsustainable agricultural practices. Instead, we infer things like, "She is thin and smiles, so she must be healthy and happy," or, "My boss is dismissive, so I must be stupid," or, "I'm single, so I must be unlovable."

In the process of trying to interpret our pain and suffering and make sense of them, we extend them. We hold on to them, sometimes momentarily, as we get curious about what they're trying to tell us, and sometimes nearly indefinitely, as we integrate the stories we created into our identities, worldviews, and so on.

Acceptance is the process of feeling what's ours to feel without pushing it away or numbing it. We let go of our stories and simply experience the sensations in our body. Our emotional experiences are the felt sense of our internal energies in motion. To be aware of what we feel is to be aware of the energy as it is without assigning any meaning to it. Bodily sensations are neither good, nor bad. They just are.

When we jump into a cold body of water, our bodies involuntarily respond to the sudden cooling. Our blood vessels constrict, decreasing blood flow to the skin to prevent heat loss, and we feel our heart pumping harder and faster to move the same amount of blood. We often start breathing rapidly. Many of us sense these bodily responses and experience them as panic.

The cold water isn't bad. Our bodily response to it isn't bad. Our translation of the sensations into the emotion, *panic!*, isn't even necessarily bad. All of it just is. As a matter of fact, studies are beginning to show cold-water immersion can have benefits to the body, such as reduced inflammation and increased immunity (Knechtle et al. 2020). But to take advantage of it, we have to get into the water. We have to subject ourselves to the things we might initially interpret as "bad" and let the experiences pass over us without bailing.

Similarly, if we were better able to let the feelings of everyday experience pass over us without immediately bailing, we might receive the self-medicine—the cure that's embedded in our pain.

To feel what's ours to feel often involves mindfulness. Jon Kabat-Zinn, the founder of Mindfulness-Based Stress Reduction—which he calls "Buddhist meditation without the Buddhism"—explains that "Mindfulness is awareness that arises through paying attention, on purpose, in the present moment, nonjudgmentally," to which he sometimes adds, "in the service of self-understanding and wisdom" (Fisher 2010; Mudit 2021). Through mindfulness practices, we add conscious awareness to whatever's happening and anything we engage in—from commuting and exercising to washing the dishes, feeling our feelings, and everything in between.

We know mindfulness and meditation can be misused as a way to pacify and exploit workers and to encourage dissociation and escape rather than action against injustice. With careful attention to intention, implementation, and context, however, we can use these practices to develop awareness, agency, and emotional regulation. By separating our experiences from the meanings we make about them, we create some of that subject-object space that helps us to see the difference between our sensations, feelings, thoughts, and stories, and to accept and honor them as valid even when they are painful. This allows us to be in choice about them. Rather than convincing ourselves things are fine, we can accept what is and learn that sometimes things feel bad because they are, in fact, bad. Along the way, we must be mindful of the tension between secular mindfulness practices and wisdom traditions that include ethics and guidance. The goal is not passive disengagement but to find the medicine embedded in the pain and use our newfound awareness as self-guidance to create change.

Instead of resisting the way my body recoils at hugs it doesn't want to be in, I receive that information. I accept there's a reason this feeling exists in my body. Rather than levying judgment, I recognize this is a sign my body doesn't feel safe. Sometimes, I get curious about why. Sometimes, I let that data be sufficient and refuse those hugs in the future. I realize there doesn't always have to be an interpretation for me to move forward differently.

In fact, our interpretations routinely convolute, complicate, and cause suffering themselves. When I think back to the stories I told myself about my coat, for instance, I see clearly that the meaning I made about the coat was far more problematic than the actual problem itself. Having a coat that doesn't fit is a technical problem with a concrete, attainable solution. Drawing a conclusion that I am a disgusting, slothful human means I'm the problem and an irredeemable one at that. How do you solve a problem like irredeemability? When the solution is to levy more shame, I'm actually the one shooting the second arrow, and on purpose, because I think it works.

The way I see it now, shame is a felt experience that tells us when we're bumping up against the edges of what we, and more often our society, are willing to accept. It doesn't mean we're bad. It means individual or collective consciousness has not extended its perception of "acceptable" to include you and has no way to relate to you other than to "other" you. Rather than internalizing shame, I now allow it to wash over me and reveal my perceptions of society: I feel shame not because I am bad but because I have a feeling some slice of society has deemed me bad. Allowing ourselves to internalize that shame means tacitly adopting that belief, too.

When we make decisions based on shame, we often take steps to reduce the shame without taking the necessary steps that would eliminate the source of the pain itself. I might scroll social media to muffle my shame around loneliness, for example, without doing anything to resolve the loneliness itself. When we practice nonjudgmental, radical acceptance, we can recognize the source of our pain and choose a different response. In the coat example, getting a new coat is the technical solution. My true pain was shame itself. Healing my relationship with my body and learning how to deal with other people's disapproval of my body would have been transformational.

Tara Brach is an American psychologist and mindfulness meditation teacher whose teachings are also heavily influenced by Buddhist philosophy. In her book *Radical Acceptance,* she defines the concept as "a willingness to experience ourselves and our life as it is." It is the antidote, she says, to self-neglect, self-judgment, and self-delusion. It's radical in the sense that it gets back to the root of who we are—a sea of boundless love having a human, bodied experience. To practice *radical* acceptance is to dissolve the story of separation, and really, all story, as we experience the coming and going of sensation, feeling, and emotion as we let life live through our awakened bodies (Brach 2003).

In *The Body Keeps the Score,* Dr. Bessel van der Kolk notes our unresolved traumas live in the body (2015). As long as they remain repressed and resisted, they live on. Through acceptance, we're able to identify them, work with them, and work through them. By practicing acceptance, we process the traumas of the past and return to our home—our bodies. We reorient ourselves to a felt sense of safety in the present and, in the process, support ourselves in opening to our pain with the compassion we need to heal.

Carl Rogers said, "The curious paradox is that when I accept myself just as I am, then I can change" (1995).

Navigating this paradox often feels confusing, unpredictable, and a bit chaotic. There's a lot to process as we unpack what we have not allowed ourselves to feel or come to terms with. Our responsibility, though, is to heal what hurts so we don't pass our baggage on to future generations and call it culture. Nature, left to her own devices, heals herself. We, too, heal ourselves, given the time, space, and conditions for healing. We cannot control the speed, degree, or path our healing will take, but we can create the conditions for healing to occur within ourselves.

Even when we heal what hurts in us, though, we're still focusing the solutions on ourselves as individuals. Social wounds, like injustice, require social healing. When we are hurt in relationship, we need to heal in relationship.

I find this requires a different kind of radical acceptance—an acceptance that gets not just at the root of who we are as individual people but the root of the collective experience. Too often, acceptance is used to avoid the second arrow suffering without seeking to help eliminate the first arrow pain for ourselves and others.

Accepting my reality, more often than not, has meant acknowledging my unenviable position in life. It has meant receiving the deep shame of inadequacy and letting it wash over me without fighting it. Releasing self-judgment and making peace with the situation didn't get me out of the social and economic situations I was in and wouldn't relieve the source of pain for others. Accepting the reality of my student debt nearly led to me ending my life. I accepted that even with income-based repayment, if I continued to live in this society, contributing in the field of education where I felt called to contribute, I'd remain in the underclass, underrespected, undervalued, and underpaid, with no end to suffering in sight.

If the cure for the pain is in the pain, I can investigate the pain to see its societal source, too. Who the hell shot that first arrow, anyway?

Radical acceptance, for me, means not only accepting I had crippling student debt but tracking the source of that pain to its roots—our unjust, predatory systems of capital that vilify poverty and make it a punishable, immoral identity; our unjust, predatory, elitist university systems that make it infinitely harder for people of lower socioeconomic status and cultural capital to gain access; the stranglehold that our economic system has on our political system, which prevents economic and educational justice. Radical acceptance means accepting it had very little—if anything at all—to do with me and that suicide would do nothing to change the system. Radical acceptance meant accepting how the system worked to implicate me, somehow, in the crime of not being born rich enough to access a human right.

When we open up to and accept the pain we feel, we often realize the cure is not in changing ourselves. It is accepting ourselves, as we are, and changing how we orient ourselves to our pain and the world around us. It is accepting that the way we live and the societies we have created inflict pain. As a result, I posit that a curious paradox, too, is that when we accept society just as it is, we can change it. Rather than repressing and resisting our collective, traumatic pasts and present, we need to practice a collective radical acceptance to process them, heal, and reorient ourselves to each other and our collective future.

Thanks to unrestricted access to the world's information, including first-hand and bystander footage of atrocities, we have been able to create visibility into the stories that don't fit dominant narratives. Centuries of public denial are being disrupted, inviting a collective opportunity for acceptance and therefore change (Souli 2020).

Over the past fifty years, at least forty-six countries have engaged in the process of collective acknowledgment and processing known as Truth and Reconciliation (Souli 2020). Unlike the retributive justice and punishment approach we associate with our justice system or the collective justice associated with the Nuremberg Trials following the Holocaust, Truth and Reconciliation prioritizes restorative justice. In restorative justice, focus is on offenders taking responsibility for their actions and repairing the harm they've caused. The most well-known Truth and Reconciliation efforts worldwide occurred in South Africa at the conclusion of the more than forty years of racial segregation and injustice known as Apartheid.

Truth and Reconciliation is, at its heart, about practicing acceptance in a way that allows perpetrators and victims to move forward differently. It's not widely practiced yet, but also not unheard of in the United States. In fact, attempts were made in 1980 after the internment of Japanese Americans and Japanese nationals during World War II and in 2004 after five protesters were killed during an anti-Ku Klux Klan rally in 1979 (Souli 2020).

Restorative justice replaces our mass punishment system with truth-telling, collective healing, and forward-facing solutions. It asks, "Who was harmed? What do they need? Whose obligation is it to meet those needs?" and produces consensus-based proposals that meet the needs of everyone impacted (Baliga 2018). Truth-telling relies on an acceptance by all parties of what happened, whose fault it was, and the pain caused. It rebalances power through dialogue and allows survivors to reconnect with their power after experiencing something that made them feel powerless.

Survivors of sexual assault typically want the person who assaulted them to claim ownership, responsibility, and understanding. They want an indication that the person who harmed them understands the impact of what they've done, that they truly get it, and won't do it again. Sometimes, other people are present to witness the truth-telling, removing the veil of shame and secrecy from the survivor, and to hold the person who caused harm accountable for doing right by the people they've harmed. In a practice of radical acceptance, root causes are also addressed—being clear to distinguish between explanations and excuses—which can provide a course of action for addressing structural inequalities and healing the unresolved trauma that led to the offending person's behavior in the first place (Baliga 2018).

Restorative justice in the realm of racism would require overcoming the widespread denial of institutionalized racism and its deep history and connections to slavery, Jim Crow, policing, and peonage. It would require a radical acceptance of who we are and who we have always been in the United States: a country of deep, structural injustice, whose wealthy have always relied on exploitation to build power. It would require truth-telling over fact-finding, ownership of impact, and responsibility-taking at scales we've never seen. It would require white people to relinquish their investment in supremacy and to acknowledge common humanity. It would enable poor people of every skin color to recognize our struggles are more similar than we'd like to admit and that the division we're conditioned into is the ruling class's way of keeping us arguing against one another rather than realizing the extent of our collective exploitation and doing something about it.

What would this look like for crimes of poverty? What does it reveal when there's no justice to be restored? When acts are beyond the measure of fault, or when it's a victimless crime? It's uncharted territory for us as a society.

Despite there being a lack of will for a centralized, organized, national truth-telling and reconciliation program in the United States, the movement to expose and resolve injustice is growing. Social media is democratizing access to information. Censorship notwithstanding, nearly four billion people use social media where they have the ability to share their stories with the rest of the world. It has the ability to amplify unheard and suppressed voices and create more transparency. Social media played a major role in mobilizing outrage against autocratic regimes during 2011's Arab Spring and led to the end of President Mubarak's thirty years of authoritarian reign (Sharma 2021).

Millennials are the first generation to not get more conservative as we age (Mahdawi 2023). We came of age during the Great Recession, and have been increasingly radicalized by the impossible cost of living and raising a family. Similarly, Gen Z has never known life without a Department of Homeland Security, or a United States not at war, and as a result, sees many of our issues without the rose-colored glasses of older generations. Together, we've watched capitalism privatize natural resources and public services for private profit, our hardworking parents lose their houses, healthcare, and hope, and politicians demonize the educated, the attuned, the aware, and the awake. We're less interested in conservatism because we're less interested in the idea of preserving hegemony.

Accepting reality means confronting that the average citizen has a near zero influence on US public policy and that even when the majority of Americans favor a particular policy change, without sustained collective activism, nothing happens (Gilens and Page 2014). Rather than lobbying on behalf of what's best for the most people, interest groups funded by a rich few shape public opinion—telling us what is good for the rich will be good for us, too—and persuade us to vote against our own best interests.

What would it mean for us to come to terms with all the systems that thrive simply because we aren't willing or able to pull back the curtain and see the roots of our discontents? What radical change would be possible if we could only practice truly radical acceptance?

Opening up that conversation requires those of us who have been hurt to accept that it's not our fault. It requires us standing in our personal, intrinsic power and using our voices to own our stories and share our experiences. It requires us standing in collective power to stand against victim blaming and victim shaming.

The #MeToo movement shifted the conversation around sexual assault, destigmatizing survivorship and revealing how rampant sexual harassment, assault, and misconduct really are. Activist Tarana Burke launched the #MeToo movement in 2007, and a decade later, it gained national awareness after a tweet from actress Alyssa Milano went viral (CBS 2017). Twelve million posts in less than twenty-four hours proved sexual harassment is neither rare nor isolated, and that victims have historically been shamed and silenced rather than supported. Since then, collective silence has turned into collective awareness, a step on the path to collective action. It was a public reckoning with the way survivors' realities are denied.

Imagine if we were able to create a public reckoning with *all* the ways our realities are denied. Imagine if we were able to normalize all the pain we're experiencing because of our stories of separation; because of the pain of disconnection and the pain of struggling for acceptance; because of all of the suffering we experience at the hands of our collective stories about who is worthy, and who deserves well-being and happiness. Imagine what it would take for us to acknowledge how exhausting it is to be fighting for our own worthiness in a society where we are all disposable; how dehumanizing it is to be a cog in the machines of our lives; how utterly unfulfilling it is to have worked so hard for so long, only to still not be happy.

What would it take for the diet industry to take responsibility for their actions? For the marketing industry to admit they're creating false hopes for the sake of selling products? For our news media to admit they've been lying and fear-mongering? For the government to take responsibility for keeping millions of its own citizens in poverty?

I imagine a person recovering from a near-fatal injury in the same room as the executive from the insurance provider who denied their reimbursement claims. Should the person who has worked hard and paid taxes their whole life apologize for being bankrupted by medical bills and unable to pay? Whose responsibility would it be to make things right? What would it take for the insurance provider to recognize the harm they've inflicted and take ownership? What would it take to get a government representative in the room and own the results of the negligence created by the systems they oversee?

I imagine detained protesters in the same room as the CEO who withheld their pay and the police chief who authorized their arrests. Who was actually harmed? Whose responsibility would it be to make things right? How do we explain to young citizens in their civics classes why it's acceptable for one CEO to harm hundreds of workers and their families through wage theft yet punishable to protest one's own exploitation?

Moving forward through truth telling requires a truly radical form of radical acceptance. It requires an acceptance of what has happened, of responsibility, ownership, and impact. It requires victims to accept they did not cause their victimization. It requires those who caused harm to accept responsibility for their actions and do everything in their power to make things right.

As much as I've tried to keep acceptance a separate chapter unto its own, I couldn't. Acceptance lies at the heart of this book. Acceptance facilitates a belonging that doesn't require you to change. Acceptance enables us to see it's not *all* our fault. In fact, this book could be described as a book of acceptance that leads us from self-help to social justice: when we accept nothing in our life is *all* our fault, we can see the interconnection of all things and create change that matters.

Only when we clearly understand our challenges and our individual and collective roles in them can we move forward in ways that will be both honest and effective. Only then can we invite ourselves and each other into real accountability. Accountability cannot happen without an acceptance of reality as it is right now, ownership, and a mutual desire for change.

CHAPTER 18

INSTITUTIONALIZING HUMANITY

One winter day, after a long, hard day at kindergarten, I came home from school to see my mother crying at the dining room table. I remember walking over, seeing tears streaming down her face, and immediately feeling overwhelmed by her sadness. I hugged her, and she held me, and I began to cry, too.

I didn't know why my mom was crying. It didn't matter. We were sad together.

Kids are born with their humanity intact. Empathy is observable as early as eighteen hours into an infant's life (Martin and Clark 1982), and babies as young as six months old reach out to victims and people who come to the defense of a victim (Dewar 2019). When met with a struggling stranger, toddlers will do their best to work out what's happening and offer a solution. We are born caring and wanting to help.

Over time, adults step in and kind of fuck it all up. In attempts to keep the peace, adults demand it, changing the nature of the experience from one of genuine empathy to one of required, performative empathy. We force kids to swallow their resentment and share rather than teaching them to compromise, negotiate, and communicate boundaries. Even when we try to positively reinforce prosocial behaviors like sharing, many children end up participating because it gets them labeled a "good kid" rather than because they genuinely want to share with their peers.

The result is that we share not because we want to be good friends but because last time we didn't, we lost the toy altogether and got yelled at. We're ordered to be good and comply "or else." Just like in the classroom, when we're punished without understanding why, we internalize shame or resent our sister because it's *her* fault we're being punished. After all, if she didn't exist, I wouldn't have to share. Let the lifelong individualism begin.

Unfortunately, too many adults have lost their innate capacity for empathy because of the trauma and myth of separation in their own lives. They end up dismissing our feelings, and we learn to dismiss them in ourselves and each other. Many of us learn that feelings are punishable offenses, and the breaking down of our capacity to feel ensues. In attempts to "prepare us for the real world," the adults in our lives harden us rather than transforming the world so it's a safe place for people to be soft, feeling, and emotive. We're trained away from awe and wonder and unrestrained expressions of love, joy, and sadness. We're trained to not care. We then head out into the world, hardened and armored up, a shell of the child we once were. We do what we need to do to survive in what we've come to learn is the big, bad, mean, unsharing, uncaring world as best we can.

If we're paying attention, we come to understand the world as inhumane. When something is inhumane, it is without compassion for misery or suffering. It is cruel. Many of us become hardened and kind of cruel just by living and existing in the systems.

When something occurs out of the ordinary, we see it as a tragedy. By the time it becomes commonplace, on the other hand, it is no longer noteworthy, and we struggle to summon the compassion, empathy, and sympathy we otherwise would. Everyday suffering is so pervasive that, like alcohol, we build up our tolerance to it over time, allowing us to consume more of it with diminishing effects. We so normalize our experience of suffering we can hardly imagine life outside of it. It's just the usual, everyday evil we're used to.

So many of us feel so small when confronted with the monstrosities of our institutions that we participate in them because they seem like the only real choice. We want help in stopping crime, so we call the police. We want enough influence to make change so we climb the corporate ladder. We have been so conditioned to believe that capitalism is the only way to live that we participate without giving it another thought.

In fact, capitalism is so ubiquitous and its players have done such a great job of convincing us it's the only viable economic model that most of us have an easier time imagining the end of the world than we do the end of capitalism. We have conflated having a free market with having capitalism. The two are not the same (Nickolas 2022). Needing the money from our jobs to live—because we've allowed ourselves to be convinced there must be a *cost to living*—we allow capitalists to derive capital from the fruits of our labor, which they then leverage into political and social power. We can hardly imagine another way.

But this was once true of the divine rights of kings, too. When we believe there is no other way, we perpetuate the only way we know.

The United States has a weird relationship with change-makers. Hero worship is deeply rooted in American culture and folklore—we are often far more familiar with the figureheads of movements than the movements themselves. As a result, many of us have a hard time seeing how "little old me" could create any change.

When change-makers are portrayed as larger-than-life heroes, they're hard to relate to and connect to. We hear about everything they overcame to achieve—or create!—the American Dream, but hear nothing about the community that built them, the people who paved the way, sacrificed on their behalf, gave them an opportunity or platform, paid their way, and did their laundry. Instead, they are portrayed as someone special, not someone like us. They don't get sad, or get tired, or need anyone's help, unlike us.

By oversimplifying how change is made, we distort our perspective of what's possible. If we aren't a once-in-a-generation orator with the charisma and power to win people over, how are we supposed to get anything done? When our change-makers are community organizers with humble beginnings and great passion, or when we know them personally, we begin to see how we could work with them, how we could get involved, and how change could come to be. We see that power is created in community. It requires relationships, plans, public accountability, and regular people with regular, everyday power who care deeply about something and build collective power, providing a platform to those orators who rally change. In a system of collective power, there's no need or pressure to be a hero—we just need you to be a leader. A leader believes a better world is possible and cares enough to use her personal power to create change and rally other people to do the same.

In a culture of hero worship, there's a good guy and a bad guy, and we seek heroic moves to take down the bad guy. We try to, for example, take down the bad guy (poverty!) through heroic moves (food stamps!) instead of understanding the multiple, complex factors that lead to poverty (discrimination, regressive tax policies, belief in meritocracy, criminalization of poverty, etc.) and changing how society delivers justice (equitable distribution of wealth, social safety nets for all humans, sustained systems that don't require intervention to deliver basic necessities). When we look for a bad guy to blame and defeat, we obfuscate systemic connections and actually make long-lasting, radically transformational change harder to create.

When we think of overthrowing a bad guy, we might think of revolutions that ousted the bad guy pulling the strings. Often, though, the "bad guy" we envision is leading a system perfectly designed to create the outcomes it produces. Systems are far greater than the sum of their parts—one bad dude does not a system make. To function, untold agents, processes, and feedback loops influence how the whole thing works.

When we approach the world through the lens of systems-thinking, we begin to see the entire ecosystem that contributes to the issue and recognize that institutions—systems so powerful they take on a life of their own—exist and do harm even when everyone within the system is ostensibly good. Consider healthcare. How do we revolutionize the healthcare system when everyone in it has already pledged to do no harm? How do we eliminate the institution and impacts of racism when no one owns up to being racist?

We tend to think of revolutions as these big, extreme events wherein a government, leader, or social order is overthrown and a new one is imposed. It's reminiscent of our hero-worship, wherein a good guy (George Washington!) takes down the bad guy (King George III!) and swiftly delivers a new world order (The Republic! Individual Rights! American Exceptionalism!). When we take a step back, however, we see it wasn't one event. It was a seven-year process that required immense public support, tremendous collective power, international support from foreign players like France, Spain, and the Netherlands, who had a vested interest in weakening a major rival's global power, and the emergence of a new set of values allies were sympathetic to. The American Revolution wasn't simply the triumph of Washington and his men over King George III and his men; it was the manifestation of the values shift from monarchy to representative democracy. It was the next iteration of the institution of government.

Revolutions are happening all the time. If we could let go of our attachments to separation, power, and war, we could see it as the natural way of things—an adaptive cycle of change from a previous way of being (not necessarily wrong) to a new way of being (not necessarily right); a previous order to a new order; the result of what the previous thing created a need and desire for.

The Industrial Revolution in particular took us away from this understanding of natural processes and revolutions as cycles. According to some scholars, the Industrial Revolution lasted from 1760–1830 (Editors of Encyclopaedia Britannica 2023). According to others, it's still going, and we're in the fourth wave (Schwab 2016). This revolution brought us dramatic innovation in the areas of science and technology, which, in some ways, dramatically improved the quality of life for folks. It also ushered in a new way of being in which we were no longer part of nature, we were a thing outside of nature that sought to control and exploit nature but not a part of nature herself. It's been a revolution in the way we orient ourselves to nature, and we've pushed the relationship to the absolute limits of exploitation and degradation.

The ironically good news, though, is that a sufficient number of us are suffering the impacts of our severed connections from ourselves, each other, and nature. The cycle is coming full circle, and we're dying to reconnect. The science cycle, too, which took us away from nature is bringing us back, showing the ways we depend on nature for our own survival. A revolution. Our blind loyalty to industrialization has run its course, and there's a renewed interest in indigenous wisdom and biocultural knowledge systems.

As many of us are waking up to our own inherent nature, our connection to the earth, and our interconnected fate, we're planting seeds for the next revolution, the next cycle, and the next iteration of life on this planet. In nature, cycles and evolution are the absolute norm. Everything in nature exists in an ecosystem and in relationship to everything else in a giant web of interconnectivity. A change in one area creates a change in other areas of the system that is perpetually in flux. When we reconnect to our understanding of systems and change as they exist in nature, we're able to learn from cycles and see that cycles are, in fact, simply the way of things.

Nothing lasts forever—no feeling, no shame, no system, no world order—nothing. The Industrial Revolution taught us to prioritize product and productivity over process and presence. In the pursuit of linear, insatiable growth, extraction, and quantity, we neglected to bring what we've always known about cycles, interconnectivity, and quality.

Nature's rules and cycles are captured in a framework of nested hierarchies known as a panarchy (Resilience Alliance 2022). The word panarchy comes from the root word *pan*, which brings two meanings to fore: *pan* meaning all things, and *Pan*, the Greek god of nature, chaos, and unpredictability. The Greek suffix *-archy* refers to rule and governance. Panarchies describe the interplay between stability and change, predictability and unpredictability, and are visualized as iterative infinity loops.

There's an initial, creative phase of reorganization and renewal, a second phase of rapid growth and exploitation, a third phase of maturity and conservation, and a final stage of collapse or release before beginning the creative phase of renewal all over again. Panarchies describe the way a change to any piece of a system, whether through mutations, experiments, or novel innovations, adds variability and diversity that destabilizes the current system, requiring it to adapt. Sometimes, the system is flexible enough to adapt and include. Other times, the system is so rigid it is destroyed under the weight of its own inflexibility, collapses, and the entities and energies within the ecosystem are required to reorganize.

Without attachment to any particular system, without being loyal to it or the power and advantages it brings us, personally, change is neutral; the natural result of feedback loops within systems, changing inputs, players, processes, and desired outcomes. We only become loyal to systems we have a vested interest in maintaining. If we could choose to see systems as neutral entities that produce humane or inhumane conditions as the output of the infinite interactions, relationships, and processes within the system, we'd be better equipped to intervene in systems change. Everything that happens in this world is the result of complex, interconnected systems. The clearer our understanding of these systems, the clearer we see that nothing exists in isolation—no person, no feeling, no injustice—for these things are not just products of systems, they are systems within themselves, too.

Nothing we experience as a static entity is, in fact, a static entity. It is merely its current position in its overall lifecycle. The book you are holding, if you are holding a book, is not just a book—it is the current iteration of existence for a number of trees, and will one day find its way into being embers, or landfill, and will eventually become the input for another cycle. You who are holding this book are the result of infinite processes and genetic adaptations while also being the input of the future. You are an infinite process. And all of us are in process with all other processes, all the time.

And not only are you an infinite process, you are a system of systems. Your bodily existence isn't even just one system—it is the result of systems of systems: your respiratory system, circulatory system, nervous system, digestive system, endocrine system, and immune system are all working together to create "you" and keep "you" in balance. Each system is made of subsystems of subsystems that work together: the circulatory system includes the heart system that pumps your blood that supports the immune system; each cell within your heart and blood is a complex system itself, always working to maintain homeostasis within itself.

In that way, both our bodies and social systems function like nested Jenga puzzles—we need a certain number of pieces to be working properly for everything to stay standing. If we don't know which pieces are relying on which other pieces to stay up, we might pull one that will take everything else down with it. On the flip side, if we're trying to take something down—whether it's our emotional eating or our unfair workplace or our corrupt police department—knowing what's holding the whole thing in place helps us to determine exactly which brick to pull to get the whole thing crashing down. What would it mean, for instance, to pull shame out of the equation? Would the self-help industry tumble if we no longer felt badly about ourselves?

Destabilization is not inherently bad. Like disruption, it is emerging as a new collective value, likely because so many of our systems have been in a conservative/conservation phase for too long and enough of us are either negatively impacted or aware of the negative impacts on others that we're finally ready for change. The system itself is producing a new outcome—the desire to disrupt and create anew.

As we lean into change on behalf of a collective embracing equality and humanity, we need to be sure we're not, yet again, leaning on "the master's tools," only to recreate a system that's inhumane in other ways (Lorde 2007). Humans are, in the grand scheme of things, an individually and socially immature species, just learning to play nice with all the other species in the sandbox. We invented hammers and suddenly saw everything in our sandbox as nails. Our planet, her systems, and her methods are far older and wiser than we give her credit for. In our immaturity and arrogance, many of our society-builders forgot to transcend *and include.* Transcendence that is born of and begets wisdom both revolts and remembers.

Nature knows all living things must work together and with their environment without destroying it and themselves (ahem: humans). This is the golden rule of regeneration: Life creates conditions conducive to life (Benyus 2009). Our current economy requires the inhumane treatment of people within its systems, requires growth and profit at the expense of people and planet, and will, unchecked and undisrupted, destroy all of it. It is not, in its current iteration, conducive to life.

Health is a qualitative condition that describes the processes, patterns, and relationships in a system. A healthy liver is not a thing in and of itself—it describes the functionality of the system and the ability of the processes of its system to adequately remove toxins from the body.

Similarly, an economy is only as healthy as its processes and the outputs it produces. Keep an eye on how people talk about the economy for a few weeks. Are they describing it based on how it works for them? How their stocks are doing? Or the degree to which it is serving life by increasing the well-being of all players in the system, not just the ones who benefit from the inequality and exploitation within it? Similarly, the "health" of our justice system is rarely considered qualitatively based on how much justice has been created—not punishment, not retribution, but fairness and equality.

Our quantitative measures of economic growth typically measure the "value" of the goods and services produced within an economy over a given year. What good are all the goods in the world when they're destroying the environment to create products that don't make us happy, break down quickly, and are thrown into landfills? What good is economic growth to a population that is being increasingly underpaid? Economic growth that requires maximum profits by minimizing labor costs in a climate of excessive consumption is simply a measurement of waste and exploitation. We measure quantities when we're not able to discern any qualitative humanity produced. It is never a qualitative measure of whether it is contributing to life itself.

As we evolve ourselves and our systems from being self-serving instruments of power, we can start to see development not in terms of linear, quantifiable growth alone but in terms of cyclical creative processes in a web of human and nonhuman communities that respect the regenerative processes of renewal that enable us to contribute to ever more healthful and humane systems. We'll prioritize fairness, abundance, and equality for all oversocialized insatiability for some; slower, better, and higher quality over faster, cheaper, and higher quantities. We'll be able to collaborate with all of nature, instead of seeing ourselves outside of her domain, existing to exploit her.

In the same way solar cells mimic plant leaves to harvest energy in ways that are infinitely regenerative, we can learn from and participate with nature. This means exploring biomimicry, ecological design, permaculture, circular economies, and so much more. It means learning from ourselves and heeding the calls of nature that exist within us—the calls to rest, recover, connect, and create.

It means letting nature exist through us—embracing our natural tendencies and desires, including the ones that will pull us into the future, the new order, the next cycle, the coming revolution—rather than conforming to societal expectations. It means recognizing that your unique genetic makeup was created just for you—an emergent reflection of the world you were born into and what's yours to do here—and letting yourself work with the genetic mutations we were given that add ever-more diversity and novelty to our species. Working with nature means honoring the consciousness that for some reason exists in us, respecting the feelings and needs that you feel, and creating the impact you're meant to have on the systems and institutions you exist within.

Your call is to respond to and honor yourself, your feelings, and your needs as a human being and in the process, create the impact you're meant to have on the systems and institutions you exist within.

Your wildest, most undomesticated self knows it is human nature to feel and to regenerate. Before she was overcivilized and oversocialized, she knew what it was like to feel her feelings, use her voice, and to let both create change. That humanity is still within you. You feel what you feel for a reason. Denying yourself is the first step to denying your humanity. Don't let "etiquette" and "professionalism" get in the way of your and others' humanity.

It's no surprise to me to see "diseases of despair" such as suicide, drug overdoses, and deaths from alcoholic liver disease on the rise (Brignone et al. 2020). What has been common in American Indian and Alaska Native communities is spilling over and affecting middle-aged white Americans (Chatterjee 2023). The astronomical inequality created by our economic systems and exacerbated by our social systems is too much. We're too disconnected from ourselves, each other, and the community that should be providing a protective barrier from pain and hardship. As Bhutan's legal code reminds us, "If the government cannot create happiness for its people, then there is no purpose for government to exist" (GNH 2023).

Depression and burnout are the natural consequences of inhumane systems. As bell hooks observed, "Who could be aware of the interrelating dynamics of domination and not be depressed?" (2022). "Healthy depression" is a natural response telling us things aren't okay right now (Gnaulati 2018). Again, *you* are not a problem, you *have* a problem.

In supportive contexts, the community steps in to be with you and offers support. When communities fail to address "healthy depression," it can lead to "debilitating depression," a sense of hopelessness, captivity, and existential questioning in the face of institutional inhumanity that never seems to change (Gnaulati 2018). As Holocaust survivor Edith Eger notes, "Depression is an existential effort—why get up? What's the purpose? For what? Why start again if it yields nothing more than the same suffering?" (2017). In the face of unrelenting pain, we are forced to grapple with questions of purpose and meaning.

It's no surprise to me we're seeing an increase in books about seeking happiness and purpose. We need something to keep us going in the midst of all of this inhumanity and suffering. Think about your own life—when do you ask, "Why am I still here?" When the party has ended and it's no longer fun; when the relationship has run its course; when the stress of the job isn't worth the money; when the stress of living outweighs the miracle of existing.

We typically don't question existence when it feels good. What if your purpose—and all our purposes—were to create a way of being that didn't require a purpose to justify? What if our pull toward purpose is an evolutionary encouragement to reflect on how absurd it is we should require a reason to live?

If you feel, today, that you require a purpose, let me offer you one: you exist to help us create a way of being that respects connection, interbeing, and planetary health while institutionalizing humanity and regeneration into all our systems. You exist to evolve us toward a more peaceful, equitable, just, and beautiful future—one that doesn't require you to change to be accepted into.

To institutionalize humanity is to create the conditions conducive to life in every process, relationship, and system. It is to practice acceptance in ways that disrupt widespread denial. It is to insert love in ways that destabilize injustice. It is to refuse to participate in systems and relationships that create barriers to social mobility and perpetuate inequality. It is refusing to participate in any system that does not improve the well-being and subjective experience of every other being in the system—including the ones who don't yet have equal power, respect, or status within the system, and including the ones not yet born. It is to recognize in what systems you have access to the keystone Jenga blocks that hold an inhumane process together and recognize your power to keep it there or pull it out and let the whole thing fall.

To institutionalize humanity is to refuse to be a cog in the current institutions of inhumanity. It is acting on morals when the rule of law is a rule of power rather than a rule of justice. It is using whatever power we have to redistribute power justly, changing policies, practices, and processes wherever we can and rallying collective power to demand change when we aren't the ones holding positional power. It is starving the inhumane systems we don't have the authoritative power to change by leveraging our collective power to strike and boycott. It is making the current systems obsolete and creating entirely new institutions that are qualitatively humane and mutually beneficial to all parties from the start.

At its core, institutionalizing humanity is about accepting our mutual fates in a vast ecosystem of interconnectedness and acknowledging that by redesigning human systems, we have the ability to dramatically improve the health of the individuals, communities, and the planet that make up the entire, broader ecosystem we exist within.

CHAPTER 19

ACCOUNTABILITY IS ALLYSHIP

When my great-grandmother moved to the United States in 1921, she relinquished all her home-country attachments. She refused to speak her native Slovenian and refused to pass her language down to her children. She abandoned her culture and heritage entirely. She understood the United States as a land of opportunity and wanted to make sure her children would be successful. She didn't want them to simply acculturate and take on some aspects of the new culture, she wanted them to assimilate. She wanted to discard her previous culture and take on a new identity, one that would help her family thrive in their new home.

She died long before I was born, when my mother was just twelve years old. My mother describes her as a deeply loving, caring, and giving person who always wore a smile, but has no real stories to pass down. I'm sad I never got to meet the kind, daring woman in my lineage who was willing to risk it all for the great-grandchildren she would never meet. I'm sad I never got to ask about life in her home country, or what we were known for in our village, or what the legacy of our women was. I never got to find out who we are, and, therefore, who I am.

Curiously, if you'd asked me about my lineage before I had my Ancestry DNA results, I would have said I was German. I studied abroad in Germany multiple times. I pursued a German major. Even my undergraduate thesis explored the idea of German ethnicity, determining if the strength of a student's ethnic identity influences his or her foreign language learning. I assumed the results would show the more German we feel, the more likely we study the language. I was dead wrong. The opposite was true—the less affirmed we are in our ethnic identity and the more we search for it, the more likely we are to learn a second language. My constant desire to connect with my German heritage revealed my underlying need to know who I was.

My great-grandmother's immigration coincided with a nationwide push for Americanization (Debska 2010). While "Americanization" has evolved as an idea since colonial times, the function has always been roughly the same: unify all members of the new country under a new culture and set of values—namely, White Anglo-Saxon Protestant (WASP) values. The United States was founded not as many other countries are, to unite a geographic region and its people, but as an idea, a philosophy, an ideal. People who existed within the geographic region were expected to conform to the ideas, not the other way around.

Whether voluntarily coming to the US, being stolen from their homeland and forced into the US, or being forced to assimilate when colonizers stole their land and sent them to boarding schools, people in the geographic region operated by the US government have been perpetually distanced from their pasts, their rich cultural heritages, diverse practices, and from their very identities. Diverse legacies, languages, and values were erased in exchange for a homogenous "American" identity and culture enforcers believed was superior to other cultures. The self-ascribed superiority of the dominant culture discriminated against those who weren't willing to assimilate and those who were visually unable to assimilate, even if they wanted to culturally. It has led to the belief that people of color are outsiders, no matter how hard they try to fit in.

With each new wave of immigrants, American society demanded, forced, and coerced assimilation. Its stability as a cohesive "American society" depended on it. Industrialization, and therefore urbanization, brought a frenzy of overcrowding cum xenophobia that galvanized nationalist groups to organize educational programs to indoctrinate foreigners into the American way of life. Students were taught patriotic loyalty, to speak English, and respect authority.

My great-grandmother renounced her heritage and identity because she was proud to be an American. But she also must have felt pressured to. She knew economic and social success in her new homeland required diving into the melting pot.

And that's the cruelest irony. When we renounce who we are for the sake of belonging, someone else gets to dictate who we get to be and what's important to us. We become agents of someone else's grand plan. We spend all our time, energy, and resources fitting into that system rather than helping that system evolve into something that works for all of us.

To move beyond caring about what we're told to care about, we have to move beyond our socialization. Most self-help keeps us working within our socialization, and navigating our oppressive, power-over systems. It is liberating to be who we are, outside of what our society tells us is acceptable. It is strangely liberating to be knowingly and unapologetically unacceptable.

Once we move beyond our socialization, we also get to evolve beyond our socially constructed identities. You get to be *you* instead of a *good* version of you. And I get to be me, the kind of woman and partner and author and business owner I want to be without someone else defining it for me. I get to define what being an American means for myself rather than let my definition, and therefore my existence, be exploited by the people in power. Moving beyond socialization does not mean moving past identity or values. On the contrary, it means moving beyond *ascribed* values and identities and choosing our values and identities for ourselves.

When we're clear on who we are and what we value aside from who we're told to be and what we're told to value, we are able to use our personal power to move closer to our personally held vision for a more beautiful world. We get to work with other people who share the same vision, regardless of whether they are part of our "in-group" or not. We get to work with people who are very different from us, who very much care about the same things.

Along the way, we come to find out we're all far more alike than we are different and have more shared dreams than we were conditioned to believe.

The success of a plutocracy masquerading as a democracy requires that collective power be so fractioned against itself and so busy trying to survive that it can't band together to create change. Thanks to today's capitalist power structures, the richest 1 percent of households have fifteen times more wealth than the entire bottom half of households *combined* (Beer 2020). They maintain their image as the bastions of the

American Dream, insisting we need them to exploit us—err, to create jobs—so we can put food on the table and pay our increasingly expensive rents and mortgages (to them). Most of us feel like we literally cannot afford to shift our focus away from our own survival.

Some studies suggest the top 1 percent holds as much wealth as the bottom 90 percent (Smith, Zidar, and Zwick 2021). The super-rich 0.01 percent of families make, on average, seven million dollars a year and have $111 million in net worth (Gold 2017). Worse still are the Waltons, the Kochs, and the Zuckerbergs; the ones with the money and resources to buy politicians and supreme court justices to swing "justice" in their favor.

Three hundred million people don't share the same wealth as the top 1 percent, and nearly 336 million people don't share the same wealth as the top 0.01 percent. That's almost everyone.

How much power do 336 million people have?

More than we could fathom.

Research used to suggest no government could survive if 5 percent of its population rose up against it. Studies show it's less than that: no campaigns fail once they've achieved active and sustained participation of just 3.5 percent of the population, and many succeed with far fewer. In the twentieth century, every movement that actively mobilized 3.5 percent of the population won (Chenoweth 2013). Every. One. And the majority have been nonviolent.

During consumer boycotts in Apartheid-era South Africa, for instance, Black citizens' refusal to buy products from companies with white owners led to an economic crisis among the white elite that contributed to the end of segregation. In 1986, nonviolent demonstrations ousted Philippine President

Ferdinand Marcos—a man who had kept himself in power via martial law for twenty years—in just four days of sustained protest (McGeown 2011). Estonians have used music as a cultural unifier and political weapon for centuries and, in 1991, won their independence from the Soviet Union in what became known as Estonia's Singing Revolution (Zunes 2009). Each of these campaigns was able to successfully and actively mobilize more than 3.5 percent of its population in nonviolent struggle.

Nonviolent campaigns are not only much easier for the general population to support, they are twice as likely to achieve their goals (Robson 2019). They tend to be more inclusive, spanning gender, race, age, class, political party, and so on. As anyone who has met a toddler knows, everyone is born with and has the personal power to resist nonviolently. When there's safety in numbers, as with civil disobedience or protests, the more risk averse join in. Public demonstrations allow folks to see there's public support for an idea, and the ambivalent are more likely to join in. The larger, more diverse, and more inclusive the movement, the more likely there are friends and family members of those in power in the crowd, and that matters. Police officers are more likely to refuse orders to shoot demonstrators when they know their kids will be in the crowd (Chenoweth 2013). When large numbers of people stop participating in oppressive systems, the systems struggle to maintain their power.

In the US, we know far more about the history of war than about the history of successful movements. That's by design. No government can withstand the sustained mobilization of 3.5 percent of its population without accommodating or disintegrating. But to rally 3.5 percent of the population requires us to come together on the basis of shared values and shared goals and do something. Together.

American historian, author, and activist Howard Zinn, author of *You Can't Be Neutral on A Moving Train: A Personal History* notes, well, you can't be neutral on a moving train (2018). Our systems are already in motion, and creating their effects. To not do anything to change the speed or the direction of the train is to be complicit in where it ends up and who it runs over on the way.

Most changemakers don't set out to be heroes or even do anything remarkable. Instead, something happens to personally activate their interest in a cause and they refuse to sit idly by. Some are simply trying to live their lives and bump up against laws that need to change to make that possible. Others come up against injustice they can't turn away from. Others still recognize their privilege and spend the rest of their lives trying to do good with it. All have chosen to do something about it and, often, garnered incredible community support and leveraged collective power to make it happen.

Nicole Maines was simply trying to live her life when her school district began regulating which bathroom she could use (Maines 2020). Recognizing she was being discriminated against, her family sued the school district to enable her to use whatever bathroom she felt comfortable in. Nicole was just a child trying to live her life. Her parents were fighting to make that possible for her. In the process, they became transgender activists and paved the way for others by establishing protections for transgender students. Since then, Nicole has gone on to become TV's first transgender superhero, portraying Dreamer on "Supergirl." She uses her platform to increase visibility and advocate for representation (Gustines 2018).

Similarly, Shannon Watts didn't set out to take on the National Rifle Association (Cox 2023). Instead, the stay-at-home mom was activated by the Sandy Hook school shooting in 2012 that killed twenty-six children and educators. She leveraged her former experiences as a communication executive to increase awareness of the issue and attract attention to the cause. Her organization, Moms Demand Action (MDA), established chapters in all fifty US states, resulting in hundreds of gun safety laws, improved corporate policies, and increased education about gun storage (Moms Demand Action 2013). In the 2022 elections, 140 MDA volunteers were elected to public office (Fowler 2022). There was no massive, preconceived plan. Instead, a mom was mobilized, invited other moms to the table, and, together, created the greatest counterbalance to the gun lobbying industry in existence. By my estimation, their membership is almost at 3.5 percent.

Finally, Stanley Levison was an attorney and supporter of left-wing causes (Stanford n.d.). Despite remaining relatively unknown, his contributions to the labor, civil rights, and peace movements made a huge difference behind the scenes. In the 1950s, he and two colleagues created In Friendship, an organization that raised money for southern civil rights activists, organizations, and movements, including the Montgomery bus boycott. Their concept of a "congress of organizations" later developed into the Southern Christian Leadership Conference. He became acquainted with Martin Luther King, Jr. in 1956 and became a close friend and advisor. Levison drafted articles and speeches on King's behalf, prepared his tax returns, raised funds, and helped him secure a book contract, all without pay. He used his privilege and power to support the collective struggle for liberation.

All three change-makers took an active role. They saw where the train was heading, who it was hurting, and did something to prevent further harm from being caused. The ecosystem created the need and motivated their activation.

They worked with others in the ecosystem to create positive change.

Our systems are hitting the limits of the inequality they can sustain. In fact, the likelihood of a system falling is in direct proportion to its failure to meet the needs of its people. As more people are disenfranchised, more of us will continue to be activated. We are activated for a variety of reasons, but crisis and personal motives often activate the passion, persistence, and sacrifice required to keep the momentum for action, especially when we'd otherwise benefit from the train's momentum. To interrupt life as usual, we need to be interested in something other than life as usual.

Knowing the facts of inequality rarely produces enough motivation for us to demand, and work toward, another way. Without the emotional attachment to it, without feeling a sense of personal connection or solidarity with an issue, it often remains a nebulous, abstract idea *out there*, and we suffer a sort of justice inertia. To garner the necessary 3.5 percent, we need to allow not just our needs but our connection to other people and real, felt empathy to unite us together in shared struggle. None of us exist outside the interlocking systems of oppression. This fight is all of ours.

The word "ally" comes from the Latin *alligare*, meaning "to bind together." Ally, meaning member of an alliance, was used to describe people who came together through marriage, political, military, or business agreements for a common purpose. Allies in war recognize a shared fate and work together. They coordinate operations, intelligence, and resources while supporting one another toward a shared outcome. In war, there needn't be a formal alliance. Fighting next to each other is enough. In fact, it is the demonstration of solidarity that makes one an ally, not the self-labeling. The same is true in social justice work.

Social justice is about recognizing our fates are interconnected, war or not, declared, official alliance or not. To recognize our interdependent fates is to recognize we're already bound together.

For some, allyship is about folks using the power they have on behalf of others, such as Stanley Levinson's support of Martin Luther King, Jr.'s leadership (Giannaki 2016). It led Nicole Maines' parents to support their daughter and Shannon Watts to activate moms in support of all children. In this way, privilege isn't inherently bad—it's a matter of how we wield our privilege and power that matters. In war, countries that can contribute more troops and resources do. Allyship in social justice contexts requires the same. It is important that those who have more time, energy, resources, or power recognize that everything contributed to the greater good benefits society as a whole.

Allies of privilege use their relative positions of power within the system to speak up and create change when it's difficult and dangerous for others to do so for themselves. It often means opening oneself up to censure and punishment from the same system that granted you power when you were willing to do their bidding. To be in solidarity can mean doing the work quietly, behind the scenes, ensuring pay equity exists in your organization and labor equity exists in your home, risking close relationships by having tough conversations, and paying reparations directly to people affected by systemic injustices, slavery, and colonialism. Other times, solidarity means standing so close to those affected by oppression that, as it has been said, you risk being hit by the stones hurled at the oppressed. It looks like white Freedom Riders protesting bus segregation alongside Black Freedom Riders, veterans enduring tear gas and rubber bullets alongside indigenous activists at Standing Rock (Tolan 2016), and religious congregations practicing civil disobedience by providing a safe haven for refugees and asylum seekers in the Sanctuary Movement.

There are a tremendous number of roles we can play in creating change. We need disruptors and activists, to be sure, who lead our system in a new direction of release and reorganization. We also need pathfinders, facilitators, connectors, and amplifiers who keep the movement going (Miemis 2010). We need observers and scribes who criticize the systems, advocate for better ones, and record what happens. There's a role for everyone.

Regardless of the role we play, to make sure we're doing the most good for the most people, we also need to make sure we're holding ourselves accountable to the people we're working on behalf of. Like the truth and reconciliation efforts of restorative justice, accountability is the expectation that individuals and organizations are responsible for the consequences of their actions.

In typical parlance, such as business settings, I hear folks talking about accountability in a transactional, asymmetrical, unilateral, and imbalanced way: one person has power over the other and wants to hold them accountable for not doing something they were told to do. Unilateral accountability means one party can be held responsible for their actions and the other party cannot. When one entity has the power in the relationship, accountability is not a two-way discussion to explore root causes. At work, that would require employers to take responsibility for setting impossible expectations. In society, it would require politicians to take responsibility for allowing the inequality that results in crimes of desperation. Instead, people are punished for advocating for themselves, defending themselves, and doing what they need to do to survive.

When someone is in control of our safety, security, and well-being, when they threaten our jobs—and therefore access to healthcare, housing, and more—we're forced to decide between our values and our employment. The "accountability" transaction is clear: I keep the power; you accept the punishment and you get to keep your job. It is a clear demonstration of inequality and breeds tension, resentment, and conflict.

Transformational accountability requires mutuality. It requires a mutual understanding and shared goals. This involves taking ownership and responsibility for actions that do not contribute to the common goal or even undermine it. Mutual accountability means rethinking power structures, expectations, how we commit to one another, and what we're building so it works for everyone. In the creation of a more beautiful future, accountability is a process that begins when we come together to discuss what we need, whether or not needs are being met, and what the collective can do to support the needs of all parties in the ecosystem.

True allyship cannot exist without accountability, and mutual accountability cannot exist without allyship—knowing our fates are bound up together. A world that works for everyone requires everyone's input to build. Participation in anything larger than oneself requires compromise but should not require the sacrificing of one's own health, happiness, values, or identity.

For generations, scientists and philosophers have tried to explain human cooperation, altruism, and generosity. It was a point of confusion for Darwinists, who described interaction through the lens of competition and fitness. People struggle to fully explain why folks cooperate, but the reality is it's essential to all domains of life and is observable across all of nature. Bees work together to maintain hives; birds collaborate via V-formations to save energy; fish coordinate movements in schools to deter predators. Similarly, homo sapiens have evolved to cooperate with one another, which is likely how we came to triumph over Neanderthals—we simply outnumbered them ten-to-one and knew how to coordinate our efforts (Collins 2011).

Over time, natural selection within cooperative groups favored genes with prosocial motives (Boyd and Richerson 2009). As a result, today, our human bodies are genetically predisposed to live and thrive in healthy relationships. Strong relationships function as protective mechanisms, significantly increasing one's likelihood of survival (Weir 2018). With strong social connections, we enjoy increased immune function, increased regulation of stress hormones, higher moods, motivation, and coping. Our bodies are marvels of nested system cooperation that respond positively to our cooperation with people in our external environment. Genes work together to activate and repress genetic expression and create our overall genome. Mitochondria communicate and cooperate both within and between cells, sharing tasks, synchronizing activities, and responding to their environments and each other (Zimmer 2021). Whether or not we can explain it, it's who we are. Cooperation is at the heart of our existence.

In some ways, the common human's plight against the wealthy mirrors homo sapiens' plight against the Neanderthals, except instead of outnumbering Neanderthals ten to one, we outnumber the ultrawealthy by more like a thousand to one. Getting to a place where we're able to work together is a matter of unlearning the stories that keep us fighting each other. It's time to stop forcing ourselves to fit into rigid identities within rigid systems and instead allow the systems to adapt to our needs. We are the diversity that will drive society's evolution.

To have the effect we were meant to have on our collectives, we need to understand that we are who we are for a reason. Perhaps we were born into privilege and retained enough empathy to make a difference. Or perhaps we were born on the fringes of society in order to invite that society into being more inclusive. The diversity within our solidarity is the necessary variety that will make our entire system adaptable enough to create and withstand the changes we demand of it.

When we have personal experience with an issue, either through our own experience or through a close friend or family member, we are more likely to support policies reducing discrimination and promoting equality—like Nicole Maines' family. Similarly, when we have a positive personal relationship with someone, we are less likely to vilify them just because someone else told us to. Drag queens are easy to vilify when they are abstract people we don't know; they are much harder to vilify when we grew up with them reading to us at the local library (Middleton 2022).

When we don't have direct personal experience, we look to people in our "in-group" to help us craft our opinions. This presents allies with a huge opportunity to make their communities more inclusive. When Green Bay Packers fans were informed hall-of-famer LeRoy Butler supported the LGBTQ community, they were significantly more likely to also support the LGBTQ community (Woo 2017). Similarly, when Barack Obama announced he was pro same-sex marriage, approval of gay marriage went up in Black American communities anywhere from 10 to 20 percent (King 2013). When it was a trusted clergy member approving, approval of hypothetical same-sex marriage ballot measures went up by a whopping 22 percent among the very religious, showing the more dissonant and unexpected the approval, the more effective it was (Harrison and Michelson 2015).

Allyship can mean helping folks to challenge stereotypes we were given. It can mean sharing our own experiences in order to create more empathy and understanding. Whether I'm being an ally by supporting anti-racist policies and politicians, encouraging my HOA to create more inclusive policies, or educating a neighbor about the importance of affordable housing and public transportation in all neighborhoods, including ours, there are several strategies I can use to be more effective. As an ally, effective persuasion means remembering we're all equal parts of the ecosystem, getting to the heart of what potential allies are interested in, hoping for, and worried about. I can practice curiosity to seek the core values they stand for and what motivates them. Once we get to a point of shared values and shared goals, we can move beyond our socialization and work together to create the effect we want to have on the world. It is to find common humanity, and from a shared goal create a shared future (Giridharadas 2022).

To create change, we need to both practice acceptance of what is—the good, the bad, and the ugly—and to be willing to speak that truth in places where it matters. As Howard Zinn is often quoted as saying, "the most revolutionary act one can engage in is… to tell the truth" (Zinn 1999).

To tell the truth and speak truth to power is to challenge the narratives that maintain the status quo. It is to share experiences and perspectives that increase transparency and visibility, the precursors to accountability. When we speak our truths about how we are negatively affected, we raise awareness. When we speak openly about the negative effects of systemic oppression, police brutality, and structural inequality, we engage in transparency that reveals a society to itself. To speak honestly is to acknowledge where we, too, are complicit and work with others to dismantle the systems that maintain privilege for the sake of equality, equity, and justice.

Truth-telling means saying, "Do you want this relationship to work for both of us or not? Cause this isn't working for me." Acceptance means not resisting the answer. Transformational accountability means taking ownership for the world we're building together and having repeated conversations to make sure it works for everyone in it.

Allyship is the dance floor where individuals and the collective meet to decide if we're working with or against each other. As individual players, we lack the emergent properties that arise when a collective system creates a whole that is greater than the sum of its parts.

It's like the murmuration of migrating birds, where the needs of each bird move the flock as a whole, creating a beautiful display of cohesion, collective power, and avian allyship. By working together toward justice and equality, we can create a sense of belonging that is not dependent on the approval of those in power but on solidarity and collective efforts to create a more just and equitable world, whether we're "birds of a feather" or not.

CHAPTER 20

WE NEED YOU

Earlier this year, I took a yoga class for the first time in more than three years. I was attending a retreat on the future of consciousness in the mountains north of San Francisco. All the participants gathered in a beautiful, spacious yurt atop a grassy hill. As we twisted and bent, I found myself slipping back into familiar, covert competition. Am I bending farther than her? Can I hold the pose longer than him? I snuck out to the bathroom to shake it off and returned to the instructor pairing up participants.

My heart sank. I knew it was coming, but knowing didn't stop the gnawing fear in my stomach. I was worried I'd become even more competitive or even more self-conscious. A man with kind eyes met my gaze and smiled. He was slender and about my height. Having done acro-yoga once before, I was immediately fearful he would have to lift me by his feet like we did as kids playing airplane. We exchanged nervous smiles and turned to face the instructor.

Our first invitation was to support our partners in their downward dogs. Our partners created A-frames with their bodies, as we placed one foot between their hands and our hands on their hips to aid the stretch.

"Make sure you're communicating!" our instructor reminded us.

I snapped out of my self-consciousness.

"How's it going down there?" I inquired.

"A little more pressure would be great," he answered. I leaned in.

Adding another human directly into my experience reminded me it wasn't—and never had to be—a competition. My existence had a purpose: to help him get the stretch he wanted for himself. As long as I was present and responsive, I was doing enough. Rather than retreating into self-consciousness or competition, I could focus my thoughts and energy on working together for a deeper stretch, a more solid foundation, and a sense of calm cooperation.

We finished our downward dogs, thanked each other for the support, and were invited to choose new partners for our next stretch. The second round was, I think, less awkward for all of us. Nervous glances and nervous giggles evolved into genuine smiles as we appreciated each other for the support.

Finally, the instructor had us gather in a circle for a collective tree pose. Each participant balanced on one foot while their other foot rested on their ankle, calf, or inner thigh. We were invited to reach our arm branches upward, connecting our palms with those of the persons next to us, connecting us all as a forest of trees.

"If you're used to giving lots of support in your life, maybe take this opportunity to receive. If you find yourself often receiving, take this opportunity to give." I felt the arms holding mine relax. I relaxed my arms, too. I watched as outstretched arms with locked elbows loosened and leaned.

Our forest of tree poses swayed but did not fall—not one of us—something unusual even in practiced yoga studios.

We held the pose at least twice as long as I'm accustomed to with half as much difficulty.

I was immediately aware of the comparative ease. By having each of us support the other, none of us had to be particularly strong. Each of us could contribute strength to our collective balance simply by being present, by existing, and in turn, fortifying our entire forest.

It turns out trees do exactly this underground, leveraging not only their root systems but the root systems of neighboring trees. Connected beneath the surface, each tree supports their neighbor. Studies found trees growing close together were much more likely to survive storms and hurricanes than trees that were alone (Kamimura et al. 2022). Each tree, strong yet flexible, is made sturdier by the presence of every other tree in the forest.

And the analogy runs deeper. Not only do trees provide necessary strength and grounding, they share resources, nutrients, and even information through massive underground fungal networks. They send signals to warn about drought, disease, and insect attacks, which allow trees to alter their behavior accordingly and maximize their chances of surviving and thriving as a group (Grant 2018; Jabr 2020). Forests share and coordinate, some going so far as to orchestrate collective blooms, ensuring each tree is able to participate together.

Trees, like you and me, are not meant to exist in isolation, or in intense, sustained competition for sunlight, resources, and acceptance. In partnership with others, we share and support, each helping the other. In collectives, we can all contribute to the systems we build, ensuring the health and well-being of each and every one of us and the longevity and integrity of the whole.

Some of us find our way into roles we don't expect.

I didn't set out to be a traitor to the self-help industry. It's a role I stumbled my way into.

I originally set out to be a profitable cog in the self-help machine. I feel tremendously grateful it didn't work the way I'd hoped—the harmful impacts were never obscured by profits. I connected with others experiencing the same, growing levels of self-consciousness and discontent, and witnessed it worsen over time. I had to opt out. Opting out created the space I needed to see clearly, to process what was happening with trusted friends, coaches, and confidantes, and to untangle how we got here and what I wanted to do about it. I had to be willing to give up the business, the platform I'd created, and the privilege of being on the inside of the industry in order to end the harm I was facilitating.

Self-help is a dangerous drug that obscures the true causes of our pain. I refuse to be a dealer.

Part of this book is a reckoning; a way of sharing everything I've learned about the self-help industry as both participant and purveyor. It is also my accountability to myself and to our collective. It's my way of taking ownership for harm I've caused while sending oppressive propaganda out into the world and owning its impacts even if no one's asking me to.

One of my mentors used to say integrity is doing the right thing even when no one is watching. I used to levy it against my students to keep them under my control, even when I wasn't standing over them. Now, I see it as both a way of exerting control *and* an invitation to right wrongs, even if no one's asking for it. This is something I need to do if I want to live by my values.

I own that I've given platforms to both liberatory and oppressive self-help. I've furthered obsessions with the self and pushed aggressive and invasive levels of self-control. Now that I know better, I'd like to do better. I invite you to do better with me. Here's how I intend to do so:

1. Invite the self-help industry and its purveyors into accountability;

2. Liberate myself from individualized oppression and invite others into the liberation journey with me;

3. Take steps to create the more beautiful world I know is possible every day and, in the process, render predatory industries obsolete;

4. Be a traitor to inequitable systems of power and the beliefs that fuel them.

I don't think self-help will ever go away, and I don't think that's even the goal. Our species is far too curious and far too dedicated to sharing what we've learned on our personal journeys. We don't need it to go away. We need it to evolve. I envision an evolution in the genre, one far more honest about the world and her systems, the sources of the pain we face, and what we can do about it.

An evolution in the genre recognizes that self-help, too, is a system in progress. It's creating the effects that it was designed to create—keeping us navigating our socialization rather than transcending it, and surviving rather than thriving. By accepting that self-help is merely in its current phase in its overall lifecycle, we can find the opportunities to inject some disruption, invite it into a new way of being, and find ways to influence the next wave, the next cycle, the next iteration.

We deserve a wave of self-help that invites us into the next stage of consciousness as a collective and into the next stage of our collective (r)evolution, transcending the self entirely and empowering individuals to recognize the interplay between the *me* and the *we*, while simultaneously embracing our role in the cocreation process. Liberatory self-help will free us from our stories, our conditioned attachments, and our shame. It will help us to feel and heal what hurts, give us ways to support ourselves and our collective, and acknowledge the best self-help is justice, institutional humanity, mutual aid, and community care.

Like all development, the next iteration of self-help will be a response to what came before it. I look forward to a wave of self-help that prioritizes better questions and nuanced complexity over hot takes and easy answers. A more mature self-help will transcend binaries and dichotomies of good/bad, right/wrong, and us/them. It will not encourage us to change as a means or an end unto itself but as a means of healing, disrupting oppressive constructs, patterns, and paradigms. It will reunite us with who we are, our inherent power, and the effects we were meant to have on the Universe. It will recognize we don't actually know how to get out of all of the complex messes we're in, but that it won't be solved by *more of the same* from the people who got us into the mess and profit from keeping us here.

Supporting this evolution means accepting self-help for what it *is* and helping to create this awareness for others before we collectively lean into what it *could be*. By now, you probably have a pretty good idea of what oppressive self-help looks like, feels like, and sounds like. If not, I've created an assessment tool you can use to discern more concretely. It can be found at www.itsnotallyourfault.com, and every submission helps us to cocreate a more robust and collaborative filtering system.

Once we've got a solid level of awareness, we can start taking responsibility and meaningful action. If you come across self-help you determine to be oppressive, you have options. You could send the book to the next iteration in its physical life cycle and use any copies you own as campfire fuel. You could leave reviews on Amazon, Goodreads, or Book Riot, inviting the author and readers into greater self-awareness by sharing the impact the book has had on you. You could pen an email to the author, inviting them to participate in cocreating a more liberatory and inclusive future instead.

Remember—we're looking to put an end to the individualization of oppression, not to attack the people who do it. It's about the behavior and its impact, not the person. The person, too, is the result of their conditioning and environment. We aren't fighting each other; we're fighting our conditioning into separation and the systems that perpetuate it. There's a legitimate chance they have no idea. If that's the case, we can let them know about the harm being caused and invite them into radical accountability. If they know and don't care or are hungry for the profits at the expense of the people they hurt, we can mitigate the effects by reducing demand for that kind of content. The market will respond to the demand.

Like the abandoned farmhouses of my youth now covered with moss and ivy, immense beauty can arise in decay and rebirth. The structures that once served to shelter families now serve as a nutrient-rich substrate and, like nurse logs, serve as the foundation for new life in the form of ivy and the seedlings of hope. Their decay is but another phase in the cycle, facilitating the transition to what comes next.

Similarly, self-help resources were once crucial in helping us to navigate the complexities and paradoxes of our socialization. Their structures provided us shelter from the discomfort of disapproval, the fears of getting it wrong, and the stressors of everyday life. As our wants and needs evolve, so too must the methods that meet them. We can build on the foundation we've created and use the positive tools we've gained along the way—increased self-awareness, self-reflection, self-control, and understanding of society's systems and structures—to usher in the next iteration of self, self-help, and society. As we seek to bring about the next phase in our collective existence, let us seek support in intentionally creating love, justice, and the institutionalization of humanity, so that we might create a way of being that is conducive to life, regeneration, shared power, true contentment, and well-being.

We have the power to create demand for personal development wherein the self is neither isolated nor problematic; a subgenre that specializes in helping us to accept ourselves unconditionally and accept that our bodies are doing exactly what they're supposed to do; a subgenre that helps us to navigate the disconnect between our bodily systems and our social systems, including the way we work, contribute meaningfully, and participate in a collective economy. We deserve support in connecting personal pain to the social and relieving both individual *and* collective pain and suffering.

I encourage you to create the demand for personal development books that support the Inner Development Goals, helping us to deepen our relationship with and compassion for ourselves and each other, break old patterns with courage and creativity, and make sense of and work with the world as one big interconnected system. Ask bookstore owners and librarians for the kind of self-help that encourages us to dream and courageously cocreate with the others in our lives, learning together as we experiment in the sandbox of life. This self-help will be holistic, emergent, iterative, transformational, and playful. It will increase our self-awareness, help us redirect our energy, and steer our collective journey in a more peaceful, just, and equitable direction.

The result of a more just self-help will be more justice.

As we pursue justice, let's reclaim our inherent curiosity, playfulness, creativity, and experimentation as we imagine a more beautiful future together. I encourage you to consider, for example, the thought experiment proposed by philosopher John Rawls: Envision a society you'd like to exist in the future (Rawls 2005). Picture its social structures and values, its economic systems and taxes, and its justice system and laws. Do so with one caveat: You don't know what role you'll play in that future. You don't know where you'll be born or to whom. You don't know what gender, skin color, social strata, religion, or sexual orientation you'll be. From this "Veil of Ignorance," we're much more inclined to empathy, to take everyone into consideration, and to design a future that works for everyone in it.

Imagine this future with such precision and clarity that you experience a nostalgia for this future you've not yet experienced. Feel its existence in your bones, in your soul, and in the webs between your fingers. Know what it will feel like, smell like, sound like, and taste like. Then get to work building the society where it's assumed you belong, just as you are. Who do you get to be? What strengths will you get to leverage? What effect do you get to have on your world? Allow the tendrils of that future to reach back and pull you forward.

The way forward doesn't actually require us all to agree on the same vision. It'd be ideal if everyone agreed, but we don't need that many, and it doesn't have to be a national movement every time. Diversity in what we care about and how we try to get there matters, too. We need some people to care about the environment and other people to care about eradicating poverty. And then we need the conditions for collaboration so we achieve our goals more effectively by working together. That's the only way to recognize the interconnectedness between all our systems, and to recognize, for example, as Chico Mendes famously stated, "Environmentalism without class struggle is gardening" (Yatharth 2021).

Find the thing that speaks to you, its societal roots, and everyone else that root is affecting. Find or build your coalition, cocreate your vision, and get to experimenting with creating a better way. Commit to using what you were born with and what makes you come alive. As Howard Thurman reminds us, "Don't ask yourself what the world needs. Ask yourself what makes you come alive, and go do that, because what the world needs is people who have come alive" (Thurman et al. 2010). Allow yourself to play and dance with the flow of the Universe. Write your more beautiful future into existence. Sing it here. Inspire it with your art, your voice, your story. Call it forth, and allow your calling to show you the way.

You were born with the exact genetic makeup you have, with the pulls you feel, for a reason. You are evolving our society in the way you were meant to. Being who you are *is* your purpose.

Being who you are means recognizing where you're conforming to someone else's standards, embracing someone else's values, and building someone else's future at the expense of your own, and choosing *your* standards, values, and vision for the future instead. To paraphrase Joseph Campbell, if you can see your path laid out in front of you, you know it's not your path—you're on someone else's. You must find your own way, step by step. That's why it's *your* path (Campbell and Moyers 1988). Fulfilling your purpose means having the effect you were meant to have on people—that's why they manifested you into their lives, after all—and contributing to the collective in ways only you can.

When you seek success along a defined and narrow path, you will inevitably find yourself in crowded competition; when you seek to be the epitome of you, you are guaranteed success.

You don't need to know where you're going, and you don't need to know how you will get there. You don't need to have your path laid out before you begin. Take the next right step and watch as your path emerges.

This book, for me, has not only been the result of answering the call to write I could no longer ignore but also my way of processing, releasing, and making sense of my experiences, my pain and suffering, and everything I've learned along the way. It was the process of my wounds transmuting themselves into wisdom and the last hurrah of my attachment to staying silent. It is my refusal to go unheard and unwitnessed and my commitment to speaking truth to power. It's the culmination of so many ideas, studies, philosophies, quotes, and images that have lodged themselves inexplicably into my memory, only to be recalled when the time was right. And it's clear that time is right now.

From my fascination with nurse logs and potential futures to the interconnection of all things, the things I can't get enough of all found their ways into these pages. Choices that didn't make logical sense and outcomes I couldn't have planned for, including this book and who she turned out to be, were emergent in every way. This book wrote herself. I am but a grateful, humble conduit.

My vision for the future changes every day as I learn more about myself, what I want, what other people want, and what's possible. I imagine yours will, too. As we heal our relationships with ourselves, we'll come to feel the extent of our personal power and what we're capable of. As we create love and justice in our relationships, we'll see the ripple effects of justice spreading like wildfire in our communities and see the way justice for us results in justice for others, too. As we reduce the demand for inhumanity, increase the demand for humanity, and make unjust systems obsolete, our entire society will be transformed.

Let us move toward our desired futures together, providing one another guidance, not solutions. Revealing obstacles, not prescribing paths. Exploring the both/and, the Third Ways, the beauty in the mystery, the complexity and emergent majesty in the chaos. Let us learn the rules and techniques so we might be in choice about when, where, why, and how to break them, change them, and transcend them.

You'd be surprised how many people will stand with you when you take a stand, and how many will contribute time, energy, and resources if you ask. When we take action to support the people around us, the people around us take action, too. Hell, if you run for office, reach out to my organization, The Center for Conscious Leadership, and we'll support you however we can.

As you grow and evolve, use what you've learned not to profit off your lessons, necessarily, or to prescribe solutions to others, but to contribute to our collective consciousness what you can for the sake of creating something new and beautiful. We can use our experiences to inspire, educate, uplift, and activate those around us. We can also share our experiences as a means of rejecting the systems of shame and silence that keep us divided and oppressed. I invite you to betray the systems by owning and sharing your story and speaking truth to power. You are in no obligation to keep secrets for the people in power, especially when they're hurting people. Throw out the stories power tells and write your own. Speaking your truth out loud just helps other people realize they're not alone, either.

As we share, we can't help but connect, and deeply. From a mutual refuge of respect and compassion, we create the conditions for healing and possibility. Together, we paint a picture of another way of being so vivid, we can't help but bring it to life. Embracing this future wholeheartedly grants us the courage of our convictions and the ability to commit acts of rebellion that are healing, cathartic, authentic, and empowering.

Whether you commit treason by going to therapy when your parents *would never!*, talk about salaries when your boss would rather you be exploited in silence, or share the ways you know your industry takes advantage of other people's vulnerability, find ways of creating change that feel liberating and authentic to you. As the saying goes, "The only way to deal with an unfree world is to become so absolutely free that your very existence is an act of rebellion."

Let yourself become the rebel-with-a-cause we desperately need.

I don't know what role this book will have played in your story or in our collective story. My hope is that it will remind us that our lives are not *all* our fault and that we have a responsibility to ourselves and each other as we create our future.

Thank you for walking this path with me. The book is complete, but the journey isn't over.

No one will ever know you better than *you* know you—your pulls, your wisdom, your gifts, and what's yours to contribute here. Trust your path. Trust in what *is* and what *will be*. Allow yourself to rewild, to return to who you are, to be who you have been all along.

You are your purpose.

The best self-help ultimately comes from within, but only when the external conditions allow our inner selves to flourish. Personal development and collective transformation are not separate and distinct; they are one and the same.

It's our collective responsibility to ensure we *all* get to be who we are and contribute what's ours to contribute.

We need you.

ACKNOWLEDGMENTS

Thank you for reading this book.

Time and energy are my favorite expressions of love, and I'm honored and grateful that you took the time and energy to sit with me in consideration of what is and what could be.

Thank you to Past Me, for finding ways to cope and make it through. Thank you to Future Me, for who you are pulling forth and encouraging to emerge; you never lost your faith in me. Thank you to Current Me, for allowing the process to be what it *is* and *wanted to be*, replacing force with flow and pressure with play. You've turned your wounds into wisdom and, in sharing your stories, done your Scariest Thing. I'm proud of us. We're throwing out the stories that power tells and writing our own. Keep writing.

Mark, you are the most beautiful human I've ever known. You are love incarnate. We are the more beautiful world my heart knows is possible.

Mom, despite your fear that I was writing a family exposé, you never attempted to dissuade me from doing what I needed to do. Your willingness to let me go forth into unchartered territory with unconditional acceptance has made me who I am.

To the friends who are a constant source of support, a safe place to land, and a salve for my insecurities, thank you, I love you. Brighid, Caitlin, Rasaja, Sandra, and Sara, I'm looking at you.

I'm grateful to my editors, especially Ace, Cass, and Chelsea, who added fuel to my fires, encouraged me to be unapologetic and stand strong in my experiences, expertise, and analysis. Your fortitude fueled my fierce. Ace, the MVP I didn't know I needed. Thanks for helping me land the plane.

I'm indebted to the thinkers and teachers who came before me, whose frameworks and reflections were foundational to my own: Dr. Barbara Love, bell hooks, Paolo Freire, and so many more. To those whose stories opened my own windows of understanding for me to realize I wasn't alone, Brené Brown, Devon Price, Glennon Doyle, and Johann Hari: your stories have made me more at home in my own. To the writers whose pages turn themselves in my hands, especially David Sedaris and Malcolm Gladwell: thank you for being the inspiration for my own. And to the folks who have gently encouraged me toward the next right step and story in my journey, especially Jess E, Jess L, Mushfiqa, Natalie, Nina, and Renee: thank you.

To the coaches who have walked alongside me as I excavated through tears, I am grateful for your questions, insights, containers, and mirroring. Laura, thank you for helping me to burn down my metaphorical barn. Lauryn, thank you for helping me to "give in," feel, and reconnect to my body. Lenora, your practical guidance made space for this project and helped me to create a new reality for myself. Meghan, thank you for holding space for me with compassion and generosity and helping me make sense of where the past meets the future. Andrea, thank you for helping me to understand that I make sense and for being my broken record of compassion. David, our conversation about aggressive self-control opened this door. Brian, you turned my office into a sacred space. Your faith emboldened mine. I love you.

To the Beta Readers and coconspirators who love me enough to be beautifully candid in your feedback, call out my bullshit, and invite me to go deeper, thank you. Jess, I'm grateful for every time you encouraged me to say the Quiet Part out loud. Renee, you made the power of collaboration over competition real. Nina, my fellow deep-sea fish, every conversation with you brings me home. Mom, Mark, Anand, and Heather, your feedback challenged me to think deeply about my ideas and how to present them in a way that would be both evocative and accessible. Nicole and Sandra, your insights were more instrumental than you know. Rasaja and Sara, every ounce of resonance reminds me we're on to something real.

To my team at The Center for Conscious Leadership, I couldn't have done it without your support. You are masterful at what you do. Caitlin and Rasaja, thank you for keeping things running smoothly while I balanced multiple projects and competing demands.

I'm thankful for my writer friends who, early mornings, late nights, and everywhere in between, create the life-giving community I need to sustain me. Jen, thank you for introducing me to LWS. Coonoor, thank you for introducing me to Eric and the Creator Institute.

I'm so appreciative of every person who invested in me and Go Love Yourself over the years. To every member of the community: I see you. I honor your journey, and I hope this resonates with you. To Emma, Heather, Jen, and Victoria, I couldn't have done it without your love, support, and company every single month. Dan and Léon, I won't forget the original kindness that made this happen. To Brighid, Lauren, Natalie, Renee, and Mark, thank you for being my sounding boards, my extra set of eyes and ears and brain cells along the way.

To everyone who preordered, you literally made this possible. Thank you for loving me and supporting this project. You turned a lifelong dream into a reality:

Alan Heymann, Alicia Ostarello, Alicia Smith, Alina Lux, Alyssa Cundari Roelans, Alyssa Goodman, Amanda Lynn Lorge, Amanda Powtir, Amanda Presgraves, Anand Boscha, Angela Tennison, Anna Boyd, Anna Schepcoff, Anne Lackritz, Ariel Sublett, Ashleigh Smith, Ashley Fontaine, Awate Idris, Becca Vanderberg, Beth Greaves, Betsy Nicchetta, Bob Peterson, Bradley Pferdehirt, Brandon Miller, Brigitte Granger, Brittany Wilson, Brittney (Shephard) Murphy, Caitlin Smith, Camilla Schaeffer, Cass Lauer, Cathy Ferris, Cerasela Cristei, Chaten Boscha, Chelsea Gaus, Christina Pierce, Christina Wegner, Cierrah West-Williams, Claire Muszalski, Colleen Johnson, Coonoor Behal, Courtney Hambell, Cristina Colquhoun, David Levinson, Deanna Ulino, Deepti Gudipati, Derek Eguae-Obazee, Diane Peterson, Eleanor Arkhipova, Elena Roberts, Emily Allen, Eric Koester, Erica Klingbeil, Erica Svendsen, Fernanda Andalaft, Heather Murphy, Heather Whelpley, Heide Cruikshank, Heidi Reed, Irv Barkley, Isabel Llerena, Jacqueline Smyth, Jaime Holmes, Jamie Baker, Jean Gasen, Jeannine Wrayno, Jeff Goldberg, Jen Welsh, Jennifer Grella, Jessica Auvenshine, Jessica Edelstein, Jessica Monterrosa, Jessica Yowonske, Jimmy Martinez, Jo Ann Casselberry, Joe Levitt, Joe Manno, Jordan Kerstetter, Julia Byrnes, Jyl D Camhi, Kailyn Henry, Kate Doherty, Kathryn Baker, Kayla Locklin, KC Kent, Kelly Forsythe, Kelly Harris Perin, Kelsey Dixon, Kenneth Boscha, Kiara Hernandez,

Kim-Ngan Nguyen, Kimberly Tomlinson, Kristiana Colleen de Leon, Kristina Kiefer, Kyle Peterson, Laura Adiletta, Laura Morrow, Lauren Ruggles, Lauren Williams, Leelynn Brady, Lenesa James, Lenora Edwards, Lisa Fain, Lisa Hope Tilstra, Maggie Owens, Mallory Grantz, Marilyn Edmunds Bowser, Mark Peterson, Megan Mastre, Melanie Martin, Melissa Ann Kerwin O'Neil, Micha Goebig, Michelle Klaty, Molly K. West, Naomi Perl, Natasha Tokowicz, Nathaniel Wetzel, Nepal O'Connor, Nicholas Farruggia, Nick Globig, Nickie Smith, Nicole Bryan, Nicole Mason, Nina Kuzniak, Noah Green, Pam Krultiz, Paula Lynch, Pete Haas, Peter Cheney, Rachel Rogowin, Rachel Van Sickle, Rasaja Hart, Rebecca Podobnik, Rebecca Sklepovich, Rebecca Torres, Renee Powers, Richard Chan, Romnee Auerbach, Ruth Gaus, Sandra Sarucia, Sara Arnett, Sara Parli, Sarah Akbar, Sarah Bergstein, Sarah Eaton, Sarita Baker, Shaelyn Watson, Shanna Stryker, Shannon Bolger, Shayna Hammond, Shereen Jegtvig, Shirley Coile, Stacy Harris, Stephanie Robey, Steve Okon, Sue Podobnik, Susan Seah, Suzanne Bozart, Suzanne Weller, Tabitha Snyder, Tish Oye, Vicky Mennare, Vicky Wong, and Vincent Loran.

Thank you.

I love you.

APPENDIX

INTRODUCTION

CapitalOne. 2020. “Big Picture Thinking Leads to the Right Money Mindset.” Accessed April 27, 2023. https://www.capitalone.com/about/newsroom/mind-over-money-survey/.

Carlson, Richard. 2006. *You Can Be Happy No Matter What: Five Principles for Keeping Life in Perspective*. Novato, CA: New World Library.

Freire, Paulo. 2014. *Pedagogy of the Oppressed: 30th Anniversary Edition*. Camden, UK: Bloomsbury Academic Publishing.

Gallup. 2022. *State of the Global Workplace 2022 Report*. Washington, DC: Gallup Workplace. https://www.gallup.com/workplace/349484/state-of-the-global-workplace.aspx.

hooks, bell. 2014. *Feminism Is for Everybody*. Oxfordshire, UK: Routledge.

Love, Barbara J. 2013. “Developing a Liberatory Consciousness.” In *Readings for Diversity and Social Justice*. Edited by Marianne Adams, Warren J. Blumenfeld, Heather W. Hackman, Madeline L. Peters, and Ximena Zuniga, 599–603. Oxfordshire, UK: Routledge.

Smolak, Linda. 2004. “Body image in children and adolescents: where do we go from here?” *Body Image* 1, no. 1: 15–27. https://doi.org10.1016/S1740-1445(03)00008-1.

CHAPTER 1: WAKING UP

Brown, Brené. 2012. “Brené Brown—Worthiness.” Sounds True. August 7, 2012. 1:05. https://www.youtube.com/watch?v=BHHghrHUGOI&ab_channel=SoundsTrue.

Coloroso, Barbara. 2003. *The Bully, the Bullied, and the Bystander: From Preschool to High School—How Parents and Teachers Can Help Break the Cycle*. New York: William Morrow Paperbacks.

Dalai Lama [Tenzin Gyatso] and Desmond Tutu. 2016. *The Book of Joy: Lasting Happiness in a Changing World.* With Douglas Abrams. New York: Avery.

Eisenstein, Charles. 2013. *The More Beautiful World Our Hearts Know Is Possible (Sacred Activism).* Berkeley, CA: North Atlantic Books.

Miller, Alice. 1979. "The drama of the gifted child and the psycho-analyst's narcissistic disturbance." *International Journal of Psychoanalysis 60*, no. 1: 47–58. https://pubmed.ncbi.nlm.nih.gov/457342/.

Weaver, Janelle. 2011. "Social before Birth: Twins First Interact With Each Other as Fetuses." *Scientific American*, January 2011. https://www.scientificamerican.com/article/social-before-birth/.

CHAPTER 2: SOCIALIZATION

Brown, Brené. 2012. "Listening to Shame—Brené Brown." TED. March 16, 2012. 20:39. https://www.youtube.com/watch?v=psN1DORYYVo&ab_channel=TED.

Cooley, Charles. 1908. *Human Nature and the Social Order.* New York: Charles Scribner's Sons.

Curran, Thomas, and Andrew Hill. 2019. "Perfectionism Is Increasing Over Time: A Meta-Analysis of Birth Cohort Differences from 1989 to 2016." *American Psychological Association* 145, no. 4: 410–429. http://dx.doi.org/10.1037/bul0000138.

Flanagan, Nancy. 2017. "When Teachers Use Shame as a Disciplinary Tool." *Opinion* (blog), *Education Week.* November 4, 2017. https://www.edweek.org/education/opinion-when-teachers-use-shame-as-a-disciplinary-tool/2017/11.

Hagerman, Margaret Ann. 2014. "White families and race: colour-blind and colour-conscious approaches to white racial socialization." *Ethnic and Racial Studies* 37, no. 14: 2598–2614. https://doi.org/10.1080/01419870.2013.848289.

Harris, Matthew A., Caroline E. Brett, Wendy Johnson, and Ian J. Deary. 2016. "Personality Stability from Age 14 to Age 77 Years." *Psychology and Aging* 31, no. 8 (December): 862–874. https://doi.org/10.1037%2Fpag0000133.

Mead, George Herbert. 1934. *Mind, Self, and Society.* Chicago: University of Chicago Press.

Okun, Tema. 1999. "White Supremacy Culture." *White Supremacy Culture.* https://www.whitesupremacyculture.info/uploads/4/3/5/7/43579015/okun_-_white_sup_culture_2020.pdf.

Robinson, Ken. 2009. *The Element: How Finding Your Passion Changes Everything.* New York: Penguin Publishing Group.

Schneiderman, Kim. 2020. "Healing the Wounds That Bind, and Why They Don't Define Us." *Psychology Today* (blog). April 20, 2022. https://www.psychologytoday.com/intl/blog/the-novel-perspective/202204/healing-the-wounds-bind-and-why-they-dont-define-us.

Schwartz, Richard. 2023. "The Larger Self." *Articles* (blog), IFS Institute. Accessed May 1, 2023. https://ifs-institute.com/resources/articles/larger-self.

CHAPTER 3: AMERICAN DREAMING

Cammett, Ann. 2014. "Deadbeat Dads and Welfare Queens: How Metaphor Shapes Poverty Law." *CUNY School of Law* 34: 233–265. https://academicworks.cuny.edu/cgi/viewcontent.cgi?article=1031&context=cl_pubs.

Ford, Brett Q., Julia O. Dmitrieva, Daniel Heller, Yulia Chentsova-Dutton, Igor Grossmann, Maya Tamir, Yukiko Uchida, Birgit Koopmann-Holm, Victoria A. Floerke, Meike Uhrig, Tatiana Bokhan, and Iris B. Mauss. 2015. "Culture shapes whether the pursuit of happiness predicts higher or lower well-being." *Journal of Experimental Psychology: General* 144, no. 6 (December): 1053–1062. https://doi.org/10.1037/xge0000108.

Isaacs, Julia. 2008. "International Comparisons of Economic Mobility." In *Getting Ahead or Losing Ground: Economic Mobility in America*. Edited by Julia Isaacs, Isabel Sawhill, and Ron Haskins, 37–46. Washington DC: Brookings.

Kristof, Nicholas. 2020. "Pull Yourself Up by Bootstraps? Go Ahead, Try It." *The New York Times*, February 19, 2020. https://www.nytimes.com/2020/02/19/opinion/economic-mobility.html.

New York University Staff. 2018. "Lack of social mobility 'more of an occupational hazard' than previously known." *Social Sciences* (blog), Phys.org. September 3, 2018. https://phys.org/news/2018-09-lack-social-mobility-occupational-hazard.html.

Peterson, Mike. 2020. "An iPhone Makes You 76% More Attractive on Dating Apps." *AppleInsider* (blog). August 28, 2020. https://appleinsider.com/articles/20/08/28/an-iphone-makes-you-76-more-attractive-on-dating-apps.

Szalavitz, Maia. 2018. "What's behind rich people pretending they're self-made?" *The Guardian*, January 28, 2018. https://www.theguardian.com/us-news/2018/jan/29/rich-people-wealth-america.

The Knot Research & Insights Team. 2023. "The Knot 2022 Real Weddings Study: Taking an in-depth Look at Weddings in 2022." *The Knot*. https://www.theknot.com/content/wedding-data-insights/real-weddings-study.

CHAPTER 4: SELF-HELP IS INEVITABLE

Carlyle, Thomas. 1831. *Sartor Resartus: The Life and Opinions of Herr Teufelsdrockh*. Salt Lake City: Project Gutenburg Literary Archive Foundation. https://www.gutenberg.org/files/1051/1051-h/1051-h.htm.

Given, Florence. 2020. *Women Don't Owe You Pretty.* London: Cassell Publishing.

Grand View Research. 2022. "Personal Development Market Size, Share & Trends Analysis Report by Instrument (Books, e-Platforms, Personal Coaching/Training), by Focus Area, by Region, and Segment Forecasts, 2022–2030." San Francisco: Grandview Research.
https://www.grandviewresearch.com/industry-analysis/personal-development-market.

Kelly, Mary. 2014. "Ask a Man." *Awful Library Books* (blog). November 18, 2014. https://awfullibrarybooks.net/ask-a-man/.

Kelly, Mary. 2019. "Homemaking as a Religious Experience." *Awful Library Books* (blog). August 7, 2019.
https://awfullibrarybooks.net/homemaking-as-a-religious-experience/.

Kerber, Linda. 1976. "The Republican Mother: Women and the Enlightenment—An American Perspective." *American Quarterly* 28, no. 2 (Summer): 187–205. https://doi.org/10.2307/2712349.

Ngozi, Chimamanda. 2014. *We Should All Be Feminists.* New York: Knopf Doubleday.

Rose, Jane E. 1995. "Conduct Books for Women, 1830–1860: A Rationale for Women's Conduct and Domestic Role in America." In *Nineteenth-Century Women Learn to Write (Feminist Issues: Practice, Policies, Theory)*, edited by Catherine Hobbs, 37–58. Charlottesville, VA: University Press of Virginia.

Salerno, Steve. 2005. *Sham: How the Self-Help Movement Made America Helpless.* New York: Crown.

Smith-Rosenburg, Caroll. 1998. "The Cult of Domesticity." In *The Reader's Companion to US Women's History*, edited by Wilma Mankiller, Gwendolyn Mink, Marysa Navarro, Barbara Smith, and Gloria Steinem, 139. New York: Houghton Mifflin Company.

Storr, Will. 2018. *Selfie: How We Became So Self-Obsessed and What It's Doing to Us.* London: Picador.

Taylor, Sonya Renee. 2018. *The Body Is Not an Apology.* Oakland, CA: Berrett-Koehler Publishers.

Welter, Barbara. 1966. "The Cult of True Womanhood: 1820–1860." *American Quarterly* 18, no. 2 (Summer): 151–174.
https://doi.org/10.2307/2712349.

CHAPTER 5: IT'S NOT WORKING

American Psychological Association. 2017. "Fat Shaming in the Doctor's Office Can Be Mentally and Physically Harmful." Accessed April 27, 2023.
https://www.apa.org/news/press/releases/2017/08/fat-shaming.

ANAD. 2023. "Eating Disorder Statistics." *National Association of Anorexia Nervosa and Associated Disorders.*
https://anad.org/eating-disorders-statistics/.

Argov, Sherry. 2002. *Why Men Love Bitches: From Doormat to Dreamgirl—A Woman's Guide to Holding Her Own in a Relationship.* New York: Simon and Schuster.

Belluz, Julia. 2016. "The problem with diet books written by doctors." *Science* (blog), *Vox*. April 27, 2016. https://www.vox.com/2016/3/24/11296168/down-with-diet-books.

Benton, David, and Hayley Young. 2017. "Reducing Calorie Intake May Not Help You Lose Body Weight." *Perspectives on Psychological Science* 12, no. 5 (September): 703–714. https://doi.org/10.1177%2F1745691617690878.

Berlant, Lauren. 2011. *Cruel Optimism*. Durham, NC: Duke University Press Books.

Cox, Josie. 2021. "Why women are more burned out than men." *BBC—Worklife* (blog), BBC. October 3, 2021. https://gdc.unicef.org/resource/why-women-are-more-burned-out-men.

de Beauvoir, Simone. 2012. *The Second Sex*. New York: Knopf Doubleday.

Devlin, Keith. 2009. "Top 10 Reasons Why the BMI Is Bogus." *Your Health* (blog), NPR. July 4, 2009. https://www.npr.org/templates/story/story.php?storyId=106268439.

Ferreira, Ana Julia. 2021. "The Minnesota Starvation Experiment—How It Happened and What It Taught Us." *Maze*, May 2021. https://maze.wp.st-andrews.ac.uk/2021/05/04/the-minnesota-starvation-experiment-how-it-happened-and-what-it-taught-us/.

Fraga, Juli. 2018. "For Many People, Especially Women—Weight Loss Is Not a Happy Ending." *Women's Wellness* (blog), *Healthline*. August 22, 2018. https://www.healthline.com/health/losing-weight-and-relationships.

Gil, Chantal. 2021. "The Starvation Experiment." *Center for Eating Disorders Blog* (blog), *DukeHealth*. Accessed April 27, 2023. https://eatingdisorders.dukehealth.org/education/resources/starvation-experiment.

Gill, Rosalind, and Ana Sofia Elias. 2014. "Awaken your incredible: Love your body discourses and postfeminist contradictions." *International Journal of Media & Cultural Politics* 10, no. 2: 179–188. https://doi.org/10.1386/macp.10.2.179_1.

Gonick, Marina. 2004. "The 'Mean Girl' Crisis: Problematizing Representations of Girls' Friendships." *Feminism & Psychology* 14: 395–400. https://doi.org/10.1177/0959353504044641.

Hemmingsson, E. 2014. "A new model of the role of psychological and emotional distress in promoting obesity: conceptual review with implications for treatment and prevention." *Obesity Reviews* 15, no. 9 (September): 769–779. https://doi.org/10.1111/obr.12197.

Krivkovich, Alexis, Wei Wei Liu, Hilary Nguyen, Ishanaa Rambachan, Nicole Robinson, Monne Williams, and Lareina Yee. 2022. "Women in the Workplace 2022." New York: McKinsey & Company. https://www.mckinsey.com/featured-insights/diversity-and-inclusion/women-in-the-workplace.

LaRosa, John. 2021. "$10.4 Billion Self-Improvement Market Pivots to Virtual Delivery During the Pandemic." *Market Research Blog* (blog), MarketResearch.com. August 2, 2021.
https://blog.marketresearch.com/10.4-billion-self-improvement-market-pivots-to-virtual-delivery-during-the-pandemic.

Lean, M.E.J., and D. Malkova. 2016. "Altered gut and adipose tissue hormones in overweight and obese individuals: cause or consequence?" *International Journal of Obesity* 40, no. 4 (April): 622–632.
https://doi.org/10.1038/ijo.2015.220.

Leigh, Suzanne. 2019. "Anorexia Nervosa Comes in All Sizes, Including Plus Size." *Research* (blog), University of California San Francisco. November 6, 2019.
https://www.ucsf.edu/news/2019/11/415871/anorexia-nervosa-comes-all-sizes-including-plus-size.

Olito, Frank. 2019. "How the divorce rate has changed over the last 150 years." *Lifestyle* (blog), *Insider*. January 30, 2019.
https://www.insider.com/divorce-rate-changes-over-time-2019-1.

Omer, Tahir. 2020. "The causes of obesity: an in-depth review." *Advances in Obesity, Weight Management & Control* 10, no. 3 (July): 90–94.
https://doi.org/10.15406/aowmc.2020.10.00312.

Orgad, Shani, and Rosalind Gill. 2022. "How Confidence Became a Cult." *The Atlantic*, March 2022.
https://www.theatlantic.com/culture/archive/2022/03/limits-women-confidence-workplace-inequality/626562/.

US Census Bureau. 2020. "US Marriage and Divorce Rates Declined in Last 10 Years." US Marriage and Divorce Rates by State. Accessed April 27, 2023.
https://www.census.gov/library/stories/2020/12/united-states-marriage-and-divorce-rates-declined-last-10-years.html.

Vogel, Lauren. 2019. "Fat shaming Is making people sicker and heavier." *Canadian Medical Association Journal* 191, no. 23 (June): 649.
https://doi.org/10.1503%2Fcmaj.109-5758.

Warner, Judith, Nora Ellmann, and Diana Boesch. 2018. *The Women's Leadership Gap: Women's Leadership by the Numbers*. Washington, DC: Center for American Progress.

Weiner, Jennifer. 2021. "The Weight-Loss Industry Is Coming for Our Post-Lockdown Bodies." *The New York Times*, May 5, 2021.
https://www.nytimes.com/2021/05/05/opinion/culture/dieting-covid-weight-loss.html.

Witcomb, Gemma. 2017. "Why people with eating disorders are often obsessed with food." *Health* (blog), *The Conversation*. May 15, 2017.
https://theconversation.com/why-people-with-eating-disorders-are-often-obsessed-with-food-77509.

Wolpert, Stuart. 2007. "Dieting does not work, UCLA researchers report." *Science + Technology* (blog), UCLA. April 3, 2007.
https://newsroom.ucla.edu/releases/Dieting-Does-Not-Work-UCLA-Researchers-7832.

CHAPTER 6: THE VULNERABILITY TRAP

Ashley, Shannon. 2021. "How Many Times Can Rachel Hollis Apologize and Still Miss the Point?" *Honestly Yours* (blog). April 7, 2021. https://medium.com/honestly-yours/how-many-times-can-rachel-hollis-apologize-yet-still-miss-the-point-f892a425ade1.

Burg, Bob. 2010. *Endless Referrals*. New York: McGraw Hill.

Elkins, Kathleen. 2015. "From poverty to a $3 billion fortune—the incredible rags-to-riches story of Oprah Winfrey." *Careers* (blog), *Insider*. May 28, 2015. https://www.businessinsider.com/rags-to-riches-story-of-oprah-winfrey-2015-5.

Gallo, Carmine. 2017. "Why We're Wired to Love Rags-to-Riches Stories." *Inc. Life* (blog), Inc. April 21, 2017. https://www.inc.com/carmine-gallo/why-were-wired-to-love-rags-to-riches-stories.html.

Grindell, Samantha. 2021. "Rachel Hollis is in hot water for comparing herself to Harriet Tubman, but it's not the self-help author's first controversy. Here's a complete timeline." *Lifestyle* (blog), *Insider*. April 30, 2021. https://www.insider.com/a-complete-timeline-of-rachel-hollis-controversies-2021-4.

Griswold, Kylee. 2021. "Rachel Hollis's Problem Isn't Privilege, It's an Anti-Christian Gospel." *Culture* (blog), *The Federalist*. May 1, 2021. https://thefederalist.com/2021/05/01/rachel-holliss-problem-isnt-privilege-its-an-anti-christian-gospel/.

Gyatso, Geshe Kelsang. 2016. *How to Transform Your Life: A Blissful Journey*. New York: Tharpa Publications.

Inc Staff. 2016. "How Tony Robbins Created an Empire by Being the Most Confident Man on Earth." *Innovate* (blog), Inc. September 21, 2016. https://www.inc.com/magazine/201610/most-confident-man-tony-robbins.html.

Itani, Omar. 2021. "It's Time You Realize That Most Self-Help Gurus Are Total Frauds." *Mind Cafe* (blog). July 30, 2021. https://medium.com/mind-cafe/its-time-you-realize-that-most-self-help-gurus-are-total-frauds-7eef026617fe.

Kiesling, Lydia. 2022. "Rags-to-Riches Stories Are Actually Kind of Disturbing." *The New York Times*, April 5, 2022. https://www.nytimes.com/2022/04/05/magazine/billionaire-books.html.

Kiyosaki, Robert. 2022. *Rich Dad Poor Dad: What the Rich Teach Their Kids About Money That the Poor and Middle Class Do Not!* Scottsdale, AZ: Plata Publishing.

Lewtan, Lisa. 2015. *Busy, Stressed, and Food Obsessed!: Calm Down, Ditch Your Inner Critic-Bitch, and Finally Figure Out What Your Body Needs to Thrive*. Healthy, Happy & Hip.

McNeal, Stephanie. 2021. "Rachel and Dave Hollis Built An Empire From Scratch. Now They Are Destroying It." *Internet Culture* (blog), *Buzzfeed News*. November 5, 2021. https://www.buzzfeednews.com/article/stephaniemcneal/rachel-hollis-dave-hollis-instagram-rant.

McNeal, Stephanie. 2020. "Rachel Hollis Has Apologized After Posting a Maya Angelou Quote Without Attribution." *Internet Culture* (blog), *Buzzfeed News*. April 27, 2020.
https://www.buzzfeednews.com/article/stephaniemcneal/rachel-hollis-apology-maya-angelou-quote.

Novak, Matt. 2016. "The Untold Story of Napoleon Hill, the Greatest Self-Help Scammer of All Time." *Tech* (blog), *Gizmodo*.
https://gizmodo.com/the-untold-story-of-napoleon-hill-the-greatest-self-he-1789385645.

Powers, Renee M. 2012. "Postfeminist social networks: Traditional femininity in life-coaching blogs and image-aggregating websites." Dissertation. Northern Illinois University.
https://www.proquest.com/openview/9ef61003a3976054684b92e216eb94f3/1?pq-origsite=gscholar&cbl=18750.

Rosman, Katherine. 2021. "Girl, Wash Your Timeline." *The New York Times*, April 29, 2021.
https://www.nytimes.com/2021/04/29/style/rachel-hollis-tiktok-video.html.

Wolfson, Sam. 2020. "'I'm living my highest purpose:' mogul monk Jay Shetty on free market teachings." *The Guardian*, September 12, 2020.
https://www.theguardian.com/lifeandstyle/2020/sep/12/im-living-my-highest-purpose-mogul-monk-jay-shetty-on-free-market-teachings.

Young, Valerie. 2021. *The Secret Thoughts of Successful Women: Why Capable People Suffer from the Imposter Syndrome and How to Thrive in Spite of It.* Sydney: Currency.

CHAPTER 7: THE PARADOX OF HOPE

Colombo, Desiree, Javier Fernandez-Alvarez, Carlos Suso-Ribera, Pietro Cipresso, Azucena Garcia-Palacios, Giuseppe Riva, and Cristina Botella. 2020. "Biased Affective Forecasting: A Potential Mechanism That Enhances Resilience and Well-Being." *Frontier Psychology* 11 (June).
https://doi.org/10.3389/fpsyg.2020.01333.

Drexler, Madeline. 2014. "The Happiness Metric: Bhutan's experiment in turning principle into policy." *Tricycle*, Fall 2014.
https://tricycle.org/magazine/bhutan-happiness-metric/.

Frank, Robert. 2012. "The Perfect Income for Happiness? It's $161,000." CNBC, November 30, 2012.
https://www.cnbc.com/id/50027184.

GNH Centre Bhutan. 2023. "History of GNH." Accessed April 27, 2023.
https://www.gnhcentrebhutan.org/history-of-gnh/.

GNH Centre Bhutan. 2023. "The 4 Pillars of GNH." Accessed April 27, 2023.
https://www.gnhcentrebhutan.org/the-4-pillars-of-gnh/.

Kahneman, Daniel, and Angus Deaton. 2010. "High income improves evaluation of life but not emotional well-being." *Proceedings of the National Academy of Sciences* 107, no. 38 (September): 16489–16493.
https://doi.org/10.1073/pnas.1011492107.

Leaver, Kate. 2018. "Finland came out on top in the 2018 World Happiness Report, but what if the Finnish people don't agree?" *BBC Travel* (blog), BBC. June 18, 2018. https://www.bbc.com/travel/article/20180617-why-the-finns-dont-want-to-be-happy.

Miller, Tarah. 2016. "6 reasons Bhutan might be the world's most liveable country." *The Journal* (blog), *Intrepid Travel.* January 11, 2016. https://www.intrepidtravel.com/adventures/bhutan-liveable/.

Morton, Caitlin. 2022. "These Are the Happiest Countries in the World." *Inspiration* (blog), *Conde Nast Traveler.* March 31, 2022. https://www.cntraveler.com/gallery/the-10-happiest-countries-in-the-world.

National Conservation Division. 2004. *A Landscape Conservation Plan: a way forward.* Thimpu, Bhutan: Department of Forestry Services. https://wwfasia.awsassets.panda.org/downloads/b2c2_20landscapeconservation_20plan.pdf.

Price, Devon. 2021. *Laziness Does Not Exist: A Defense of the Exhausted, Exploited, and Overworked.* New York: Atria Books.

Tam, Ruth, and Michelle Aslam. 2022. "If your spending is eating your savings, you might be experiencing 'lifestyle creep.'" *Life Kit* (blog), NPR. July 15, 2022. https://www.npr.org/2022/07/13/1111300716/lifestyle-creep-definition.

WWF. 2021. "Bhutan Biological Conservation Complex." Accessed April 27, 2023. https://www.wwfbhutan.org.bt/projects_/bhutan_biological_conservation_complex/.

Yu, Jessica. 2023. "Why Are Nordic Countries So Happy?" *Community* (blog), *Business Review at Berkeley.* March 7, 2023. https://businessreview.berkeley.edu/why-are-nordic-countries-so-happy/.

CHAPTER 8: WINDOWS OF UNDERSTANDING

Agrawal, Miki. 2015. *Do Cool Sh*t: Quit Your Day Job, Start Your Own Business, and Live Happily Ever After.* New York: Harper Business.

Bateson, Gregory, Don Jackson, Jay Haley, and John Weakland. 1956. "Toward a theory of schizophrenia." *Behavioral Science* 1, no. 4: 251–264. https://doi.org/10.1002/bs.3830010402.

Cameron, Julia. 2002. *The Artist's Way.* Los Angeles: TarcherPerigee.

Doyle, Glennon. 2020. *Untamed.* New York: The Dial Press.

Eriksen, Karen. 2007. "Counseling the 'Imperial' Client: Translating Robert Kegan." *Family Journal: Counseling and Therapy for Couples and Families* 15, no. 2 (April): 174–182.
http://dx.doi.org/10.1177/1066480706298919.

Kegan, Robert. 1982. *The Evolving Self: Problem and Process in Human Development.* Cambridge, MA: Harvard University Press.

LaPorte, Danielle. 2014. *The Desire Map: A Guide to Creating Goals with Soul.* Louisville, CO: Sounds True.

Mallel, Natali. 2017a. "Part 1: How to Be An Adult—Kegan's Theory of Adult Development." *Natali Mallel (Morad)* (blog). September 28, 2017. https://medium.com/@NataliMorad/how-to-be-an-adult-kegans-theory-of-adult-development-d63f4311b553.

Mallel, Natali. 2017b. "Part 2: How to Be An Adult—Kegan's Theory of Adult Development." *Natali Mallel (Morad)* (blog). November 20, 2017. https://medium.com/@NataliMorad/part-2-how-to-be-an-adult-kegans-theory-of-adult-development-ddf057b4517b.

Mallel, Natali. 2020. "Part 3: How to Be An Adult—Kegan's Theory of Adult Development." *Natali Mallel (Morad)* (blog). April 23, 2020. https://medium.com/@NataliMorad/part-3-how-to-be-an-adult-kegans-theory-of-adult-development-3ed9f2340f9f.

Pruyn, Peter. 2010. "An Overview of Constructive Developmental Theory (CDT): How do adults grow?" *Peter Pryun* (blog). June 8, 2010. https://peterpruyn.medium.com/an-overview-of-constructive-developmental-theory-cdt-667f3e015cc1.

Sincero, Jen. 2013. *You Are a Badass: How to Stop Doubting Your Greatness and Start Living an Awesome Life.* Philadelphia: Running Press.

CHAPTER 9: NAVIGATING OPPRESSION

Armstrong, Elizabeth A., Laura Hamilton, Elizabeth M. Armstrong, and J. Lotus Seeley. 2014. "'Good Girls:' Gender, Social Class, and Slut Discourse on Campus." *Social Psychology Quarterly* 77, no. 2 (May): 100–122. https://doi.org/10.1177/0190272514521220.

Asare, Janice Gassam. 2022. "Exploring the Ways Internalized Oppression Shows Up in the Workplace." *Diversity, Equity & Inclusion* (blog), *Forbes.* January 28, 2022. https://www.forbes.com/sites/janicegassam/2022/01/28/exploring-the-ways-internalized-oppression-shows-up-in-the-workplace/?sh=527eb1d95f09.

Carlsson, Magnus, and Stefan Eriksson. 2019. "Age discrimination in hiring decisions: Evidence from a field experiment in the labor market." *Labour Economics* 59 (August): 173–183. https://doi.org/10.1016/j.labeco.2019.03.002.

Crenshaw, Kimberlé. 1989. "Demarginalizing the Intersection of Race and Sex: A Black Feminist Critique of Antidiscrimination Doctrine, Feminist Theory and Antiracist Politics." *University of Chicago Legal Forum* 1, no. 8: 139–167. https://chicagounbound.uchicago.edu/cgi/viewcontent.cgi?article=1052&context=uclf.

David, E.J.R., and Annie Derthick. 2013. "What Is Internalized Oppression, and So What?" In *Internalized Oppression: The Psychology of Marginalized Groups*, edited by E.J.R. David. New York: Springer Publishing Company.

Doyle, Glennon. 2020. *Untamed.* New York: The Dial Press.

Doyle, Laura. 2001. *The Surrendered Wife: A Practical Guide to Finding Intimacy, Passion, and Peace.* Chicago: Touchstone.

Frankel, Lois. 2014. *Nice Girls Don't Get the Corner Office: Unconscious Mistakes Women Make That Sabotage Their Careers*. New York: Balance.

Gray, John. 2009. *Men Are from Mars, Women Are from Venus: The Classic Guide to Understanding the Opposite Sex*. New York: HarperCollins.

Harvey, Steve. 2014. *Act Like a Lady, Think Like a Man, Expanded Edition: What Men Really Think About Love, Relationships, Intimacy, and Commitment*. New York: Amistad.

Hollis, Rachel. 2018. *Girl, Wash Your Face: Stop Believing the Lies About Who You Are so You Can Become Who You Were Meant to Be*. Nashville, TN: Thomas Nelson.

Nagoski, Emily, and Amelia Nagoski. 2019. *Burnout: The Secret to Unlocking the Stress Cycle*. New York: Ballantine Books.

Nieto, Leticia, and Margot Boyer. 2006. "Understanding Oppression: Strategies in Addressing Power and Privilege." *Colors NW Magazine*, March 2006. https://beyondinclusionbeyondempowerment.com/wp-content/uploads/2019/12/nieto-articles-understanding-oppression-2006.pdf.

Oh, DongWon, Eldar Shafir, and Alexander Todorov. 2020. "Economic status cues from clothes affect perceived competence from faces." *Nature Human Behavior* 4, no. 3 (March): 287–293.
https://doi.org/10.1038/s41562-019-0782-4.

Sandberg, Sheryl. 2013. *Lean In: Women, Work, and the Will to Lead*. New York: Knopf Doubleday.

CHAPTER 10: SELF-HELP IS A CAPITALIST RELIGION

Bergoglio, Jorge Mario. 2016. "Untitled speech during mass at Casa Santa Marta." Speech delivered May 2016 in Vatican City.

Bowles, Nellie. 2020. "God Is Dead. So Is the Office. These People Want to Save Both." *The New York Times*, August 28, 2020.
https://www.nytimes.com/2020/08/28/business/remote-work-spiritual-consultants.html.

Bucholz, Rogene A. 1983. "The Protestant Ethic as an Ideological Justification of Capitalism." *Journal of Business Ethics* 2, no 1 (February): 51–60.
https://doi.org/10.1007/BF00382713.

Byrne, Rhonda. 2006. *The Secret*. New York: Atria Books.

Carrette, Jeremy and Richard King. 2004. *Selling Spirituality: The Silent Takeover of Religion*. Oxfordshire, UK: Routledge.

Chodron, Pema. 2023. "How to Practice Tonglen." *Lion's Roar*, January 2023.
https://www.lionsroar.com/how-to-practice-tonglen/.

Christian Publishing House Staff. 2022. "PROSPERITY THEOLOGY: Does God Want You to Be Rich?" *Christian Publishing House Blog* (blog). October 6, 2022.
https://christianpublishinghouse.co/2022/10/06/prosperity-theology-does-god-want-you-to-be-rich/.

Copeland, Kenneth. 2012. *The Laws of Prosperity.* Fort Worth: Kenneth Copeland Ministries.

Covey, Steven. 2004. *The 7 Habits of Highly Effective People: Powerful Lessons in Personal Change.* New York: Free Press.

Covey, Steven. 2004. *The Divine Center.* Salt Lake City: Deseret Book Company.

Crispin, Jessa. 2020. "Thought capitalism couldn't get worse? Meet the workplace 'spiritual consultants.'" *The Guardian*, September 6, 2020. https://www.theguardian.com/commentisfree/2020/sep/06/office-spiritual-consultants-capitalism.

Fosslien, Liz, and Mollie West Duffy. 2022. "Stop Telling Employees to Be Resilient." *MITSloan Management Review*, April 2022. https://sloanreview.mit.edu/article/stop-telling-employees-to-be-resilient/.

Hicks, Esther, and Jerry Hicks. 2004. *Ask and It Is Given: Learning to Manifest Your Desires.* Carlsbad, CA: Hay House.

Marx, Karl. 1844. "A Contribution to the Critique of Hegel's Philosophy of Right." *Deutsch-Französische Jahrbücher* 7 and 10 (February). https://www.marxists.org/archive/marx/works/1843/critique-hpr/intro.htm.

Mascari, John. 2006. "US Conscientious Objectors in World War II." *Friends Journal* (blog). December 1, 2006. https://www.friendsjournal.org/u-s-conscientious-objectors-world-war-ii/.

Murphy, Justin. 2017. "Quakers fought for women's suffrage and to abolish slavery." *Extras* (blog), *Democrat & Chronicle*. April 23, 2017. https://www.democratandchronicle.com/story/insider/extras/2017/04/23/quakers-abolitionism-and-suffrage/100648372/.

McSloy, Steven Paul. 2018. "'Because the Bible tells me so': Manifest Destiny and American Indians." *Archives* (blog), ICT News. September 12, 2018. https://ictnews.org/archive/because-the-bible-tells-me-so-manifest-destiny-and-american-indians.

Peale, Norman Vincent. 2003. *The Power of Positive Thinking.* Chicago: Touchstone Books.

Peale, Norman Vincent. 2007. *A Guide to Confident Living.* Chicago: Touchstone Books.

Peale, Norman Vincent. 2022. *You Can if You Think You Can.* Mumbai, India: Grapevine India.

Rae, Noel. 2018. "How Christian Slaveholders Used the Bible to Justify Slavery." Adapted from The Great Stain: Witnessing American Slavery, edited by The Overlook Press, Peter Mayer Publishers, Inc., and Time. New York: Abrams Books. https://time.com/5171819/christianity-slavery-book-excerpt/.

Robertson, Pat. 2017. *The Secret Kingdom: Your Path to Peace, Love, and Financial Security.* Self-published.

Ruether, Rosemary Radford. 2014. "Sexism and Misogyny in the Christian Tradition: Liberating Alternatives." *Buddhist-Christian Studies* 34: 83–94. https://doi.org/10.1353/bcs.2014.0020.

Tilton, Robert. 1988. *The Power to Create Wealth.* Tulsa, OK: Robert Tilton Ministries.

Waldrep, Bob. 1998. "The Shifting Paradigms of Stephen Covey." *New Age* (blog), Watchman Fellowship. November 1998. http://web.archive.org/web/20111121063212/ http://www.wfial.org/index.cfm?fuseaction=artNewAge.article_2.

Williams, Anthony Alan John. 2016. *Christian Socialism as Political Ideology: The Formation of the British Christian Left, 1877–1945.* London: Bloomsbury.

CHAPTER 11: PRIVATIZING THE SELF

Alcohol and Drug Foundation. 2021. "MDMA-assisted therapy for PTSD edges closer." Accessed April 27, 2023. https://adf.org.au/insights/mdma-ptsd/.

Almohammed, Omar A., Abdulaziz A Alsalem, Abdullah A. Almangour, Lama H. Alotaibi, Majed S. Al Yami, Leanne Lai. 2022. "Antidepressants and health-related quality of life (HRQoL) for patients with depression: Analysis of the medical expenditure panel survey from the United States." *PLOS ONE* 17, no. 4 (April). https://doi.org/10.1371/journal.pone.0265928.

Carrette, Jeremy, and Richard King. 2004. *Selling Spirituality: The Silent Takeover of Religion.* Oxfordshire, UK: Routledge.

Charlton, James I. 2000. *Nothing about Us Without Us: Disability Oppression and Empowerment.* Berkeley, CA: University of California Press.

Cleveland Clinic. 2022. "Gamma-Aminobutyric Acid (GABA)." Accessed April 25, 2022. https://my.clevelandclinic.org/health/articles/22857-gamma-aminobutyric-acid-gaba.

Hari, Johann. 2018. *Lost Connections: Why You're Depressed and How to Find Hope.* London: Bloomsbury.

Harrogate, Franki. 2019. "Psychology Is for White People: How White Supremacy Is Built into Our Discipline." Preprint. Athabasca University. https://www.researchgate.net/publication/333093236_Psychology_is_for_White_People_How_White_Supremacy_is_Built_Into_Our_Discipline.

Harvard University. 2023. "Scientific Racism." *Harvard Library.* https://library.harvard.edu/confronting-anti-black-racism/scientific-racism.

Henrich, Joseph, Steven J. Heine, and Ara Norenzayan. 2010. "The weirdest people in the world?" *Behavioral Brain Science* 33, no. 2–3 (June): 61–83. https://doi.org/10.1017/s0140525x0999152x.

Kaplan, Abraham. 1998. *The Conduct of Inquiry: Methodology for Behavioral Science.* Oxfordshire, UK: Routledge.

Kirsch, Irving, and Guy Sapirstein. 1998. "Listening to Prozac but hearing placebo: A meta-analysis of antidepressant medication." *Prevention & Treatment* 1, no. 2 (June). https://psycnet.apa.org/doi/10.1037/1522-3736.1.1.12a.

Knaak, Stephanie, Ed Mantler, and Andrew Szeto. 2017. "Mental illness-related stigma in healthcare." *Healthcare Management Forum* 30, no. 2 (March): 111–116. https://doi.org/10.1177%2F0840470416679413.

Ktitowsky. 2017. "Phrenology and 'Scientific Racism' in the 19th Century." *Real Archaeology* (blog). March 5, 2017. https://pages.vassar.edu/realarchaeology/2017/03/05/phrenology-and-scientific-racism-in-the-19th-century/.

Lockett, Eleesha. 2022. "How We Can Change the Stigma Around Mental Health." *Healthline* (blog). October 26, 2022. https://www.healthline.com/health/mental-health/mental-health-stigma-examples.

Maslow, Abraham. 1954. *Motivation and Personality*. New York: Harper & Row.

Maslow, Abraham. 1962. "Lessons from the Peak—Experiences 1." *Journal of Humanistic Psychology* 2, no. 1 (January): 10. https://www.deepdyve.com/lp/sage/lessons-from-the-peak-experiences1-otbp4M95NR.

Maslow, Abraham. 1967. "The Farther Reaches of Human Nature." Lecture delivered at Brandeis University on September 14, 1967. https://atpweb.org/jtparchive/trps-01-69-01-001.pdf.

Maust, Donovan T., Lewei A. Lin, Frederic C. Blow. 2018. "Benzodiazepine Use and Misuse Among Adults in the United States." *American Psychiatric Association Psychiatric Services* 70, no. 2 (December): 97–106. https://doi.org/10.1176/appi.ps.201800321.

McLeod, Saul. 2018. *Maslow's Hierarchy of Needs*. London: Simply Psychology. https://canadacollege.edu/dreamers/docs/Maslows-Hierarchy-of-Needs.pdf.

Menand, Louis. 2017. "Why Freud Survives." *The New Yorker*, August 2017. https://www.newyorker.com/magazine/2017/08/28/why-freud-survives.

Milenkovic, Milja. 2019. "42 Worrying Workplace Stress Statistics." *Daily Life* (blog), The American Institute of Stress. September 25, 2019. https://www.stress.org/42-worrying-workplace-stress-statistics.

Nisbett, Richard E. 2004. *The Geography of Thought: How Asians and Westerners Think Differently... and Why*. New York: Free Press.

Nordt, Carlos, Wulf Rossler, and Christoph Lauber. 2006. "Attitudes of Mental Health Professionals Toward People with Schizophrenia and Major Depression." *Schizophrenia Bulletin* 32, no. 4 (October): 709–714. https://doi.org/10.1093%2Fschbul%2Fsbj065.

Price, Leah. 2013. "When doctors prescribe books to heal the mind." *The Boston Globe*, December 22, 2013.

https://www.bostonglobe.com/ideas/2013/12/22/when-doctors-prescribe-books-heal-mind/H2mbhLnTJ3Gy96BS8TUgiL/story.html.

Reddy, Ajitha. 2008. "The Eugenic Origins of IQ Testing: Implications for Post Atkins Litigation." *DePaul Law Review* 57, no. 3: 667–678. https://via.library.depaul.edu/cgi/viewcontent.cgi?article=1270&context=law-review.

Rossler, Wulf. 2016. "The stigma of mental disorders: A millennia-long history of social exclusion and prejudices." *EMBO Reports* 17, no. 9: 1250–1253. https://doi.org/10.15252%2Fembr.201643041.

Sexual Assault Centre of Edmonton (SACE). 2023. "Victim Blaming." *Learn* (blog), Sexual Assault Centre of Edmonton. Accessed April 28, 2023. https://www.sace.ca/learn/victim-blaming/.

Vine, Nicholas. 2009. "Psychology Under the Third Reich." August 10, 2009. https://web.wpi.edu/Pubs/E-project/Available/E-project-102609-144251/unrestricted/PsychologyUndertheThirdReich.pdf.

Yadav, Riya. 2018. "Freud and penis envy—a failure of courage?" *The Psychologist* (blog), The British Psychological Society. https://www.bps.org.uk/psychologist/freud-and-penis-envy-failure-courage.

CHAPTER 12: FAULT OBSCURES RESPONSIBILITY

Brown, Brené. 2012. "Listening to Shame—Brené Brown." TED. March 16, 2012. 20:39. https://www.youtube.com/watch?v=psN1DORYYV0.

DFW Child Editors. 2022. "Stress: The Trickle-Down Effect." *Self + Wellness* (blog), *DFW Child*. April 25, 2022. https://dfwchild.com/stress-the-trickle-down-effect/.

Douglass, Frederick. 1852. "Oration, Delivered in Corinthian Hall, Rochester." Speech delivered July 1852 in Rochester New York. https://classroom.monticello.org/view/74287/.

Douglass, Frederick. 1872. "Self-Made Men." Speech delivered 1872 in unknown location. https://www.leeannhunter.com/english/wp-content/uploads/2015/01/Douglass_SelfMadeMan1872.pdf.

Gillette, Hope. 2022. "What Is Guilt and How Do You Manage It?" *PsychCentral* (blog). October 18, 2022. https://psychcentral.com/health/what-is-guilt.

Leaver, Kate. 2018. "Finland came out on top in the 2018 World Happiness Report, but what if the Finnish people don't agree?" *BBC Travel* (blog), BBC. June 18, 2018. https://www.bbc.com/travel/article/20180617-why-the-finns-dont-want-to-be-happy.

Miller, Tarah. 2016. "6 reasons Bhutan might be the world's most liveable country." *The Journal* (blog), *Intrepid Travel*. January 11, 2016. https://www.intrepidtravel.com/adventures/bhutan-liveable/.

Morton, Caitlin. 2022. "These Are the Happiest Countries in the World." *Inspiration* (blog), *Conde Nast Traveler.* March 31, 2022. https://www.cntraveler.com/gallery/the-10-happiest-countries-in-the-world.

Nieto, Leticia, and Margot Boyer. 2006. "Understanding Oppression: Strategies in Addressing Power and Privilege." *Colors NW Magazine*, March 2006. https://beyondinclusionbeyondempowerment.com/wp-content/uploads/2019/12/nieto-articles-understanding-oppression-2006.pdf.

Price, Devon. 2022. "An Autistic Social Butterfly's Guide to Making Friends" *Autistic Advice* (blog). January 26, 2022. https://medium.com/autistic-advice/an-autistic-social-butterflys-guide-to-making-friends-40bf4f9377f.

Promise Neighborhoods Institute. 2010. "Creating Promise Neighborhoods." *PolicyLink*. July 13, 2010. https://web.archive.org/web/20100713152718/http:/www.policylink.org/site/c.lkIXLbMNJrE/b.5136647/k.3BB1/Creating_Promise_Neighborhoods.htm.

VanScoy, Holly. 2016. "Shame: The Quintessential Emotion." *PsychCentral* (blog). May 17, 2016. https://psychcentral.com/lib/shame-the-quintessential-emotion#1.

CHAPTER 13: RETHINKING ACTION

Behal, Coonoor. 2021. *I Quit! The Life-Affirming Joy of Giving Up.* Washington DC: New Degree Press.

Bloem, Craig. 2018. "Successful people like Barack Obama and Mark Zuckerberg wear the same thing every day—and it's not a coincidence." *Strategy Contributors* (blog), *Insider.* February 28, 2018. https://www.businessinsider.com/successful-people-like-barack-obama-wear-the-same-thing-every-day-2018-2.

brown, adrienne maree. 2017. *Emergent Strategy: Shaping Change, Changing Worlds.* Chico, CA: AK Press.

Engler, Mark, and Paul Engler. 2021. "Andre Gorz's Non-Reformist Reforms Show How We Can Transform the World Today." *Politics* (blog), *Jacobin.* July 22, 2021. https://jacobin.com/2021/07/andre-gorz-non-reformist-reforms-revolution-political-theory.

Gilbert, Elizabeth. 2007. *Eat, Pray, Love: One Woman's Search for Everything Across Italy, India and Indonesia.* New York: Riverhead Books.

Goldsmith, Marshall, and Mark Reiter. 2007. *What Got You Here Won't Get You There: How Successful People Become Even More Successful.* New York: Hachette Books.

Heifetz, Ronald A., and Donald L. Laurie. 1997. "The Work of Leadership." *Managing People* (blog), *Harvard Business Review.* December 2001. https://hbr.org/2001/12/the-work-of-leadership.

Heifetz, Ronald A., and Marty Linsky. 2002. *Leadership on the Line.* Cambridge, MA: Harvard Business School Press.

Hodgkinson, G.P., J. Langan-Fox, and E. Sadler-Smith. 2008. "Intuition: A fundamental bridging construct in the behavioral sciences." *British Journal of Psychology* 99, no. 1: 1–27.
https://doi.org/10.1348/000712607x216666.

Julmi, Christian. 2019. "When rational decision-making becomes irrational: a critical assessment and re-conceptualization of intuition effectiveness." *Business Research* 12, no. 1 (April): 291–314.
https://doi.org/10.1007/s40685-019-0096-4.

Lorde, Audre. 2007. *Sister Outsider.* New York: Crossing Press.

Lufityanto, Galang, Chris Donkin, and Joel Pearson. 2016. "Measuring Intuition: Nonconscious Emotional Information Boosts Decision Accuracy and Confidence." *Psychological Science* 27, no. 5 (April): 622–634.
https://doi.org/10.1177/0956797616629403.

Marcus, Bonnie. 2015. "Intuition Is an Essential Leadership Tool." *ForbesWomen* (blog), *Forbes.* September 1, 2015.
https://www.forbes.com/sites/bonniemarcus/2015/09/01/intuiton-is-an-essential-leadership-tool/?sh=466862271c18.

CHAPTER 14: SPIRALING UP

Brown, Brene. 2017. *Rising Strong: How the Ability to Reset Transforms the Way We Live, Love, Parent, and Lead.* New York: Random House.

Cullors, Patrisse. 2022. *An Abolitionist's Handbook: 12 Steps to Changing Yourself and the World.* New York: St. Martin's Press.

Doyle, Glennon. 2020. *Untamed.* New York: The Dial Press.

Freedman, Rory, and Kim Barnouin. 2005. *Skinny Bitch: A no-nonsense, tough-love guide for savvy girls who want to stop eating crap and start looking fabulous!* Philadelphia: Running Press.

Grace, Annie. 2015. *This Naked Mind: Control Alcohol, Find Freedom, Discover Happiness & Change Your Life.* New York: Avery.

Guidi, Jenny, Marcella Lucente, Nicoletta Sonino, and Giovanni A. Fava. 2021. "Allostatic Load and Its Impact on Health: A Systematic Review." *Psychotherapy and Psychosomatics* 90, no. 1: 11–27.
https://doi.org/10.1159/000510696.

Hamer, Fannie Lou. 1964. "I'm Sick and Tired of Being Sick and Tired." Speech delivered December 1964 in Harlem, New York.
https://awpc.cattcenter.iastate.edu/2019/08/09/im-sick-and-tired-of-being-sick-and-tired-dec-20-1964/.

Hübl, Thomas, and Julie Jordan Avritt. 2020. *Healing Collective Trauma: A Process for Integrating Our Intergenerational and Cultural Wounds*. Louisville, CO: Sounds True.

Lazarus, R.S., and S. Folkman. 1984. *Stress, Appraisal, and Coping*. New York: Springer.

Loeb, Paul Rogat. 2004. *The Impossible Will Take a Little While: A Citizen's Guide to Hope in a Time of Fear*. New York: Basic Books.

Philips LLC. 2019. *Philips Global Sleep Survey*. Cambridge, MA: Philips USA. https://www.usa.philips.com/c-dam/b2c/master/experience/smartsleep/world-sleep-day/2019/2019-philips-world-sleep-day-survey-results.pdf.

Rodriguez, Erik J., Edward N. Kim, Anne E. Sumner, Anna M. Napoles, and Eliseo J. Perez-Stable. 2019. "Allostatic Load: Importance, Markers, and Score Determination in Minority and Disparity Populations." *Journal of Urban Health* 96, no. 1 (March): 3–11. https://doi.org/10.1007%2Fs11524-019-00345-5.

The American Institute of Stress. 2022. "What Is Stress?" Stress.org. Accessed April 27, 2023.
https://www.stress.org/daily-life.

van der Kolk, Bessel. 2015. *The Body Keeps the Score: Brain, Mind, and Body in the Healing of Trauma*. New York: Penguin Publishing Group.

Wheaton, Anne, Sherry Everett Jones, Adina C. Cooper, and Janet B. Croft. 2015. "Short Sleep Duration among Middle and High School Students." Centers for Disease Control and Prevention.
https://www.cdc.gov/mmwr/volumes/67/wr/mm6703a1.htm?s_cid=mm6703a1_w.

Weil, Andrew. 2013. "US manages disease, not health." *CNN Opinion* (blog), CNN. March 10, 2013.
https://www.cnn.com/2013/03/08/opinion/weil-health-care/index.html.

williams, angel Kyodo, Lama Rod Owens, and Jasmine Syedullah. 2016. *Radical Dharma: Talking Race, Love, and Liberation*. Berkeley, CA: North Atlantic Books.

Williams, David R., Naomi Priest, and Norman Anderson. 2016. "Understanding Associations between Race, Socioeconomic Status, and Health: Patterns and Prospects." *Health Psychology* 35, no. 4: 407–411.
https://doi.org/10.1037%2Fhea0000242.

CHAPTER 15: WRITING A NEW STORY

Anderson, Bob. 2021. *The Spirit of Leadership*. Utah: The Leadership Circle. https://leadershipcircle.com/wp-content/uploads/2021/07/Spirit-of-Leadership-Whitepaper-2021-07.pdf.

Beck, Don Edward, and Christopher C. Cowan. 2005. *Spiral Dynamics: Mastering Values, Leadership and Change*. Hoboken, NJ: Wiley-Blackwell.

Defund the Police. 2023. "Enough Is Enough. Let's Take Action Now." *Defund the Police*. Accessed March 27, 2023.
https://defundthepolice.org/about/.

Du Bois, W.E.B. 1935. *Black Reconstruction in America*. New York: Russel & Russel.

Eisenstein, Charles. 2013. *The More Beautiful World Our Hearts Know Is Possible (Sacred Activism)*. Berkeley, CA: North Atlantic Books.

Fuller, Doris A., H. Richard Lamb, Michael Biasotti, and John Snook. 2015. *Overlooked in the Undercounted: The Role of Mental Illness in Fatal Law Enforcement Encounters*. Arlington, VA: Treatment Advocacy Center.

Fuller, Buckminster. 1981. *Critical Path*. New York: St. Martin's Press.

Hübl, Thomas, and Julie Jordan Avritt. 2020. *Healing Collective Trauma: A Process for Integrating Our Intergenerational and Cultural Wounds*. Louisville, CO: Sounds True.

Inner Development Goals. 2021. *Inner Development Goals: Background, method and the IDG framework*. Sweden: Inner Development Goals. https://static1.squarespace.com/static/600d80b3387b98582a60354a/t/61aa2f96dfd3fb39c4fc4283/1638543258249/211201_IDG_Report_Full.pdf.

Kaba, Mariame. 2021. *We Do This 'Til We Free Us: Abolitionist Organizing and Transforming Justice*. Chicago: Haymarket Books.

Maher, Geo. 2021. *A World Without Police: How Strong Communities Make Cops Obsolete*. New York: Verso Books.

Mendez, Marisa. 2020. "Snoop Dogg's Latest Meme: No One Ever Made a Song Called 'Fuck the Fire Department.'" *Hip Hop DX News* (blog). June 10, 2020. https://hiphopdx.com/news/id.56310/title.snoop-doggs-latest-meme-no-one-ever-made-a-song-called-fuck-the-fire-department.

Mummolo, Jonathan. 2018. "Militarization fails to enhance police safety or reduce crime but may harm police reputation." *Proceedings of the National Academy of Sciences* 115, no. 37 (September): 9181–9186. https://doi.org/10.1073/pnas.1805161115.

Nin, Anaïs. 1961. *Seduction of the Minotaur*. Athens, OH: Swallow Press.

Pearl, Betsy, and Maritza Perez. 2018. "Ending the War on Drugs." *American Progress*. June 27, 2018. https://www.americanprogress.org/article/ending-war-drugs/.

Sherman, Stephen Averill. 2020. "Many cities are rethinking the police, but what are the alternatives?" *Urban Edge* (blog), Rice University. July 22, 2020. https://kinder.rice.edu/urbanedge/many-cities-are-rethinking-police-what-are-alternatives.

United Nations. 2015. "The 17 Goals." Sustainable Development Goals. Accessed April 27, 2023. https://sdgs.un.org/goals.

van der Kolk, Bessel. 2015. *The Body Keeps the Score: Brain, Mind, and Body in the Healing of Trauma*. New York: Penguin Publishing Group.

Wheatley, Margaret J. 2006. *Leadership and the New Science: Discovering Order in a Chaotic World*. Oakland: Berrett-Koehler Publishers.

CHAPTER 16: CREATING JUSTICE

Anderson, Bob. 2018. *Leadership Circle: Profile*. Utah: The Leadership Circle. https://leadershipcircle.com/wp-content/uploads/2018/03/LCP_Breakthrough.pdf.

Brady, Louise. 2021. "K'ASHEECHTLAA—LOUISE BRADY on Restoring the Sacred /230." For the Wild. Released April 14, 2021. 58:30. https://forthewild.world/listen/kasheechtlaa-louise-brady-on-restoring-the-sacred-230.

brown, adrienne maree. 2019. *Pleasure Activism: The Politics of Feeling Good*. Chico: AK Press.

Casey, J. Tyson. 2021. "Regenerative Power." *Perspectives* (blog), *Anarchist Studies*. January 25, 2021. https://anarchiststudies.org/regenerative-power-by-j-tyson-casey/.

Carlsen, Audrey, Maya Salam, Claire Cain Miller, Denise Lu, Ash Ngu, Jugal Patel, Zach Wichter. 2018. "#MeToo Brought Down 201 Powerful Men. Nearly Half of Their Replacements Are Women." *The New York Times*, October 29, 2018. https://www.nytimes.com/interactive/2018/10/23/us/metoo-replacements.html.

Crenshaw, Kimberlé. 1989. "Demarginalizing the Intersection of Race and Sex: A Black Feminist Critique of Antidiscrimination Doctrine, Feminist Theory and Antiracist Politics." *University of Chicago Legal Forum* 1, no. 8: 139–167. https://chicagounbound.uchicago.edu/cgi/viewcontent.cgi?article=1052&context=uclf.

Cullors, Patrisse. 2022. *An Abolitionist's Handbook: 12 Steps to Changing Yourself and the World*. New York: St. Martin's Press.

Goode, William. 1959. "The Theoretical Importance of Love." *American Sociological Review* 24, no. 1 (February): 38–47. https://doi.org/10.2307/2089581.

Hampton Institute (@HamptonThink). 2020. "A 10-day General Strike would accomplish more for the working-class majority than a century's worth of elections. It would represent an immediate momentum shift by bringing the capitalist behemoth to its knees. Our true power is in our collective labor, not in a voting booth." Twitter. February 9, 2020, 5:24 p.m.

Hübl, Thomas, and Julie Jordan Avritt. 2020. *Healing Collective Trauma: A Process for Integrating Our Intergenerational and Cultural Wounds*. Louisville, CO: Sounds True.

Kendi, Ibram X. 2019. *How to Be an Antiracist*. London: Oneworld Publications.

Levin, David. 2017. "The 1997 UPS Strike: Beating Big Business & Business Unionism." *LaborNotes* (blog). August 15, 2017. https://labornotes.org/2017/08/1997-ups-strike-beating-big-business-business-unionism.

Lorde, Audre. 2018. *Master's Tools Will Never Dismantle the Master's House.* London: Penguin Books.

Love, Barbara J. 2013. "Developing a Liberatory Consciousness." In R*eadings for Diversity and Social Justice*. Edited by Marianne Adams, Warren J. Blumenfeld, Heather W. Hackman, Madeline L. Peters, and Ximena Zuniga, 599–603. Oxfordshire: Routledge.

Orbey, Eren. 2019. "The Victims of Larry Nassar Who Dared to Come Forward First." *The New Yorker*, May 2019. https://www.newyorker.com/culture/culture-desk/the-victims-of-larry-nassar-who-dared-to-come-forward-first.

Soul Fire Farm. 2023. "Mission." *Soul Fire Farm*. Accessed April 30, 2023. https://www.soulfirefarm.org/.

West, Cornel. 2011. "Cornel West: Justice Is What Love Looks Like in Public." Supernegromantic. April 17, 2011. 1:00:00. https://youtu.be/nGqP7S_WO6o.

williams, angel Kyodo, Lama Rod Owens, and Jasmine Syedullah. 2016. *Radical Dharma: Talking Race, Love, and Liberation*. Berkeley, CA: North Atlantic Books.

World Justice Project. 2022. "WJP Rule of Law Index." World Justice Project. Accessed April 28, 2023. https://worldjusticeproject.org/rule-of-law-index/global/2022/ranking.

CHAPTER 17: A MORE RADICAL ACCEPTANCE

Baliga, Sujatha. 2018. "A different path for confronting sexual assault." *Politics* (blog), *Vox*. October 10, 2018. https://www.vox.com/first-person/2018/10/10/17953016/what-is-restorative-justice-definition-questions-circle.

Brach, Tara. 2003. *Radical Acceptance: Embracing Your Life with the Heart of a Buddha*. New York: Random House.

Chauncey, Sarah. 2017. "The Lifespan of an Emotion." *Living the Mess* (blog). March 6, 2017. https://www.livingthemess.com/the-lifespan-of-an-emotion/.

CBS. 2017. "More than 12M "Me Too" Facebook posts, comments, reactions in 24 hours." CBS News, October 17, 2017. https://www.cbsnews.com/news/metoo-more-than-12-million-facebook-posts-comments-reactions-24-hours/.

Fisher, Danny. 2010 "Mindfulness and the cessation of suffering: An exclusive new interview with mindfulness pioneer Jon Kabat-Zinn." *Lion's Roar*. October 7, 2010.

Gilens, Martin, and Benjamin Page. 2014. "Testing Theories of American Politics: Elites, Interest Groups, and Average Citizens." *American Political Science Association* 12, no. 3 (September): 564–581. https://doi.org/10.1017/S1537592714001595.

Kelner, Simon. 2014. "Perception is reality: The facts won't matter in next year's general election." *Voices* (blog), *The Independent*. October 30, 2014. https://www.independent.co.uk/voices/comment/perception-is-reality-the-facts-won-t-matter-in-next-year-s-general-election-9829132.html.

Knechtle, Beat, Zbigniew Waskiewicz, Caio Victor Sousa, Lee Hill, and Pantelis Nikolaidis. 2020. "Cold Water Swimming—Benefits and Risks: A Narrative Review." *International Journal of Environmental Research and Public Health* 17, no. 23 (December): 8984.
https://doi.org/10.3390%2Fijerph17238984.

Mudit. 2021. "What Is Mindfulness?" *Mindful Mudit* (blog). July 1, 2021. https://mindfulmudit.com/what-is-mindfulness/.

Mahdawi, Arwa. 2023. "Millennials aren't getting more rightwing with age. I suspect I know why." *The Guardian*, January 2, 2023.
https://www.theguardian.com/commentisfree/2023/jan/03/millennials-radicalism-not-getting-more-rightwing-with-age.

Rogers, Carl R. 1995. *On Becoming a Person: A Therapist's View of Psychotherapy.* San Francisco: Harper One.

Rumi, Jalal al-Din. 2004. *The Essential Rumi, New Expanded Edition*. Translated by Coleman Barks. San Francisco: Harper One.

Sharma, Yash. 2021. "Social Media, Democracy and Democratization." *Diplomatist* (blog), *Extraordinary and Plenipotentiary Diplomatist*. August 13, 2021. https://diplomatist.com/2021/08/13/social-media-democracy-and-democratization/.

Souli, Sarah. 2020. "Does America Need a Truth and Reconciliation Commission?" *Politico*, August 2020.
https://www.politico.com/news/magazine/2020/08/16/does-america-need-a-truth-and-reconciliation-commission-395332.

van der Kolk, Bessel. 2015. *The Body Keeps the Score: Brain, Mind, and Body in the Healing of Trauma*. New York: Penguin Publishing Group.

CHAPTER 18: INSTITUTIONALIZING HUMANITY

Benyus, Janine. 2009. "Biomimicry in action | Janine Benyus." TED. August 6, 2009. 20:14.
https://www.youtube.com/watch?v=k_GFq12w5WU.

Brignone, Emily, Daniel George, Lawrence Sinoway, Curren Katz, Charity Sauder, Andrea Murray, Robert Gladden, Jennifer Kraschnewski. 2020. "Trends in the diagnosis of diseases of despair in the United States, 2009–2018: a retrospective cohort study." *BMJ Open* 10, no. 10 (November).
https://doi.org/10.1136/bmjopen-2020-037679.

Chatterjee, Rhitu. 2023. "Native Americans left out of 'deaths of despair' research." *Health News* (blog), NPR. February 1, 2023.
https://www.npr.org/sections/health-shots/2023/02/01/1152222968/native-americans-left-out-of-deaths-of-despair-research.

Dewar, Gwen. 2019. "Moral sense: Babies prefer underdogs and do-gooders." *Babies* (blog), *Parenting Science*. September 19, 2019. https://parentingscience.com/do-babies-know-right-from-wrong/.

The Editors of Encyclopaedia Britannica. 2023. *Industrial Revolution*. Chicago: Encyclopaedia Britannica. https://www.britannica.com/event/Industrial-Revolution.

Eger, Edith Eva. 2017. *The Choice: Escaping the Past and Embracing the Possible.* Read by Tovah Feldshuh. New York: Simon & Schuster Audio. Audible Audio ed., 12 hr. 26 min.

Gnaulati, Enrico. 2018. "In Defense of Healthy Depression." *MIA Reports* (blog), *Mad in America*. July 8, 2018. https://www.madinamerica.com/2018/07/defense-healthy-depression/.

GNH Centre Bhutan. 2023. "History of GNH." Accessed April 27, 2023. https://www.gnhcentrebhutan.org/history-of-gnh/.

hooks, bell. 2022. *Sisters of the Yam (2nd Edition): Black Women and Self-Recovery.* Narrated by Adenrele Ojo. Old Saybrook, CT: Tantor Media. Audible audio ed., 6 hr. 55 min.

Lorde, Audre. 2007. *Sister Outsider.* New York: Crossing Press.

Martin, G.B., and R.D. Clark. 1982. "Distress crying in neonates: Species and peer specificity." *Developmental Psychology* 18, no. 1: 3–9. https://psycnet.apa.org/doi/10.1037/0012-1649.18.1.3.

Nickolas, Steven. 2022. "How Is a Capitalist System Different Than a Free Market System?" *Economy* (blog), Investopedia. August 15, 2022. https://www.investopedia.com/ask/answers/042215/what-difference-between-capitalist-system-and-free-market-system.asp.

Resilience Alliance. 2002. "Panarchy." Resilience Alliance. https://www.resalliance.org/panarchy.

Schwab, Klaus. 2016. "The Fourth Industrial Revolution: what it means, how to respond." *Agenda* (blog), *World Economic Forum*. January 14, 2016. https://www.weforum.org/agenda/2016/01/the-fourth-industrial-revolution-what-it-means-and-how-to-respond/.

CHAPTER 19: ACCOUNTABILITY IS ALLYSHIP

Beer, Tommy. 2020. "Top 1% of US Households Hold 15 Times More Wealth Than Bottom 50% Combined." *Business* (blog), *Forbes*. October 8, 2020. https://www.forbes.com/sites/tommybeer/2020/10/08/top-1-of-us-households-hold-15-times-more-wealth-than-bottom-50-combined/?sh=4b310cc75179.

Boyd, Robert and Peter J. Richerson. 2009. "Culture and the evolution of human cooperation." *Philosophical Transactions of the Royal Society of London. Series B, Biological Sciences* 364, no. 1533 (November): 3281–3288. https://doi.org/10.1098%2Frstb.2009.0134.

Chenoweth, Erica. 2013. "The success of nonviolent civil resistance: Erica Chenoweth at TEDxBoulder." TEDx Talks. November 4, 2013. 12:33. https://www.youtube.com/watch?v=YJSehRlU34w&ab_channel=TEDxTalks.

Collins, Nick. 2011. "Neanderthals overrun by early humans." *The Telegraph*, July 28, 2011. https://www.telegraph.co.uk/news/science/evolution/8668713/Neanderthals-overrun-by-early-humans.html.

Cox, John Woodrow. 2023. "Moms Demand Action founder, Shannon Watts, who took on the NRA, to retire from group she created." *The Washington Post*, January 9, 2023. https://www.washingtonpost.com/dc-md-va/2023/01/09/shannon-watts-retire-moms-demand-action/.

Debska, Marta. 2010. "A Brief History of Americanization." *Krakowskie Studia Miedzynarodowe* 2, no. 2: 13–32. https://repozytorium.ka.edu.pl/bitstream/handle/11315/23463/DEBSKA_A_brief_history_of_americanization_2010.pdf?sequence=1&isAllowed=y.

Fowler, Sarah. 2022. "She founded Moms Demand Action for gun reform. 140 of its volunteers won office." *The Washington Post*, December 8, 2022. https://www.washingtonpost.com/parenting/2022/12/08/shannon-watts-moms-demand-action/.

Giannaki, Angeliki Fanouria. 2016. "The Role of 'Privileged' Allies in the Struggle for Social Justice." *Knowledge Resources* (blog), Humanity in Action. October 2016. https://humanityinaction.org/knowledge_detail/jlf-16-the-role-of-privileged-allies-in-the-struggle-for-social-justice/.

Giridharadas, Anand. 2022. *The Persuaders: At the Front Lines of the Fight for Hearts, Minds, and Democracy*. New York: Knopf Doubleday.

Gold, Howard. 2017. "Never Mind the 1 Percent. Let's Talk About the 0.01 Percent." *Economics* (blog), *Chicago Booth Review*. November 29, 2017. https://www.chicagobooth.edu/review/never-mind-1-percent-lets-talk-about-001-percent.

Gustines, George Gene. 2018. "Nicole Maines on Becoming TV's First Transgender Superhero." *The New York Times*, October 12, 2018. https://www.nytimes.com/2018/10/12/arts/television/nicole-maines-supergirl-transgender-interview.html.

Harrison, Brian F., and Melissa R. Michelson. 2015. "God and Marriage: The Impact of Religious Identity Priming on Attitudes Toward Same-Sex Marriage." *Social Science Quarterly* 96, no. 5 (November): 1411–1423. https://www.jstor.org/stable/26612284.

King, James. 2013. "Catalyst of Change? President Obama's Impact on Public Opinion of Same-Sex Marriage." Dissertation. Kent State University Honors College. https://etd.ohiolink.edu/apexprod/rws_etd/send_file/send?accession=ksuhonors1384887236&disposition=inline.

Maines, Nicole. 2020. "Speaking Truth to Youth: Nicole Maines." *Americans Who Tell the Truth*. August 10, 2020. 15:39.

https://www.youtube.com/watch?v=NQMS7lRyET4&ab_channel=AmericansWhoTelltheTruth.

McGeown, Kate. 2011. "People Power at 25: Long Road to Philippine democracy." BBC. February 25, 2011.
https://www.bbc.com/news/world-asia-pacific-12567320.

Middleton, Lucy. 2022. "EXPLAINER-What Is Drag Queen Story Hour and why are the events under attack?" *Openly News* (blog), Thomas Reuters Foundation. September 2, 2022.
https://www.openlynews.com/i/?id=01d49b89-4e91-48fd-91d9-d589fa5576ed.

Miemis, Venessa. 2010. "Conceptual Framework for Online Identity Roles." *Emergent by Design* (blog). August 4, 2010.
https://emergentbydesign.com/2010/08/04/conceptual-framework-for-online-identity-roles/.

Moms Demand Action. 2013. "Mayors Against Illegal Guns and Moms Demand Action to Join Forces, Unite a National Movement to Protect Communities and Save Lives." *Moms Demand Action for Gun Sense In America*. December 19, 2023.
https://momsdemandaction.org/mayors-illegal-guns-moms-demand-action-join-forces-unite-national-movement-protect-communities-save-lives/.

Robson, David. 2019. "The '3.5% rule': How a small minority can change the world." *BBC Future* (blog), BBC. May 13, 2019.
https://www.bbc.com/future/article/20190513-it-only-takes-35-of-people-to-change-the-world.

Smith, Matthew, Owen Zidar, and Eric Zwick. 2021. "Top Wealth in America: New Estimates under Heterogeneous Returns." Working Paper at Princeton University, Princeton, New Jersey, October 2021.
https://economics.princeton.edu/working-papers/top-wealth-in-america-new-estimates-under-heterogenous-returns/.

Stanford University. n.d. "Levison, Stanley David." The Martin Luther King, Jr. Research and Education Institute. Accessed April 28, 2023.
https://kinginstitute.stanford.edu/encyclopedia/levison-stanley-david.

Tolan, Sandy. 2016. "Veterans came to North Dakota to protest a pipeline. But they also found healing and forgiveness." *Los Angeles Times*, December 10, 2016.
https://www.latimes.com/nation/la-na-north-dakota-20161210-story.html.

Weir, Kirsten. 2018. "Life-saving relationships: New research details how important close emotional connections are for health and well-being, prompting psychologists to call for making strong relationships a public health priority." *American Psychological Association* 49, no. 3: 46.
https://apa.org/monitor/2018/03/life-saving-relationships.

Woo, Sofia. 2017. "Dissonant priming: Poli-sci prof presents new theory on how to change hateful attitudes toward…" *News* (blog), *The Lowell*. March 25, 2017.
https://thelowell.org/328/news/dissonant-priming-poli-sci-prof-presents-new-theory-on-how-to-change-hateful-attitudes-toward/.

Zimmer, Katarina. 2021. "'Social' Mitochondria, Whispering Between Cells, Influence Health." *Quantamagazine*, July 2021.

https://www.quantamagazine.org/social-mitochondria-whispering-between-cells-influence-health-20210706/.

Zinn, Howard. 2018. *You Can't Be Neutral on a Moving Train: A Personal History.* Boston: Beacon Press.

Zinn, Howard. 1999. *Marx in Soho: A Play on History.* Boston: South End Press.

Zunes, Stephen. 2009. *Estonia's Singing Revolution (1986–1991).* Washington DC: International Center on Nonviolent Conflict. https://www.nonviolent-conflict.org/estonias-singing-revolution-1986-1991.

CHAPTER 20: WE NEED YOU

Campbell, Joseph, and Bill Moyers. 1988. *The Power of Myth.* New York: Doubleday.

Grant, Richard. 2018. "Do Trees Talk to Each Other?" *Science* (blog), *Smithsonian Magazine.* March 2018. https://www.smithsonianmag.com/science-nature/the-whispering-trees-180968084/.

Jabr, Ferris. 2020. "The Social Life of Trees." *The New York Times,* December 2, 2020. https://www.nytimes.com/interactive/2020/12/02/magazine/tree-communication-mycorrhiza.html.

Kamimura, Kana, Kazuki Nanko, Asako Matsumoto, Saneyoshi Ueno, James Gardiner, and Barry Gardiner. 2022. "Tree dynamic response and survival in a category-5 tropical cyclone: The case of super typhoon Trami." *American Association for the Advancement of Science* 8, no. 10 (March). https://doi.org/10.1126/sciadv.abm7891.

Rawls, John. 2005. *A Theory of Justice.* Cambridge, MA: Belknap Press.

Thurman, Howard, Vincent Harding, Michael Bernard Beckwith, and Alice Walker. 2010. *The Living Wisdom of Howard Thurman: A Visionary for Our Time.* Louisville, CO: Sounds True.

Yatharth. 2021. "Environmentalism without Class Struggle Is Gardening." *Political Economy* (blog), *Yatharth Magazine.* December 27, 2021. https://yatharthmag.com/2021/12/27/environmentalism-without-class-struggle-is-gardening/.